To: Jan
With best Wishes,
and a Happy Future!

Mick

THE MAGIC SEASONING

THE MAGIC SEASONING

A Global Search For Flavor

BY DAVID W. RUSSELL

Mill City Press Books

Mill City Press, Inc.
2301 Lucien Way #415
Maitland, FL 32751
407.339.4217
www.millcitypress.net

Printed in the United States of America

ISBN-13: 9781545616154

For Midori

Table of Contents

Introduction

For as long as I can remember, I have enjoyed puzzles. Not crosswords and the like, but more conceptual puzzles — historical oddities, mysteries, and so on that can be solved through solid research and detective work. Maybe that's why I also like company stories — it's interesting to dig into the past and find out how a company in the nineteenth century, for instance, was restructured over and over and became something quite different in the twentieth century, and lives on today in yet a different guise in the twenty-first century. Finally, on our full-disclosure list of personal foibles, I admit to having a deep fondness for Japan. I lived there for several years as a business journalist, and I still find the country and its culture fascinating.

When the stars are in proper alignment, all of these traits come together and I find myself able to work on a project that involves digging into both the past and present operations of some global Japanese business to unravel an intriguing story that has piqued my interest. Several years ago, a casual lunch with a Wall St. friend sparked an interest in a Japanese financial services company that I had never heard of. As I began to pull on that thread, it led to a bigger and bigger story and a journey around the world. I discovered how the company had grown from nothing into a giant conglomerate with operations across the U.S. and around the globe, all within the founder's lifetime. Solving that puzzle yielded a fascinating book (*GOOD RISKS*, John Wiley & Sons, 2014).

Recently, another puzzle presented itself and another journey began. As before, it started in New York City in the most innocuous and unassuming way but soon led me around the world in search of answers. This time, the quest did not begin as a search for a company, but instead, a flavor, a taste that I recognized but wasn't aware of. As I prepared to set out on this journey, I was advised by an expert in the field to focus on one company's products. Fortunately, I had no difficulty locating them, as they seemed to be on the shelves of every supermarket, grocery, and gourmet food store on the planet. This in itself helped to answer my initial question about how important this flavoring is to humankind, which led to the question of how a small, unknown Japanese firm had in such a short span of time made its signature product an indispensable item in every celebrity chef's kitchen, as well as in most of the restaurants and millions of private kitchens around the world. That larger puzzle soon led me down a familiar rabbit hole, and I began to investigate Kikkoman, one of the most traditional and at the same time innovative of Japan's major companies.

I immediately discovered commonalities between Kikkoman and the other company I had investigated a few years before, ORIX Corporation: both of their dynamo top executives, the men who had turned these companies into global leaders, happened to be born in the same year, and both had studied abroad and received MBAs from American universities at a time when such a thing was almost unheard-of in Japan. Both leaders had come back from the U.S. with new ideas and new perspectives that turbo-charged their companies' growth. But there the similarity ends.

ORIX is a "new" company, founded in 1964, so it is barely a half-century old, a sapling in the redwood forest of Japanese business. Kikkoman, on the other hand, has a history dating back centuries, making it one of oldest continuing businesses in Japan. In fact, the company's history extends so far back that some of it is wrapped in legend as much as fact, and no one will ever know all the details.

More significantly, ORIX began by copying a U.S. business model and actively importing it to Japan, then cultivating a domestic market where none yet existed. Kikkoman's business was just the opposite — it had existed in one form or another since before George Washington was born, and its main product was used by every Japanese housewife. Rather than importing from abroad, it exported a traditional Japanese product, making it not only well known but widely accepted around the world. Japan's industrial giants, companies such as Toyota, Canon, Sony and others, grew mostly by exporting repackaged versions of Western products back to the countries that had originally made them popular, competing on size, features, price, etc. Kikkoman, on the other hand, exported something virtually unknown in the West and launched decades-long campaigns to educate Western consumers about their product. To me, that — much more than the exploits of Japan's auto, electronics, and camera giants — is a highly significant achievement.

I will frankly admit that my research stance changed as I continued my journey, shifting from objectively dispassionate to keenly interested to overtly impressed. I discovered a unique "corporate DNA" and an extremely effective approach to globalization that is, if not unique, at least extremely rare. Kikkoman's global growth deserves to be studied in business schools and boardrooms around the world as a case study in how to successfully blend into local communities, defuse potential anti-foreign sentiment, and become accepted as a local, rather than a transplanted business. Moreover, everywhere I went — in North America, Europe, and Asia — I discovered that the company had instilled a level of loyalty and familial identity in both its employees and its key stakeholders that I have never witnessed anywhere else.

Acknowledgements

This book would not have been possible without the help of many people around the world, in fact, far too many to list up here. Just to mention the tip of the iceberg, I would like to extend my deep personal thanks to Ronald Yates, Barb Stuckey, Mick Neshek, Dan Miller, Jayne Formen, Steve Siegelman, Martin Brink, Han Willems, Peter Deeg, Kazuo Shimizu, Takeshi Miki, Masa Shimada, Masashi Kasuga, Junichi Sawano, Rika Tabei, and, most of all, Mr. Yuzaburo Mogi. All of these people, and many more, contributed in a major way to assist me in understanding Kikkoman and completing both my research and writing. I am indebted to you, one and all. I also want to give a hat-tip to the nice people at Mill City Press who helped to edit and produce this volume: Cindy, Sasha, Jose, Christopher, Michelle.

Last but not least, a special shout-out to Toshiaki Iizuka, my loyal business partner and traveling companion.

And I cannot close without saying how deeply I am indebted to the amazing Shizuko K. She was my muse, she inspired me much more than she knows, and she made me unbelievably happy in the months when I was working on this manuscript. She appeared suddenly and disappeared even more suddenly, but I have thanked God for bringing her into my life. A truly remarkable woman, she will always be my very special S.E.G.

Author's Note: In visiting so many companies and talking to dozens of people from various countries, all with different versions of English, I undoubtedly misunderstood a few things along the way. I apologize in advance if anyone feels misquoted or misrepresented. Needless to say, I am solely responsible for any mistakes of fact or interpretation in this text.

New York

*I*t all started with food. Doesn't it always?

I was visiting old friends on the Upper West Side of Manhattan one Saturday night last spring. Rob is a retired New York City employee and devoted part-time rock musician with a couple of CDs to his credit; his wife, Laurie is a professional videographer and a card-carrying foodie of the nicest sort. Although I love them both dearly, I never fail to marvel at the unfathomable glue that holds a good marriage together.

Rob's idea of *haute cuisine* is a hot dog at Grey's Papaya, while Laurie prefers to entrust her taste buds to the newest, as-yet-undiscovered chef of the moment. Having studied cooking and even apprenticed briefly with a published chef, she now enjoys seeking out whatever unusual cuisines New York has to offer. If Rob heard her raving about some Haitian refugee with a food truck in Chelsea who miraculously combines avant-garde Peruvian appetizers with faux-Mongolian grilled yak entrees seasoned with just a dash of the latest nouvelle Tasmanian sauces, his response would be to turn down the volume on the ballgame momentarily and say, "Fabulous, honey. Does he make a good cheeseburger?"

Frankly, my tastes fall in the middle of these two extremes, and so I am thankful that Laurie, who has forgotten more about fine dining than I will ever know, often lets her love for the culinary arts take a back seat to her love for her husband, and sups on more plebeian fare, at least when I come to visit. Fortunately, this was one of those occasions.

I love food but am no expert — a devotee of all cuisines, master of none — but my palate is nowhere near as exotic as Laurie's, and so the finer things in life would most likely be wasted on me. Thus, when I dropped in one evening to visit my old friends, I had to suppress a smile when Rob drew a cold bottle of craft beer from the fridge and announced to his wife upstairs, "Hon, David's here. Let's take him out for a slice!" I may have involuntarily winced when I thought about the reaction upstairs.

We locked up the apartment and set off across Broadway, then over to Amsterdam Ave. We walked a few blocks and almost immediately Rob spotted the oasis he was searching for — Numero 28. We had no trouble getting a table, and in no time at all Laurie was ordering appetizers that I couldn't even pronounce. Rob and I had the old standbys and ordered a couple of special pizzas for the three of us to enjoy. I ordered a bottle of meaty Italian red wine, big on body but easy on the wallet.

It was over dinner that we started talking about food. Rob kept quiet and focused on the excellent Capricciosa he was demolishing at a rate that would impress a college freshman, while Laurie and I talked about all manner of world cuisines that she had investigated recently. At one point she brought up the topic of *umami*, the now-famous "fifth taste" that didn't even exist in the traditional sweet-salty-sour-bitter paradigm that was gospel back when I was growing up.

Of course, I had heard and read plenty about umami. All the cool chefs in New York experimented with it years ago, and some, like David Chang, who started the Momofuku group that now operates on three continents, had actually created laboratories full of fermenting foods, always searching for a new and unique umami taste. What I did not want to admit was that I had very little idea what umami really was. Yes, I knew the definition: a brothy or meaty taste, salty but not salt... but what did that really mean?

While I was pondering this, Laurie waxed lyrical about some Tribecca chef's brilliant presentation of the subtleness of umami. Okay, I could deal with that. Old story, new main character. To be honest, I was probably paying more attention to my wine than to her description of the newest rage in downtown cuisine. Then something she said caught my attention.

"...which explains humans' innate craving for umami."

What? What did she say? A *craving* for umami? How could we need some taste we didn't even know existed twenty years ago? That sounded like PR for some fancy-ass chef who wanted to get his name in *The New York Times*. I made a comment under my breath and she immediately sensed that I was skeptical.

"Absolutely!" she replied, switching to didactic mode. "Umami is part of life! Human breast milk is high in it. We all start our lives understanding that taste and we unconsciously crave it one way or another. People are naturally drawn to the taste of umami."

"I'm not," I said with mock bravado, casting a brotherly glance at Rob. Instead of support, he rolled his eyes to warn me that I'd just stepped on a land mine.

"Oh, so you don't like umami?" she said, one eyebrow arching. "You don't enjoy eating foods with umami?"

Once again, I do not pretend to be an expert on food, and the whole umami "thing" of the past decade seemed to me a food fad confined to overpriced restaurants and celebrity chefs. But Laurie was about to set me straight.

"Look at that umami bomb you're shoving in your mouth." Now she was grinning at me.

"What are you talking about, 'umami bomb'? This isn't one of your downtown iron-chef-made-for-TV creations. This is a solid, old-fashioned, manly American pizza!"

Once again I looked at Rob — after all, I was standing up for his worldview here -- but he just shook his head silently, as if to say, "Too late. I tried to warn you..."

"Right," she said emphatically. "Just a pizza. Look what you've got there! Tomato sauce — umami assault weapon. Three kinds of aged cheese — umami heavy artillery. And look at all that spicy pepperoni you've loaded it with — those are umami nukes. Are you getting the picture? Pizza is an umami explosion!"

I stopped eating and looked at the slice in my hand. Something wasn't right here. Umami was something that high-paid chefs in Michelin two-star restaurants liked to blend into exotic dishes, right? Who had snuck that imported, high-brow taste into my all-American pizza?

She must have enjoyed my totally perplexed look as I stared at the once-familiar food that had suddenly morphed into an unrecognizable alien replica of a pizza.

"Yes, you get it. Pizza is all about umami. And so is spaghetti sauce, and the steak sauce I've seen you drench your hamburgers in. It's all umami. And so's the Worcestershire sauce in your Bloody Mary. It's all around you; you don't need to go to fancy restaurants to find it, and the fact is, you *love* that taste. You want it. If someone could put you on a diet without any umami, your body would crave it in no time. It's that *basic!*"

I was stunned. Not because Laurie had educated me about things I knew little about — that was a regular occurrence — but because I now saw a huge cognitive dissonance between my image of this rarified, "foreign" taste and the reality that I'd been eating it and enjoying it all my life.

We talked some more about all sorts of foods, finished our meal and headed back to their apartment on West End Avenue. On the way, Laurie invited me to join her to hear some famous food guru talk about exactly the kinds of things we had been discussing. Normally, you could not have dragged me to a lecture about food, but something about tonight's discussion (and the better part of a bottle of Montepulciano) had put me in an unusually receptive mood, and I found myself accepting her offer. We would meet again on Monday the following week and go up to Columbia to hear some big-name author talk about... food, of course.

When Monday came, I dragged myself over to the subway and uptown to 116th St. and Broadway just as evening fell. She was already standing there in front of the big black iron gates of Columbia University, waiting for me.

"Brings back memories, doesn't it?" she said with a smile. I had half-forgotten that Rob, Laurie and I had actually met at Columbia many years ago, each of us working on a different graduate program. I had studied journalism, Laurie did fine arts, and Rob majored in graduate-level beer drinking. Although I lived in Manhattan, I almost never went back to the school.

Tonight's talk was at Uris Hall, home of the world-renowned Columbia School of Business, and judging by the signs I saw on the way in, this presentation was more of a big deal than I had imagined. What's going on? I thought. After all, it's only *food*, right? Why is a foodie lecturing at the B school anyway?

I voiced these thoughts in a slightly more polite fashion, and Laurie quickly informed me that the speaker we were going to hear was a prominent businesswoman. "She happens to be the President of Mattson International, the leading independent food consultant in the United States," she said. She went on to explain that Mattson[1] is the company that dozens of famous food brands turn to for help in revitalizing the flavors of yesterday's hit products and devising new tastes for tomorrow's hit products. The speaker's name was Barb Stuckey (stuck-ee), and she was apparently a leading light in the field of food appreciation. I noticed that Laurie carried a green-covered paperback about an inch thick called *Taste*. Yes, it was written by the same Barb Stuckey, and Laurie was hoping to get it autographed. OMG, I thought, now we have foodie groupies.

We took our seats along with a hundred or so other people, and applauded as Barb stepped up to speak. She was short, slim, blonde, and loaded with energy. A well-practiced speaker, she talked fast and kept everyone's attention, including mine, which is no small feat when you're talking about food.

She discussed all sorts of things I'd never heard before, like Oxford University research proving that sound affects our experience of food: The scientists proved that the same food tastes vastly different when different music is played in the background. She explained how smell accounts for most of what we normally consider "taste," and how research shows that people choose their life partners in part based on smell, so if you're on a first date in a restaurant and you don't like what you smell, maybe you're with the wrong person. You're definitely with the wrong entree. She railed against the American norm of nonstop, high-speed eating, mindless eating, eating without tasting, and so on. I had to admit that I enjoyed her whole talk. (Please don't tell any of my friends. I still have a reputation to think of.)

After the talk, I accompanied Laurie up to the front of the room to meet Barb, who was chatting with a bunch of people, and I noticed Laurie pointing discreetly at one of them, a guy even a Philistine such as myself recognized from the pages of the *Times* Food section as the popular owner-chef of a posh midtown eatery. As best I could tell, he and Barb were talking about variations on certain recipes. We waited patiently until almost everyone had left, then Laurie rushed up, held out her copy of *Taste* and asked Barb to sign it. She smiled a genuinely friendly smile and asked what parts Laurie had liked the most.

"The part about the roots of umami and our human need to enjoy those tastes," she said, lightly elbowing me in the ribs at the same time, and in a moment the two of them were jabbering back and forth about something I didn't understand.

Finally, noticing that I was just standing there, looking like some dumb jerk who had foolishly accompanied his foodie wife to one of these events, Barb looked up sympathetically, and said, "Don't worry. There is plenty of room in the world for burgers and pizza, and there's nothing wrong with either." I told her that comment came as a genuine relief, since I expected that such a high-brow taste-tester as herself would literally turn up her nose at the sight of a double cheeseburger.

"Not at all," she said, still smiling. "I came to this business late in the game. I loved food, but I couldn't verbalize the nuances I was experiencing between dozens of similar flavors, and I certainly didn't understand the importance of the processes that make food taste a certain way. It was a long journey, but a very enjoyable one. And that's really what I'm trying to convey to people at talks like this: learning about food is just like learning about wine. You can memorize tons of arcane information just to impress people, or you can learn a little bit and discover that it helps you to *enjoy* the experience more than you ever did before. And then you want to learn a little more. It's all about increasing your awareness of what you're tasting and in the process increasing your enjoyment."

"So you're really not telling me to give up pizza?" I asked half-jokingly, shooting a glance at Laurie.

"Absolutely not! What I'm telling you is to enjoy every mouthful of that pizza, slowly and carefully. Appreciate it, and try to identify some of the subtle flavors you are experiencing."

"Mindfulness training for foodies?" I quipped.

"Actually, that's not far off. I think we all eat too much, too fast, and we don't really pay attention to what we're eating. We have access to more food and to a broader range of food than any civilization in history, but we inhale it while we're staring at our cell phones or glued to our computer screens... It's almost criminal. I actually proposed writing laws — only half in jest — to restrict the times when people are allowed to eat. Letting kids eat and drink all day in school classrooms is crazy, and letting people drive with a burger in one hand and a giant-size soda in the other is equally crazy." She paused, took a breath, and regained her composure. "Food should be savored, not ingested, and part of my mission is to convince people that they have enormous potential to enjoy food more, even the same foods they have always eaten. Once you start learning about taste, you discover so many things you were never aware of, even though they were right there on your tongue all along."

While I considered this, she and Laurie chatted some more, and then I remembered the thing that had brought me to this talk in the first place.

"Barb," I interjected familiarly, because she was the kind of person who made you feel like an old friend right away, "what can you tell me about umami? I know it's been a fad for big-city chefs for over a decade, and everybody talks about adding umami to their recipes, but what actually *is* it?"

She grinned. "What is salt? Try to tell me what salty food tastes like without using 'salt' or 'salty' in the definition. The reason that's difficult is because the whole concept of salt and the substance we think of as salt are so basic, not only to our diets, but even to our body chemistry. Umami is the same."

That was the point I wanted to clarify. We didn't even consider umami a basic taste just a few years ago, and now people say that it's one of the five most fundamental tastes humans can recognize. How is that possible?

"First of all, you have to understand that chefs have been experimenting with umami since the discovery of fire. Most of the world has known about umami and appreciated its taste and used it intentionally in cooking for at least two millennia. How long have tomato-based dishes been around in Europe? How long have people eaten aged cheeses? How long have Chinese fermented sauces to flavor their foods? Just because we didn't have a word for it doesn't mean the taste wasn't there, and it certainly doesn't mean that we didn't understand this flavor and use it actively in cooking. We didn't create umami or discover umami, we just woke up to the fact that it's been there all along but we never put a name to it. Now we do have a name for it — precisely because we recognize the taste, and it really does deserve a separate identity to set it apart from the Big 4 of yesteryear."

That made sense, and I thanked her for such a clear explanation. Then I told her, with a know-it-all smirk at Laurie, that a friend was recently telling me some crazy idea about a human craving, a *need* for umami.

"Absolutely!" she said. "No doubt about it. We have data on people who were deprived of umami-rich foods for long periods of time, and when they were able to eat a normal range of things again they over-weighted umami-based foods. In other words, they were naturally drawn to things that had umami flavors. Humans want umami, and yes, they need umami. Trust me, if someone put you on an ultra-bland diet, you would actually come to *crave* umami."

"Crave umami? C'mon, you're exaggerating."

"No, not a bit. Remember, umami is in the amniotic fluid inside the womb and it's also in breast milk. We all spend the first nine months of our lives swimming around in umami, then, as soon as we're born, we start right in drinking it. It's certainly one of the most fundamental tastes we know, from long before birth. Umami is one of the Basic Tastes, a primary sensation that you recognized before you left the womb."

Laurie was nodding in agreement, much too polite to give me that "I told you so" look that I deserved. But I felt like a total idiot. This was the first I'd ever heard that we are born and raised tasting umami, and we naturally want it as we grow older. The whole world, West and East, has been aware of the taste for thousands of years, but only got around to naming it fairly recently. Now I was growing more curious.

"If I wanted to learn more about this, if I wanted to experiment with the flavor, what should I do?" I asked, half-dreading the response.

"Well, the fastest way to OD on umami would be to put a little grated, aged Parmesan cheese on everything you eat. That has a huge umami quotient." She was smiling as I jotted this down in my little journalist's notebook. "But there aren't many types of food you'd want to add aged Parmesan to. A much easier and more practical way is to use more *shoyu*."

Show you? I looked puzzled.

"You know, soy sauce. It's loaded with umami and it's a must-have in your kitchen. No Japanese housewife would cook without a bottle of *shoyu* on the counter, nor would any top chef I know even think of working in a kitchen without it. It's one of the most basic seasonings in the world, an easy way to add umami to almost anything."

Wait, we're talking about soy sauce, right? The black, inky stuff that I use to waterboard my sushi whenever I go to Japanese restaurants?

"Yes, that's the stuff. And you're right, it works beautifully with sushi and sashimi, but trust me when I tell you that they both will taste a *lot* better if you don't try to drown them in the sauce. With shoyu, less really is more. A little bit is enough to add just the flavor you want."

She smiled, almost apologetic for correcting my John Wayne-like approach to sushi, and continued.

"But if you're thinking that soy sauce equals sushi, you're making a BIG mistake. Shoyu works on *so* many things. If you want to experiment with the taste of umami — and I suggest you do — you can't do better than to buy a bottle of good soy sauce and try adding it to everything you cook."

Everything? You mean, like all kinds of Japanese food?

"No, I mean *everything*. Add a dash to your spaghetti sauce, your steak sauce, yes, even your pizza. I occasionally put a few drops of shoyu on vanilla ice cream—"

Whoa! Just the thought of putting that sushi sauce on my ice cream made me shiver.

"No, seriously, it's good. Soy sauce actually enhances the flavor of just about anything. You might think it would cover up other flavors, like the sweetness of the ice cream, but it does just the opposite. It brings out flavors and makes them taste richer instead of sharper. Don't believe me, get a bottle and try it for yourself."

I looked at Laurie, who nodded and said, "I've got a bottle in my kitchen cabinet somewhere."

Barb turned to her. "How long have you had it?"

"Oh, about a year. I tried making *makizushi* at home a while ago," she said proudly. "It was delicious, but Rob — that's my husband — wouldn't touch it."

"Well, throw that bottle away," Barb said with a wave of her hand. "Go buy some fresh shoyu, and don't buy the cheap junk. Even really good shoyu is not expensive. Make sure you get the naturally brewed, fermented kind. Non-fermented, chemical soy sauce is garbage."

Laurie had found a pen and was making notes in the back of her copy of *Taste*. I was impressed.

"So what should I buy?" she asked.

"I like Kikkoman. It's very natural, it doesn't overpower food, and you can get it anywhere. What's more, they make a wide range of different sauces, so you can experiment — low salt, gluten-free, trust me, there's a soy sauce just for you." She was smiling now, and Laurie was scribbling.

We talked for a while longer. Barb gave us her email address and invited us to get in touch any time. I was impressed, both with her knowledge and her friendliness. I could see why Mattson was doing such good business. And what she said had actually piqued my interest in soy sauce, or as she called it, *shoyu*, the Japanese word for the same thing. As we walked out, I found myself thanking Laurie for dragging me to this event. I had actually learned a lot and enjoyed it. And I had really enjoyed meeting Barb Stuckey. I was almost ready to go buy her book and read it for myself.

On the way out of Uris Hall, I was feeling impressed with tonight's program, and absent-mindedly picked up a pamphlet describing the Business School's lecture series. I was skimming it mindlessly as we walked back toward Broadway, and then one name jumped out at me. A presentation about the keys to success in international business by someone named Yuzaburo Mogi. His byline said, "Chairman, Kikkoman Corporation. (MBA '61)."

That stopped me in my tracks. We were just talking about *shoyu* and Barb had mentioned Kikkoman, and now here was a photo of the elderly chairman of that company, and it said he got an MBA at Columbia back in 1961. My brain went into overdrive. Were they serious? 1961? I wasn't sure they even had electricity on the campus back then. A quick calculation for my numerically challenged brain revealed that Mogi was a student there less than fifteen years after the end of World War II. How many Japanese exchange students were studying in the whole U.S. back then? When he was still in grade school in Japan, the U.S. government was herding American-born Japanese into concentration camps. A little over a decade later, this guy Mogi was wandering around New York City as an exchange student.

Columbia was always famous for being more international than other universities, and the "B" School was even more well-known and difficult to get into back then than it is today, so he must have been very smart, very determined, and more than a little brave to take on America back in the good old days.

Unfortunately, it turned out that I'd missed Mr. Mogi's presentation. It was a few weeks earlier, when I was still unenlightened about the virtues of his product. Oh, well, I thought, no big deal. But I resolved to do a little research on his company and its products. I like digging into things, especially company histories, and especially the stories of Asian companies, which for some reason always fascinate me.

Years ago I had lived in Japan for a while, working in financial journalism. I learned to speak the language a little bit, and even read and write it badly, and I definitely fell in love with the culture. I had long ago left Japan and returned to the States to live, but I could still rhapsodize about Japan and its natural beauty, wonderful food, and charming, cultured people at the drop of a hat, something my friends had long since grown weary of. Despite occasional longings and nostalgic memories, I had left that part of my life in the past. Now look at me! I was going to lectures about food! What had happened to me?

"Wow, that was interesting," I said to Laurie, quite seriously.

"You're not just saying that?" She looked dubious.

"No. Barb is a really interesting person, and anyone who can keep me awake for over an hour talking about food has got to be some kind of genius. We should talk to her again."

"How about we try her advice first?" she said.

"You mean, like experimenting with soy sauce in various dishes? I'm game. Maybe we should use my kitchen so Rob doesn't freak out," I suggested.

"And share the sink with cockroaches and last week's pizza boxes and fast food wrappers?" She winced.

"Hey, that's a cheap shot! My place isn't *that* disgusting." Even as I said it, an image of my sink this afternoon floated up in my mind. "Okay, maybe you're right. Let's use your place. I'll keep a bottle of beer in one hand at all times to convince Rob that I'm only observing, not taking part in this foodie-in-the-kitchen nonsense."

She laughed, and we made a deal. We both would shop, I would pay, she would cook, we both would eat. Sounded good to me.

A few days later, we met at a local food store, and as Barb had suggested, I looked for Kikkoman soy sauce. There was a surprising variety to choose from, including the reduced salt and gluten-free versions she had mentioned, and a lot more. They all said "fermented" prominently on the bottle. There were also Kikkoman teriyaki sauces and other items that looked interesting, but what I really wanted was the plain old-fashioned soy sauce. And then I saw it — the little five-ounce teardrop bottle with the red cap that had twin pouring spouts, exactly like I'd seen in a hundred good restaurants both here and in Tokyo. That was the iconic Kikkoman bottle I remembered. I bought it on the spot.

Over the next several days, I visited Rob and Laurie's place a few times and we experimented with all sorts of dishes. Almost immediately I saw what Barb was talking about. Everything seemed to taste a little better when we added *shoyu* to it. For some things, a splash was good; for others, a teaspoon or two; and for others, just a few drops did the job. Nothing came out tasting like soy sauce, and everything really did taste better. I found it was awesomely good with meat dishes and anything with tomato sauce. The *shoyu* was bringing out flavors I hadn't really paid attention to before.

A couple of times, Rob wandered into the kitchen to make fun of me. Laurie winked at me and asked him if he'd like a hamburger to keep his beer company while he watched a basketball game.

"Bring it on!" he said, and ambled back to the living room.

She quickly set about making a hamburger, being sure to shake a little *shoyu* into the meat before she cooked it. When it was done, she put a little more *shoyu* on top, put it on a plate and took it into the living room. We waited a few minutes in the kitchen.

"Wow, honey, this is really good! What did you do to it?"

"Nothing special. Just a little flavor pick-me-up."

I grabbed the bottle of Kikkoman and stared at the label. The clouds had parted and I was beginning to see why this unassuming little bottle, or something just like it, was on the counter in tens, no, hundreds of millions of kitchens around the world. This plain, dark liquid that I had always taken as inseparable from Japanese cuisine was turning out to be good on a whole range of foods that had never been to the Orient. I was actually getting to like it.

"I bet a lot of big-name chefs use this to perk up all sorts of dishes," I said to no one in particular.

17

"I think that's a safe bet," Laurie said. "I know several that do. It's not like a secret or anything. Good chefs use it all the time; they know when and how much to use."

"And the customers?"

She laughed. "I bet if you told most people there was soy sauce in their two-star French cuisine, they wouldn't believe you."

I was beginning to see the story — *shoyu* couldn't make a bad chef into a good one or a good one into a great one, but it certainly could make a wide variety of dishes taste *better*, and that was the kind of magic that chefs everywhere wanted to have.

So just what was this magical sauce, used around the world since reptiles first crawled on land, but unknown to me until quite recently? And who was this company that seemed to dominate the market for high-quality soy sauce-based products? It was time to do what I'm good at: research.

—§—

The next day I went back to the Columbia business school. The big library on the first floor is named for Thomas J. Watson, the founder of IBM, and a dour-looking portrait of old Tom glares out over the big reading room with its dozens of wooden tables and chairs. In some ways, it hasn't changed since I was a student at Columbia (if I remember correctly, John Adams was in the White House). But some of it has. All the kids have smartphones on the tables in front of them, about half of them are listening to something (I doubt it's Warren Buffet lectures) on earphones, and there are rows of computer terminals over on one side of the room.

Despite the advent of the Internet and the modern generation's understandable preference for digital data over dead tree
media, I am still very much an Old School guy. When I want to
find out something involving judgment rather than data sorting,
my first stop is not Google, but my nearest friendly librarian.
Yes, I know that I can get all the same advice — crowd-sourced
or cloud-sourced — on the Web, but there is something about
asking fellow human beings for advice face-to-face and getting
useful answers that appeals to my nineteenth century brain.

So I ambled up to the central desk next to the entranceway
and caught the attention of one of the librarians. I was greeted
by a bright-eyed, friendly guy who told me his name was Raza,
and he was a third-year student from Pakistan. We chatted a
bit and then I asked him if he could help me find a book about
a particular company.

"Absolutely, sir. I will be very glad to help you if I can." I'm
sure he was looking at my suit and thinking I would be asking
about U.S. Steel or Standard Oil or something from the Dark
Ages. When I mentioned Kikkoman, his face did a slight down-
ward scrunch. Aha! I had stumped the local offline data base.

"It's a Japanese food company," I offered. "They make soy
sauce. And their chairman went to this school a l-o-n-g time ago."

He put one forefinger to his lower lip, walked around in a
small half-circle, then back to me.

"Wait here a moment. I think I know just what you want."

As expected, he stepped over to a keyboard, typed in a few
search terms, and in no time at all he was back at the counter
in front of me.

"Yes, we do have it. I could try to direct you to it, but you might have a hard time finding it. If you don't mind waiting here, I would be happy to go get it for you."

How could I refuse an offer like that, I thought. Mr. Raza disappeared, and in a few moments he was back again, holding a hardcover book with a somewhat frayed, yellowed dust jacket. He passed it to me with two hands, ceremoniously.

I took a look at the cover: *The Kikkoman Chronicles.*[2] By somebody named Ronald Yates, whom the cover informed me was a *Chicago Tribune* writer. Interesting. I skimmed the table of contents and flipped a few pages. This looked like a serious history of the company, its products, and its management. To some kid doing a case study for his MBA, perhaps a bit off the mark, but for me, right now, interested to learn more about soy sauce and the companies that make it, it was perfect. I thanked him, checked out the book, and headed back downtown to read.

What I discovered was an amazing story. Kikkoman, as it turns out, is almost 400 years old! It must be one of the oldest continuously operating companies in the world. The guy whose picture I saw, Mr. Mogi, comes from one of the original families that guided the enterprise more than a century ago. The Mogis have been running Kikkoman for a long time, not to perpetuate a dynasty but to guarantee that brewing methods don't change, quality doesn't change, and taste doesn't change. If I got the drift of the book correctly, Kikkoman *shoyu* has been made pretty much the same way for four centuries. And from everything I could sense about the family, it will be made the same way four centuries from now, even if it's made in a factory on the Moon. *Shoyu* is sacred, and that means no shortcuts, no additives, no messing with the process or the recipe.

How many things in the modern world hold to that mission? The only ones I can think of are pretty small businesses. Kikkoman has been a major company listed on the Tokyo Stock Exchange for over half a century. This was becoming a more and more interesting story. I asked myself: How could any company with a 400-year-old recipe stay in business without changing it? How could they ramp up production from supplying their own little village to supplying a giant city (Tokyo was the biggest city in the world three centuries ago) to making enough to meet global demand, and still not vary the taste? And how could anyone keep up that level of quality control with a brewed product?

Distilled liquors (vodka, gin, whisky, etc.) are another whole story — controlling the taste of the output is a lot more scientific. But fermenting means bringing in Mother Nature as a full equity partner, working with live fungi and molds, and somehow accounting for all the variables that a living, growing thing adds to the final mix that will become your product. From the little I gleaned from reading the book, making *shoyu* really looks like a 17th century all-natural process that could go horribly wrong at any of several stages, resulting in wild variations in taste. And that seemed to be the one thing that Kikkoman will not tolerate. — always the same taste, always the same quality, regardless of where it is made. I actually looked up from the book a couple of times and shook my head. Hard to believe. Someone must really be fanatical about making *shoyu* in order to pull this off.

If you'll pardon the phrase, the story fermented in my brain overnight, and in the morning I resolved to track down the author of *Kikkoman Chronicles* and see what he could tell me. This time I relied on the speed and efficiency of the Internet, and in no time at all I had located ex-*Chicago Tribune* writer Ron Yates. Apparently he had retired from the Trib long ago, moved out of Chicago, and settled in southern California — a common enough story.

I sent him a mail, asking a few questions about the book, about *shoyu*, and about Kikkoman. His reply was prompt, friendly, and detailed. Once a writer, always a writer! We exchanged a couple more mails, then he included a phone number and I rang him up.

We chatted for about twenty minutes. I complimented him on his book and said I still had a lot of questions. He surprised me by remembering so much about a story he wrote almost twenty years ago. "They were a good company, and it was a damn good story," he said. "I enjoyed working on that book and working together with Kikkoman to research it. But there's a lot more to say. I sometimes think I should write a sequel, but..."

I told him I was becoming seriously interested in investigating *shoyu*, and more than that, with the one company whose name was synonymous with top-quality *shoyu* worldwide. And I had lots of questions before I could even begin to take this seriously as a writing project. Ron was way ahead of me.

"Well, why don't we get off the damn phone and talk about this over a bottle of wine?" he said. Now he was talking my language! I'm always happy to talk to another professional writer, especially one with published books to his name, and before I knew it I had agreed to fly out to the West Coast and meet with Ron to learn a little more about the *shoyu* business.

Wine Country

2

*R*on Yates had been so informative and friendly on the phone that I decided I could afford to take a couple of days to go talk to him. I had no deep purpose in mind, just the knowledge that he's a writer and I'm a writer, and we've both published multiple books, so we would definitely have things to talk about. I also figured he was my "1-stop shop" for information on *shoyu* and Kikkoman. I got a good sense of the guy from our phone chat and I knew we would get along, so a trip to California seemed worthwhile.

Ron said he lived in a small town called Temecula, about halfway between LA and San Diego, and I could travel from either one, but that I might find the latter a more relaxing drive. I knew he was right, having fought my way in and out of LA too many times.

So it was that on a bright Sunday morning in late May I arrived in San Diego. I picked up a rental car and started driving north, towards LA. It was a gorgeous sunny day, and the air felt like Hawaii – warm and moist but not heavy. Just a comfortable cocoon of warmth to envelop you as you walked or drove. And since this was California, everybody drove.

I was moving at high speed, glad that I'd opted for a bigger car than I usually reserve. Californians think their freeways are local versions of the Autobahn, and speed limit signs are posted mostly as humorous conversation pieces. I sailed past Escondido doing 70 mph, yet cars were passing me by as if I were pedaling instead of driving.

What Ron hadn't told me about his location was that Temecula is part of what is known as the South Coast wine country. This was news to me. Napa-Sonoma was old hat, an area I knew quite well, and recently I was getting to know the Central Coast wineries. I like exploring and searching for interesting wines that are neither insanely popular nor ridiculously expensive. You can still do that in Sonoma County, though Napa is a lost cause. But in all my meanderings around California's zillions of acres of vineyards, I had never heard that there were any decent wineries south of LA. I was about to get a schooling.

Ron had kindly reserved a room for me at some place called the South Coast Winery Resort and Spa. I assumed it was a fancy name for an inexpensive roadside motel. When I pulled up to the front gate, though, my jaw almost dropped. Beyond an attractive stone entrance lay a huge estate comprised of several buildings, including a multi-story hotel in the middle, and gorgeous green vineyards wrapping around both sides. I drove up to the hotel and parked my car. At the front desk, a cheery blonde receptionist was expecting me. I said I didn't need anyone to help with my luggage, I was traveling light and could bring my own bags up to my room.

"Oh, you're not staying in the hotel, Mr. Russell," she said coyly.

"But you just told me my reservation was confirmed in your system..."

"Yes, sir. But not for the hotel. You'll be staying in one of our villas." She reached under the counter and produced a key and a map.

"Just drive around the back of the hotel, along the vineyard road. You'll pass a line of villas." She ran an artistically decorated fingernail around one side of the little map. "They all have numbers on the roof. You'll be in No. 24, which is almost at the end of the line. I hope you enjoy your stay!"

The energy and enthusiasm in the last remark, which would have been uttered in a deadpan monotone in most Manhattan hotels, was like a slap in the face, waking me up. OMG! I'm in SoCal again! Everyone is cheery and healthy and blonde and full of Happy Energy. A friend who grew up not far from here once assured me the state of California puts drugs in the water supply to keep everyone smiling day after day. Looking at the hotel staff, I believed him.

The so-called villas turned out to be two dozen cloverleaf-shaped units with four individual villas each. It sounds small, but each individual "villa" turned out to be very generously proportioned. I stepped inside No. 24, which was pleasantly air conditioned in anticipation of my arrival, and immediately spied on the little dining table a bottle of red wine and two glasses. The wine bore the label of the South Coast Winery. Obviously, a complimentary bottle of the cheapest house wine, something they could easily afford to give away to guests. House plonk, as my friends Down Under would say. It was an unusual blend, too, Syrah, Granache and Mourvedre, or something like that. There was a corkscrew right on the table, so just thirty seconds inside my new lodgings, I opened a bottle of the local swill. If this was to be an educational trip, let the education begin!

I poured myself a generous glass, then wandered into the spacious bedroom and opened the curtains. In front of me stretched several acres of green vineyards sloping down a sun-drenched hillside. It looked like an oil painting. Thoughts of vines and grapes brought me back to the glass in my hand. Preparing for the worst, I took a sip. And then another, and then finished off the glass in short order. Unbelievable! This was really good! Not "free bottle of cheap grape juice you find in your hotel room" good, but "I would definitely order this in a restaurant" good. This trip was starting to look better already.

I pulled the phone from my pocket and rang Ron Yates.

"Are you settled in?" he said, and asked how I liked the hotel.

I told him I had only been there two minutes but was already prepared to stay for a month or so, provided they kept stocking my room with fresh bottles of wine every day.

"I'll talk to the management and see what they can do," he said with a laugh.

We agreed to meet for a late lunch. I asked if there was a good restaurant around and he laughed. "People drive an hour or more to dine at your hotel. You wouldn't want to miss the food." For a late-afternoon meal, he suggested the terrace at the Vineyard Rose a hundred yards or so from where I'd checked in. He said we wouldn't even be able to get tables there if it were a Saturday, but as it was past noon on a Sunday, most of the guests would be heading home to San Diego or Los Angeles.

As the appointed hour approached, I dug out the little map the girl had given me at the front desk and found my way to the Vineyard Rose restaurant. I found the main entrance and stepped inside, out of the sun and into a cool, airy expanse with one high-ceilinged room after the next, some of them decorated with framed wine awards, jeroboam bottles from famous wineries, and a huge American flag hanging high in the rafters. I tentatively mentioned to the maitre d' that I was coming to meet a friend, a Mr. Yates, and—. He brightened immediately at the mention of Ron's name and guided me outside to the terrace in the back, where he pointed to a distinguished-looking fellow comfortably seated in a wicker armchair.

Ron Yates, I realized, was a glimpse of what I would look like in a few years. He seemed totally relaxed in a classy blue polo shirt, sunglasses and shorts, with a light green ball cap that said "U.S. Virgin Islands" and a weathered smile that looked right at home in the southern California sun. He stood up with unexpected energy and greeted me warmly; we shook hands and sat down.

"They have a good Gewurtztraminer here," he said without preamble. "You like wine, right?"

Was that a trick question? I reminded him that I had been a working journalist myself. Beyond that, I assured him that I loved wine. Were we about to enjoy some special version of that distinctive Alsatian wine?

Not at all, he corrected with a big smile. We were in California, he said. We could get cited by the local police for

27

ordering out-of-state wine. With that, he called a waiter over and ordered two glasses of the local Gewurtztraminer.

We set about talking right away, even before the drinks arrived and long before the food showed up. Ron had worked for the *Chicago Tribune* for a quarter of a century, as a foreign correspondent, national correspondent, and financial writer. Back in the day, he had covered Asia when every journalist worth his martini wanted to be there. He'd covered the fall of Saigon in '75 and the Tiananmen Square massacre in '89. He lived in Japan for ten years, twice as the *Trib's* Tokyo Bureau Chief. He'd also worked the Latin American beat, coving revolutions in Nicaragua, El Salvador and Guatemala. My respect for the guy across the table was soaring and we hadn't even started in on the wine yet.

Having spent several years in Japan myself, I was eager to touch base with him on a number of points. It soon became apparent that Ron Yates had been his paper's point man in Tokyo at a time when Internet journalism did not exist and foreign journalists — at least those from papers like the NY and LA *Times*, the *Washington Post* and the *Chicago Tribune* — were treated with a level of respect and courtesy that did not survive the transition to the new millennium.

After many years abroad, Ron came back to Chicago to rejoin the paper's home office, and also to teach journalism at the University of Illinois' College of Media, where he became a professor and later on, dean.

Back on a writer's desk in Chicago, he tackled a range of stories, but one in particular caught his eye: a famous Japanese food company he remembered from Tokyo had set up a plant a couple of hours away in southern Wisconsin. And not on the outskirts of a major city, like Milwaukee or Madison, but in the middle of nowhere, in a very rural part of a rural state. The word was they were making soy sauce there with local labor. That in itself was a story: Local farmhands who might have found work in one of the state's hundreds of breweries a couple of decades ago were now brewing soy sauce. But most interesting of all, he noticed, the company was getting rave reviews from the small town where it was located, the larger community in which it operated, and even the state government that was showcasing it.

In 1991 he attended a meeting of the Japan-Midwest Society in Milwaukee and met the head of Kikkoman Corporation, Mr. Yuzaburo Mogi — the same guy whose speech I had missed in New York several weeks ago. Yates said he remembered soy sauce fondly from his years in Japan and that he always preferred Kikkoman to all other brands of *shoyu*. As he remembers it, Mr. Mogi smiled and said in perfect English, "Of course. Because it's the best!" They chatted a bit, and Mogi told him about the centuries-old natural brewing process that Kikkoman had brought to the U.S., and said they were very proud of their growing success in America. In Ron's words, "I decided that this was a company ripe for a cover story in the *Chicago Tribune* Sunday Magazine."

So he made a few trips up to little Walworth, WI, population 1,800 at that time. He interviewed managers, employees, and outside contractors of the Kikkoman plant, then talked to people in the community about Kikkoman as a corporate citizen. Back in Chicago, he eventually wrote up a long pictorial feature on the Japanese company in our midst, which was published in 1993.

Having been in Japan in the 1990s, I happened to know something about this period from first-hand experience. The early part of that decade was the height of trade friction between the U.S. and Japan. U.S. senators were smashing Japanese boom boxes on the steps of the Capitol with sledgehammers, Detroit carmakers were banning workers from parking Japanese-brand cars in their lots, and corporate raider T. Boone Pickens grabbed a microphone to argue that he was being discriminated against in Tokyo. Soon American business was up in arms over what they saw as the exclusionist policies of Japanese corporate organizations called *keiretsu*. As I remembered it, that was not a good time to be a Japanese business operating in the U.S.

"Quite right," Ron replied. "There was still a lot of anti-Japanese sentiment around, especially in Detroit and other big manufacturing towns in the early nineties. But not in Walworth, Wisconsin, that's for sure. And probably a lot of the nonsense being written about Japanese business back then contributed to the wave of positive response my article produced. It turned into one of the most popular stories I'd ever done. Mail just kept pouring in. People knew the Kikkoman name and they knew the product, and they thought the story of how this foreign company had bent over backwards to fit into the landscape of rural America and become a truly good neighbor was inspirational and a good model for other firms, domestic included."

Of course, the Japanese executives at Kikkoman's plant in Walworth sent the *Tribune* feature back to President Mogi in Tokyo, and it was not long before Ron's phone was ringing. One of the local execs in Walworth asked if he'd like to dig a little deeper into their company's history and current operations and write about it in greater detail. That led to the book I had picked up in New York, which came out just before the end of the decade.

To me, a lover of history in general and the history of Japanese business in particular, *Kikkoman Chronicles* is a fascinating book — a good study of the company's almost 400-year history, from its origins to the opening of its second U.S. factory in 1996, as well as a first-ever inside look at how real, natural *shoyu* is made. It is well written, authoritative, and highly informative. I told Ron exactly what I thought, and he thanked me.

"In some ways, it's just as accurate today as it was when McGraw-Hill first put it out," he said. We were both on our third or fourth glass of wine now and finishing excellent entrees. I could see why the restaurant was so famous. Ron continued, "The basics at Kikkoman don't change, probably will never change. So the book is still accurate, and yet, in another sense, it's a bit out of date."

I asked why.

"Because it focuses almost entirely on the U.S., and Kikkoman is no longer a U.S.-oriented business. It's a global business, with huge operations in Europe and Asia outside of Japan. In fact, Kikkoman is one of the best examples I know of a truly global company."

We ate and drank and talked some more. I asked him lots of questions about the people he had met, the corporate culture he had seen, and the parent company itself. All of his answers drew me further and further into a wild idea that had begun forming even as I read his book on the plane to San Diego.

"Ron, on the phone you mentioned something about doing a follow-up to your book. Do you really think there's enough information to warrant another in-depth look at Kikkoman, looking at it now as a global company?

He paused maybe a nanosecond.

"More than enough. Not only has the company grown and expanded around the world, but there are so many good stories to tell. If I had the time, I would love to do a second book on Kikkoman and focus more on its corporate culture, talk less about the history and try to get at the essence of the firm in different places around the world."

"So why don't you?" I wondered out loud.

"Frankly, I don't have the time. It would take several months to fly around the world and get some grasp of the company's global operations, then write up the results into a really readable book. That would be fun, but…" He paused. "I'm caught up in another project."

He held up a copy of *Finding Billy Battles*, the first volume in a trilogy of historical novels he was writing. This, he said, was his main job now, and it would be some time before he would finish the last one. However, at my suggestion that perhaps if he were busy and unable to do a book on Kikkoman, that I might try it myself, he was two-thumbs-up. "Go for it!" he said. "Fabulous company, great people, and I know there's a lot more material out there than I squeezed into *Chronicles*. Go out and find it."

We talked about it a little more and Ron encouraged me to take on the project and do a good job.

Up until that point, I had only been curious about Kikkoman and its main product and had not seriously entertained the idea of turning this into a new book project. And yet, I knew the idea was percolating in my subconscious, otherwise, why would I have come all this way to talk to Ron? I wanted his personal and professional evaluation of the merit behind this crazy idea. Go investigate Kikkoman? After an American author had already done so once? But he said yes, it made sense, there was still a good story out there to explore, and even just an update to *Chronicles* was a good idea. Sitting there on the sunlit patio of a hotel restaurant in the southern California wine country, much closer to Mexico than to Napa and several sheets to the wind, I began to take this project seriously. After all, I hadn't done a new book for years, and my wife insists I'm always happier when I have a book project in hand. Maybe she's just happier when I'm on the road for weeks at a time, who knows?

I asked Ron if he still had any connections with the company, and he said yes, one or two. Then I asked if he could use those connections to get a back-channel okay for me to work on this book. I told him I didn't want support, I really wanted to approach this story as an independent writer, looking at it as a journalist would, from the outside. On the other hand, I didn't want to show up at one of Kikkoman's overseas offices and find the doors locked in my face. As I had done with other corporate investigations in the past, I wanted cooperation in exchange for the promise of a fair story. That was my commitment: I would paint a fair picture, warts and all — if there were warts to show

— but a fair, balanced picture no matter what. All I wanted was a chance to talk to people.

He agreed, we shook hands, and ordered another bottle of wine. What was I getting into?

Airplane Reading

I enjoyed my visit with Ron Yates very much. I enjoyed the resort he introduced me to, and I enjoyed the food and wine immensely. But most of all, I enjoyed a new feeling of accomplishment, because a chance conversation in New York City about umami had led me to meet one of America's experts on food, and her suggestion had ultimately led me to discover Ron's book. I could have skimmed it and learned what I needed to know about soy sauce very quickly, but instead, I read it carefully, and it deepened my interest in the Rolls Royce of *shoyu*, a company called Kikkoman. That curiosity had taken me to California and a face-to-face meeting with the author.

I think Ron could sense that I was a book author in search of a book project, whether my conscious mind realized that or not. Now I had finally found something solid to investigate — not food (which is not my strong suit anyway), but a Japan-born global company, a centuries-old corporate legacy, and a cross-cultural business venture, all things that are right up my alley. Now I had more than an interesting story about searching out the world's No. 1 producer of high-quality soy sauce. I had a new book project that involved digging into a company's past and present to discover its essence — what makes it tick, and most importantly, what makes it successful in different cultures.

Back in Temecula, I'd asked Ron how he would do this research if he were to take on the task I'd just set for myself. He thought a moment, then replied in a steady, measured tone: "I would start at the same place I did twenty years ago, Walworth, Wisconsin. That's still the flagship, the biggest *shoyu* plant outside of Japan, and it's where Kikkoman got started in the U.S. Then you should visit Folsom here in California, where they built a second plant, which was too late to be covered in my book. Then I'd probably go to Holland to see their European factory, and maybe Germany, where they have a big trading company, and finally, to Asia. There are a few Kikkoman operations in China, and if you have enough time and budget, you should go see them. But they basically serve local markets there, not all of Asia. If it were me, I'd go to Taiwan or maybe to Singapore... Singapore would probably give you the best idea of how Kikkoman is developing its business in the Asian markets."

All that sounded like good advice from a guy who had spent years in Asia and knew Kikkoman a lot better than I did. For the moment, anyway.

I flew back to New York to make my preparations for what Ron had assured me would be a round-the-world trip if I decided to do approach it seriously, and that's the only way I approach a book project. I also wanted to wait for word that Kikkoman would grant me access to their facilities wherever I went. I was only half-finished packing when Ron's mail arrived with a big "OK" emoji and an admonition to have fun, talk to lots of people, not only Kikkoman execs, and pass along his best wishes to anyone who might still remember him.

I went online that evening and booked a flight to Chicago for the following day and a rental car to take me to Wisconsin.

During the flight from New York to Chicago, I finished *Kikkoman Chronicles* and read some other research materials I'd collected.

There was so much to study about the company, its history, the process of making *shoyu*, and what the hell *shoyu* was in the first place. Being much more methodical about work than about my personal life, I organized my thick stack of print-outs on the empty seat next to me, and sorted through the collection of digital documents stored in my laptop, and settled down to get acquainted with the material.

Where to start? Before the beginning, as one of my professors used to say. Not with *shoyu*, but with its key ingredient: soy. I discovered that soybeans have been providing humankind with nutrition for more than 2,000 years. First cultivated in China and later in Korea and Japan, soy in various forms has been used as a part of Asian diets across the millennia. Among other roles, it supplies much of the protein that Western peoples obtained from meat and milk, but soy supplies this protein from a healthier, plant-based source. Protein aside, soybeans are loaded with nutrients, some of which are well known and some of which modern science is just beginning to understand.

One point seems clear: fermenting soybeans turbo-charges their nutritional value. It breaks down their chemical structure, changing complex carbohydrates and various proteins into more digestible forms. It also improves the bioavailability of half a dozen important minerals and isoflavones that are present in raw soybeans. Recent medical studies have shown that fermented soy products can help protect against cancer, lower blood cholesterol (I discovered that for decades the Italian government has been supplying free soy protein to doctors who are treating patients for high cholesterol), and improve the health of the intestinal tract (you read a lot these days about the bacteria in the gut being so important to our overall health, yet so poorly understood; soy seems to be one of the things that help your gut). In short, fermented soy products — such as tofu, *natto*, tempeh, *miso*, and yes, soy sauce or *shoyu* — are generally healthy things to be consuming. That was interesting, because I'd always heard about tofu and *natto* being good for you, but I didn't eat much of either after I left Japan.

What was particularly interesting to me was that this "wonder food" that has been a key player in maintaining health throughout half the world for 2,000 years is now grown widely outside Asia. In fact, the world's No. 1 producer of soybeans is the United States. If that's the case, you might expect Americans to be a lot healthier than they are, but a cursory investigation shows that almost none of America's 83 million metric tonnes of soybeans is used for human food. Instead, there is a massive, $20 billion industry turning almost the entire annual crop into other, far less healthy products that can be traded easily, such as soy meal for animal feed. Unless your local grocer stocks tofu or *edamame* green beans, it is rare to find any food in the U.S. that is made from whole soybeans.

With that disappointing realization, I turned to *shoyu*, a product of soybean fermentation only recently introduced to North America. It, too, has a history stretching back thousands of years, and for that reason is sometimes called "the oldest condiment." But the origins of *shoyu* are murky, spiced with legend, and like all stories of food or wine from the ancient world, impossible to verify, in part because we cannot taste the different products that might qualify as ancestors of the modern versions we have come to know. Roman wine was famous all across the continent before Julius Caesar was born, but what did it taste like? Would we love it or spit it out? No one knows for certain.

There are no records of the first production of *shoyu*'s long-lost ancestor, but we think it may have happened in China somewhere around the third or fourth century CE. That doesn't give the average Western reader much of a handle on the time period. Noting that this was the period after the fall of the Han Dynasty and the beginning of the Six Kingdoms era doesn't help much. But if I told you that this was around the time that Constantine became emperor and the Nicene Creed was composed, even a high school student might get a general sense that this happened way before Twitter appeared. This was, like, you know, a long time ago.

It's important to note that all the histories of "soy sauce" are talking about a very early concoction, nothing at all like the tasty liquid we call by that name today. Roughly 2,000 years ago, the Chinese had a fermented, meat-based sauce called *jiang* that is often identified as the earliest ancestor of *shoyu*, but I'm willing to bet it tasted pretty nasty. It was very salty, and its original role was to preserve foods. Fermenting fish with soybeans was another mouth-watering pastime, and over the centuries these various ways to preserve food matured and changed, and at some point fermented soybeans became the main ingredient instead of a side player. This preservative ultimately made its way to Japan, where it was known as *hishio.* We have written records of *hishio* dating back to about 700. But did *hishio* become *shoyu*, and how did *shoyu* become popular?

"Who cares?" you say, but just hang on. The history gets a lot more interesting very soon. It was another Chinese import, Buddhism, that helped to boost *shoyu*'s popularity. From about the sixth century onward, Buddhism spread in Japan, espousing among other things an essentially vegetarian lifestyle. As Japanese cuisine gradually shifted from meat-based dishes to vegetable-based dishes, so did people's preference for seasonings and condiments. One story says that around 1300, a Zen monk returned from his studies in China (classical China was like the ancient world's Wikipedia), and brought back the art of making *miso* paste. Legend has it that he noticed the liquid running off from the *miso* was pretty tasty. Thus, *tamari* soy sauce was born. (*Tamari* is basically soy sauce made without wheat.)

The main point here is that some version of soy sauce has been around for centuries. The story becomes more interesting around 1700, when we find multiple families making early versions of *shoyu* in Japan (tough as the work is, making shoyu was probably easier than working in the rice fields all day). Some of these families produced not just enough for themselves and their relatives and neighbors, but an excess amount that could be sold in their village and beyond. Since the constant warring

of an earlier era had come to an end, a vibrant commercial culture was growing in places like Osaka and Edo (today's Tokyo).
Shoyu was obviously a mainstream commodity in Osaka by
1600, and in Edo a few decades later. By 1700, there was so
much *shoyu* being produced that it could be exported. Yes, we
have written records from the Dutch East India Company (the
only ships allowed to trade with Japan at that time), and one of
their cargo manifests from 1737 lists seventh-five large barrels
of *shoyu*. In that day, a "large" barrel could be as big as a house,
so we don't really know how much *shoyu* was exported, but we
do know that thirty-five barrels of the sauce were sent back to
the Netherlands. It is an absolute certainty that some portion of
such an unusual and precious cargo from the mysterious Orient
would have made its way directly to the Imperial Palace, where
it would be consumed by royalty and also packaged as gifts to
other royals around Europe. By the late 1700s, many well-to-do
Europeans (and those who cooked for them) were familiar with
this mysterious sauce from the East and interested enough in
its origins that in 1781, a Dutch scholar who had lived in Japan
actually wrote a book explaining how *shoyu* was made.

From this period onwards, *shoyu* production in Japan really
took off, but now we need to backtrack a little bit and splice
in the Kikkoman story. The full history is told in detail in Ron
Yates' excellent book, and I don't want to spoil that for you, but
some readers may want a shortened, fast food version that they
can consume right now. For those too impatient to find and
read Ron's book, and at the risk of repeating some of what he
says there, let me provide a simple overview to this fascinating

history. Kikkoman is one company where history truly matters: In a sense, the company *is* its history.

The story of Kikkoman's origins is rich in drama, easily good material for a major film, except that Hollywood doesn't do many samurai epics. And this starts as a real samurai epic, with bloody battles, life-threatening suspense, and a mother's determination to protect her son. It dates back to the early 1600s, a time when the very first European settlers were coming to the New World they called America. In Japan, it was a time of constantly feuding warlords, shifting allegiances, and political power plays. Our heroine, Shige Maki (*she-gay mah-key*), lived with her husband and young son inside Osaka Castle, where her husband was a samurai in the service of the local warlord. Another warlord, the man who would soon become the most famous shogun (supreme general) in the country, laid siege to the castle, and in the battle thousands of people died, including Maki's husband. She knew that once the shogun's army entered the castle grounds she and her young son would be put to the sword. While that might have been seen as a noble and proper end for a samurai's wife, she had no desire to see their young son chopped to pieces for a crime he knew nothing of. And so she determined to do the unthinkable, the virtually impossible — escape. She disguised herself and her son as peasants — again, something few women of samurai birth would consider under any circumstances — and used the chaos of the battle as cover for their escape.

But fleeing certain death at the hands of her husband's enemies was only the beginning of her journey. Still dressed as peasants, they wandered hundreds of miles northeast toward the capital city of Edo and then beyond, eventually settling in a small community about 30 miles (roughly 50 km) east of Edo in what is now a narrow corner of Chiba Prefecture. Knowing that her son's life would always be in jeopardy if he retained his father's name or samurai ways, she changed her family name from Maki to Mogi, took up rice farming (the work of most peasants) and tried to blend in with the quiet village life in the small hamlet of Noda over the next few decades.

Although for many years Maki devoted herself to cultivating rice, we must assume that she somehow encountered and then set about learning another trade. For it was during this time that she learned the secret arts of making *shoyu*, a process handed down by oral tradition for centuries in Japan, and as we noted, many centuries before that in China. It was the Japanese who discovered that adding wheat to the mixture (i.e., changing *tamari* into *shoyu*) improved the flavor considerably, and the stage was set for hundreds of families in villages across the country to produce small batches of *shoyu* for themselves and their neighbors.

As Fate would have it, one of the best places in Japan to make *shoyu* turns out to be the little village of Noda, where Maki, now Mogi, had gone into hiding. Clean water is essential for *shoyu* production, and Noda is blessed with two rivers that gave it not only fresh water, but also easy access to the fields of soybeans and wheat that grew nearby on the Kanto plain. The Edo River not only transported these raw materials from inland to Noda, but also led to the sea, where other families produced salt, the other essential ingredient. Thanks to its excellent location, many families in and around Noda were already making small batches, and over the next century the area would become home to scores of *shoyu* producers of various sizes.

We can only imagine why the former wife of a samurai, who now lived as a lowly peasant, doing the back-breaking work of rice farming day after day, became interested in the process of making *shoyu*. Perhaps one of her friends showed her their family's big pots of fermenting mash and invited Mogi to taste it, or perhaps she helped out a friend whose father had fallen ill and she spent one season learning to produce *shoyu* instead of growing rice. Whatever the occasion that brought Mogi and *shoyu*-making together did more than change business in the little town of Noda. It fundamentally changed Japanese culture, and eventually changed the world as well.

Mogi learned that by properly mixing simple ingredients — soybeans, wheat, water, and salt — one could make good-tasting *shoyu*. It was a slow, time-consuming process that depended on natural fermentation, which meant that much could go wrong. Even slight variations in temperature during a months-long process could spoil the mix. But if done right, the results were impressive.

Not being the dutiful daughter of a centuries-old *shoyu*-making family, Mogi must have felt more free to experiment with the traditional recipe she encountered, and in time she made individual changes to the process, which resulted in a noticeably richer taste. She went into production for herself, and in time the brand that she and her descendants created began to gain fans. The rest, as they say, is history.

There were already many prominent *shoyu* producers in the Noda area, and one of them was the Takanashi family. By the time the original Mogi had passed on and her son and grandchildren had taken over the business, the Mogis and Takanashis had intermarried and shared their production knowledge and their secrets about the mysteries of fermentation. Remember that there was nothing like modern science at the time; people believed that spirits caused the soy and wheat to ferment and produce *shoyu*, as if by magic. But the successful families knew how to help the spirits along, and they gradually became prominent *shoyu* producers in an area already famous for the quality of the sauce they were making.

Both of their businesses grew rapidly. Gradually, the Mogi and Takahashi families became leaders not only of *shoyu* production in the Noda area, but of the Noda economy in general. As their reputations expanded, so did their business. Production volume increased, and soon they were shipping larger barrels of *shoyu* downriver to Edo, the capital of this now-peaceful land. Edo merchants were becoming a powerful new social class themselves, competing to sell the finest foods and dry goods to well-to-do households in the capital. In time, Mogi's *shoyu* became one of those sought-after products, and much later would be selected as the only *shoyu* to be served to the Emperor himself.

In 1867, the era of shoguns ended, Edo became Tokyo, and Japan's modern era began. The dominant *shoyu* makers of Noda were ready to meet the challenges of the new era. In

1887, they formed the Noda Shoyu Brewers' Association, a pioneering industry group of some of the best producers in the area. Among its other activities, the Association bought raw materials in larger quantities than any of its individual members could afford and controlled the quality of the *shoyu* produced under its name. This brought even greater recognition to the high quality of the soy sauce made in Noda, and guaranteed them a significant share of the Tokyo market. Of course, *shoyu* was produced all over Japan; there were well over 10,000 registered makers and probably as many more very small, unregistered producers.

Then, as now, people in the western side of the country (from Kyoto to Kyushu) and the eastern side of the country (from Tokyo to the northern provinces) were fiercely proud of their disparate cultural heritages, of which diet has always been one of the most prominent features. Among their various disagreements on taste, the "proper" style of *shoyu* was a point of contention. Western *shoyu* did not taste the same as Eastern *shoyu*, the latter having gradually come to be identified with Noda-produced *shoyu*. However, as the first railroads spread out from Tokyo and rail networks spanned the nation from the late nineteenth to early twentieth centuries, it became cheaper and easier to ship goods nationwide. Soon "Edo-style" *shoyu* was available everywhere, and the taste of the Noda sauce won the day. By roughly the time of World War I, the Noda Shoyu Brewers' Association had developed a national market for its products.

At about this time, the market focus also shifted, from wholesalers to individual consumers, and the packaging shifted accordingly, from 18-liter (a bit less than five gallons) wooden barrels to smaller glass bottles, which didn't leak and were easier to store in the kitchen. The expanding market and the increasing focus on consumers put pressure on the Noda makers to further improve quality and to demand that their own suppliers deliver world-class, often imported raw materials. This should have had a disastrous effect on sales, pushing retail prices skyward, but by buying as an industry group and controlling costs, the Noda makers were able to offer consumers superior quality for a reasonable price. This only further sealed their already strong reputation.

Probably most of the *shoyu* that was sold over the centuries in old Edo had no name. Large barrels of unbranded *shoyu* were exactly what the wholesalers wanted. They retained the rights to market it as they pleased and brand it with their own house brands if they so chose. But by the time Edo had changed its name to Tokyo and trade with Western nations began to flourish, a few producer brands were gaining recognition. One of the handful that became popular was the Mogi family's premier brand, Kikkoman.

The famous logo that has been in use for many generations now shows a hexagonal shape, representing a tortoise shell (*kikko*), inside of which is a stylized version the symbol for 10,000 (*man*). In ancient China, the character for 10,000 was used to denote the infinite or something too large to count. Similarly, an old Japanese proverb said that a tortoise lives for 10,000 years. Thus, the image of the character *man* imposed over a *kikko* (tortoise shell) symbolized a long (and healthy) life.

Soon this distinctive logo was soon finding its way across the seas on Western merchant ships. As we noted earlier, Dutch traders who visited the port of Nagasaki regularly from the 1600s onward took home amphora-like ceramic pots of *shoyu*, which became a prized flavoring at royal kitchens across Europe. We don't know for sure if Kikkoman-brand *shoyu* was included among these early exports, but Europe's experience with the taste of soy sauce certainly set the stage for the tremendous reception it won at world's fairs in the late nineteenth century. Later in my travels I would be shown a gold medal awarded to Kikkoman *shoyu* at the Paris World's Fair of 1900, merely one in a long line of awards the brand acquired during this period.

The years after World War I were not good for Japan. As in most other countries, the war brought inflation, leading to riots and strikes and increasing turmoil throughout the economy, encouraging sensible businessmen to look for financial structures that promised stability. This was the background for the 1917 formation of the Noda Shoyu Company, one of the nation's new joint-stock enterprises that would serve as a kind of holding company for the principal business assets of two of the greatest Noda families, Mogi and Takanashi. The new company encompassed multiple businesses, from *shoyu* production to transportation, marketing, and even finance.

Noda Shoyu sold its main product under almost three dozen different brand names. However, the gold standard among them was still the Kikkoman brand, which had been gaining reputation and market share in Tokyo for decades and was already well known to consumers through its very early and active advertising campaigns. In a wise marketing move, the new company decided to consolidate its identity around one flagship brand, and Kikkoman was the natural choice.

In a very real sense, then, the creation of the Noda Shoyu Company marked the beginning of the company we know today as Kikkoman, although the product itself goes back to the widow Maki, who came to Noda in disguise and eventually learned to make *shoyu* her own way back in the 1600s.

The Noda Shoyu enterprise was a perfect mirror of the times in which it was created, intent on preserving honored traditions while at the same time taking advantage of all that Western science had to offer. Thus, the company continued to make *shoyu* in the same basic way that it had before, but actively tried out new manufacturing techniques, modernizing its production plants with mechanical conveyors and elevators to move raw materials, hydraulic presses, and modern boilers. It also invested heavily in research and development. Remember that this was the 1920s, yet the company was already active in R&D. It also moved to take its distribution and marketing out of the hands of regional and local wholesalers, and manage the whole operation from Noda, also a fairly radical step at the time. The company became not only the main business in Noda, but also its benefactor and the leading contributor to the city's growth, helping to build local schools, the town hospital, library, town hall, and much more.

One last thing of note from this era was the company's concerted efforts at what we would now call "employee relations." Unlike the many factories springing up all over Japan, where working conditions were every bit as harsh as in Dickensian London, the Noda Shoyu Company made it clear to employees that they, the managers, and even the owners were all part of one family (*ikka*), dedicated to making the very best *shoyu* in Japan. This approach in a modern, automated factory today would be considered overly progressive. In the 1920s it was unbelievable. And yet, as I was soon to discover, the *ikka* spirit is perhaps the single most recognizable quality of what defines Kikkoman around the world.

Noda Shoyu continued to expand its production capacity by buying up rival firms in its area and began to expand internationally as well. The company made *shoyu* in China and other countries for a time. The name of its main brand, Kikkoman, was easy for foreigners to pronounce. By the 1930s, the company was already exporting about 10 percent of its total output, roughly half to Asia and half to North America (Hawaii and California), most of it to meet demand from Japanese people living abroad. And most of what was exported had the Kikkoman brand.

Seeing a growing opportunity to sell all sorts of products to Japanese overseas, the company set up sales offices in China and Korea to sell *shoyu*, miso, and sake. In other words, by the dawn of WWII, Noda Shoyu was already one of the leading companies in its field in Japan, was producing *shoyu* overseas, and had established sales offices overseas to market Japanese foods internationally.

As with every other business, the war brought a sudden end to all overseas operations and had a severe impact on the domestic one as well. It is fortunate that the main plant at Noda survived the war. Being outside Tokyo, it was never at risk from aerial bombing, but other threats were just as real. In the final months of the conflict, anything resembling iron or steel was confiscated by the military to melt down for the war effort, and the tons of machinery at Noda Shoyu must have looked very tempting. If the plant had not been making condiments for the Emperor's table, it very likely would not have survived.

Reading over all this history on the airplane, the thing that struck me most was not the sudden rollback of business that the Second World War brought about — that was expected. Rather, it was that the war seemed an aberration, a temporary break in the company's steady growth and expansion, including its expansion overseas. Prior to WWII, Noda Shoyu was already doing exactly the kinds of things that its descendent, Kikkoman, would become famous for — building international factories, setting up marketing offices to support them, and representing a variety of Japanese foods, not just *shoyu*, to customers in other lands. But the effect of the war was a Great Leap Backwards, a retrenchment of Kikkoman's operations to a purely domestic sphere. Moreover, the post-war period saw a shift in eating habits, moving away from the traditional Japanese diet and moving in the direction of Western foods. Because the domestic market for *shoyu* would not grow indefinitely, sooner or later the company would have to turn its attention to international markets once again.

That's just about where I was reading when the jet touched down at O'Hare Airport. At least I felt I had used these few hours in a noisy tin can productively. I was about to start the most important part of my research — the fact-to-face part

— and if it went well and got me even more seriously interested in telling this story, then I would soon be back at O'Hare and beginning a trip around the world.

The Miracle in Walworth

4

When the plane landed in Chicago, I stashed my historical reading material in my briefcase, collected my luggage, and found my rental car. A few minutes later I was behind the wheel of a late-model American sedan, heading north on a modern six-lane highway towards the Badger State. Yet my head was still filled with images of seventeenth and eighteenth century Japan, of samurai and peasants and workers loading casks of soy sauce onto boats for the trip downriver to the old capital of Edo.

The contrast between the powerful images of Kikkoman's history and the stark reality of its modern growth was almost too much to accept. If the company had decided to come to America in the 1960s or '70s, as so many Japanese firms later did, that would be unsurprising — assuming of course that it set up shop in San Francisco or Los Angeles, or even for that matter, somewhere near New York. But it did not. Either by chance or design, Japan's first company to build a factory on American soil had chosen a quiet little town in a sleepy rural community in southern Wisconsin. How did that make sense?

It was a beautiful sunny morning, and my car quickly devoured the miles of Illinois highway heading north. The urban sprawl of Chicago disappeared quickly, and more rural landscapes came into view. I reached the state line and turned off the divided highway to see what I was missing. Sure enough, on both sides of the state road, endless stretches of farmland and pastureland spread out before me, mile after mile of green fields beneath gorgeous blue skies, the landscape dotted with barns and silos, here and there horses and cattle. *Toto*, I thought, *I have a feeling we're not in Chicago any more.*

I'd set the rental car's GPS for the address of the Kikkoman plant in Walworth, Wisconsin, but I wondered if even the global satellite system might not have trouble finding a little town out here in the Big Foot Prairie. My research said the whole town was only about thirty square miles (about 76 sq. km), with a total population of fewer than 2,000. At the speed I was going, I would probably miss it if I looked down to change the radio station.

Fortunately, the GPS system was a good deal smarter than I was, and before I knew it I saw what looked like a bunch of aluminum airplane hangars appear out of the green field ahead. I pulled up to the main gate and announced myself to the little speaker box there. I was immediately welcomed by name and invited in. I pulled the car, now considerably dustier than when I'd checked it out, into a parking lot right in front of the main entrance. I saw an opening next to a big, black GMC Sierra pick-up and swung in a little too fast, almost putting a sizable gash in the door of the truck. Probably not a good idea, I thought, as the pick-up no doubt belonged to some 7-foot-tall,

Paul Bunyan-esque line worker who bench-pressed Buicks, ate two-pound steaks for breakfast, and would happily rip my head off if I dinged his pick-up.

Getting out of the car, I noticed that it was already growing warm, so I was glad to step inside the cool, air conditioned offices of Kikkoman Foods, Inc., which I soon discovered everyone called KFI. Standing in the lobby to greet me was a fit-looking man of about forty in a beige company jacket. He had a big smile and hair cropped short enough to make a Marine recruit look shaggy. The name tag on his jacket said, "Dick Jenkins."

"Glad to see you parked right next to me," he said, still smiling and gesturing towards the pick-up. So much for my idiotic stereotypes of folks in the Midwest.

Dick and I shook hands warmly and he guided me down the hall to a small conference room. While pouring me a cup of coffee, he officially welcomed me to KFI and said he would be my personal tour guide for as long as I planned to stay. I pointed out that the business card he'd just handed me said, "Vice President, Administration." Did Kikkoman always assign vice-presidents to show uninvited guests around?

"At this facility, yes," he said with the ever-present smile. "I'm officially the VP of Administration, but in our corporate structure that covers human resources, purchasing, shipping, risk management, regulatory compliance, a bit of customer relations, and anything else that needs to be done. We don't have a corporate communications officer, so I do that, too."

I pointed out half-jokingly that such a vague job description sounded like a catch-all for everything that wasn't specifically manufacturing, engineering or finance.

"Exactly," he said. "My real job is to do whatever I can do to help the company." Still smiling. "And I wouldn't have it any other way."

Dick looked like the kind of guy who'd played football in high school, but knew he would never get serious about it. He wasn't tall but was solidly built. He spoke in a soft, easy-going tone, never stuck for words, and his smile really did seem to be a permanent fixture. I quickly discovered that he wasn't just being polite to me; that was really the kind of guy he was. He always said nice things about his co-workers, his company, and his community, and the only time I heard him criticize something, it was in a muted voice with multiple qualifying adjectives. After talking to him for fifteen minutes, I had no doubt that he was known in the community as a good husband and father and was an active member of his local church.

Getting to know the people who really manage companies is always one of my goals when I am researching a project such as this. I am a firm believer that people, not money or technology or property, are the single biggest asset class for any company. In an era where technological superiority is fleeting at best, human resources are the ultimate competitive edge. So I think it's important to see who gets hired, who gets promoted, and who is chosen to lead an enterprise. In my experience examining companies around the world, I have found that, without exception, the firms that outperform their rivals are those with outstanding managers, people who genuinely care about both their companies and their employees.

From that perspective, meeting Dick Jenkins as soon as I walked through the door of KFI was a very good sign. After simply sharing a cup of coffee, I felt that I could trust him completely, that he would answer any question honestly, even if it reflected negatively on his company or himself, and he would not hide anything from me as we inspected the plant.

I thanked him for the coffee and said I was ready to take that "vice-president tour" he'd promised. Dick laughed, tapped the table with his fist, and said, "All right, then. Let's go!"

First, he told me to hang up my sport jacket and leave my shoulder bag in the conference room. I wouldn't be needing those inside the plant. Then he took me down the hall and into a small room, where he handed me what looked like a lightweight white lab coat, a white hard hat, a hair net, and a pair of shoe coverings.

"Food business," he explained. "Everything is ultra-clean inside. We can't have people tracking in dirt or bringing all sorts of pests or contaminants inside, either on their clothes or their hair. Those aren't Kikkoman rules — it's the same for any food-related business. It's just common sense." He quickly donned his own white suit and helmet, opened a heavy metal door, and guided me inside. Soon I found myself in a long, wide, but totally empty hallway, the expanse of blank walls occasionally broken by large metal doors. There were small, almost discreet signs marking the different rooms we passed, but otherwise the cinder block walls were empty. I wondered where were the big motivational posters you would expect to see in any large American office or factory (*There's no "I" in TEAM!*; *Pitch In for Kikkoman*, *We're Brewing Quality!*, and similar nonsense). Here there was nothing. Maybe employee motivation wasn't so much of a problem.

As we walked on, we passed a few workmen, also dressed in white coats, with hairnets and helmets. They were big, stocky fellows, some much bigger than Dick, and many with beards. Yet even these gruff-looking lumberjacks all wore white hairnets to cover their beards. I was impressed. Each of them greeted Dick warmly, not the kind of stiff greeting you would give to a supervisor or a manager, just a friendly hello. And he returned each greeting in his usual, genuinely friendly manner.

"Do you know all the workers that well?" I asked.

"Well I know them all, some better than others," he said.

"They don't seem to look at you like a vice-president," I noted.

"Actually, that's probably one of the reasons the company hired me. Although I'm an officer of KFI, I sometimes feel more like the people working in the plant than the senior managers in the offices. Honestly, I'm a lot like these guys. I grew up in Wisconsin and I live here in the community, so I share a lot of their values... I like to hunt and fish, and in a lot of ways I guess I think like these guys do. It helps when the workforce feels more of a connection to the company and less of a gap between them and management."

While we were walking and talking, two more guys came out of a side room and waved to Dick. He waved back and we kept on walking.

I told him that I didn't want to learn all the ins and outs of making soy sauce, but I did want a quick crash course, just enough so that I'd understand the process and be able to talk to people I met in the plant.

"Just what I'm going to give you."

As we walked, he explained the various steps of the process and showed me the various holding tanks for raw materials, the mixing vats, fermentation tanks, pressing room, bottling operation, etc. I noticed two things about this plant (and every other Kikkoman plant I visited afterwards): they all have the same heavy, musty smell from the *shoyu* production, and the air is always warm inside.

As I walked, I kept looking at this very large facility, with its long, spotlessly clean corridors leading to gigantic rooms, each with a different purpose, but each like the others, clean and full of machinery. Some of the machinery looked state-of-the-art, and some of it looked much older. But all of it looked clean and well cared for. As we walked through one area, I noticed a fenced-off section marked DANGER - HIGH VOLTAGE - KEEP OUT. A small sign informed me that this was Electric Substation No. 4.

"The plant must use a lot of power," I said, trying to sound smarter than I felt.

"A huge amount," Dick said, still walking. "We are one of the local electric utility's top customers, both in volume and priority. We don't have back-up generators, so if the power goes out for any length of time, that can ruin a batch of *shoyu*. As you can imagine, we're always striving to increase output, so having to dump our product would make everyone very unhappy."

"Does that happen?"

"Almost never. But this is Wisconsin; we do have real winters up here... We've been hit by lightning lots of times, and once we had a utility pole go down and take out power to the whole plant. But in almost every case we get things back up and running right away."

He spotted a guy coming out a door right in front of us, his sandy hair mostly hidden beneath his helmet, and a pair of glasses dangling on a strap across the front of his blue work shirt. I noticed a Motorola microphone clipped to his shirt collar and a radio on his tool belt.

"You asked about power," Dick said in a louder voice. "This is Bud. He's our head electrician. He's the guy who keeps everything running."

We shook hands. Bud was one of those guys who could be sixty-five but would still look thirty-five. Big smile, boyish looks, easygoing manner.

"Bud Carlson. What can I do for you?"

Dick explained why I was there, and I asked Bud if I could talk to him for just a moment. He readily agreed.

"I just saw that power substation there," I said, pointing my thumb at the unit we'd just passed. "Is that your department?"

"Yup. We've got six of 'em indoors, plus switching gear outside."

"And your job is to make sure that everything runs smoothly and fix whatever breaks down?" I ventured.

"Well, if you ask the guys on the floor, that's probably what they'll tell you. But the way I see it, my job is to fix things *before* they break. I'm supposed to maintain the production equipment, and that means getting ahead of problems. We bring in outside contractors to bend the pipes and pull the wires, but my job is to keep the equipment running day in and day out. We have four electricians including me, and all of us have the same goal — solve problems before they become problems. That way things don't break down."

I looked at Dick.

"How big is this plant?" I asked.

"700,000 square feet." He was smiling because he knew where I was going with this.

"And from what I've seen, it's chock full of heavy machinery, enough that you need six power substations to run it? And to manage all that you have **four** electricians?"

He was nodding now, trying to conceal pride in the efficiency of his company's operations.

"That's because we have people like Bud here—" he clapped him on the shoulder, "—who keep everything running smoothly."

I made a few notes in my little book and then asked Bud why he was carrying a laptop in addition to all his other tools.

"Because the machinery is so complex now, you can't solve the problems easily without a computer. All the diagnostics are run automatically now. You want to know why this valve isn't firing? You go online, you check with the machine's diagnostic program, and the equipment will tell you where to look."

Times have really changed, I thought. It seemed a fast CPU was more useful than a set of pipe wrenches and screwdrivers.

"Look, we've got some really high tech equipment here, and a lot of the production is automated. We don't need a whole lot of people to run this plant, but we do need to keep the machinery running," he explained. "Now, that's a whole different mindset from when I started here twenty-one years ago. Back then the equipment was pretty old and much simpler." He looked down at the floor, rubbing his jaw with a beefy hand, remembering the challenges of a different era.

"I've been fortunate to see it all change. We're programming the human-machine interfaces now. Ten years ago we would have had to contract people to come in and tweak those HMIs, but now we do it all in-house; it's no big deal. If somebody tells us he wants some new message to appear on a screen, or wants pushbuttons added to some system, we go ahead and make that change. And that's another fun part — making something new or making something better than it was."

I asked him if he liked the work. Was this a good job? Would he recommend it to friends if they asked?

"Hell yeah!" he shot back with a grin. "It's been fun for me to watch this place grow and bring on so much new, fully automated machinery. Kikkoman has bought really good equipment, some pretty sophisticated stuff. And it's fun to work on. Sure, it's a challenge sometimes, but the biggest challenge is staying ahead of it. Fortunately, I've been doing this for a long time, so I know where the weak points are. If somebody calls and says this conveyor stopped, it's not my first rodeo. I've seen it before, I know where to look, and I can tell them to check certain things before I even get there. But fixing things after they break is never as good as preventing them from breaking down in the first place."

I apologized for keeping him away from his job. I knew he didn't expect to be grabbed in a hallway and grilled by someone from outside the company. I guessed it was only thanks to Dick's presence that Bud knew everything was okay. Still, while I had the chance I wanted to direct the conversation away from electrical machinery and towards my main interest — finding out if there was something that makes Kikkoman special. I pointed out that Bud had been with the company for over twenty years; he had a valuable skill set and could probably get hired at any factory in the Midwest before the week was out, maybe with a serious boost in salary as well. Didn't he ever think about moving on?[3]

Bud grinned again, not exactly the reaction I was expecting. "I worked for [he named a very famous American brewing company] before I came here. They're a good company and all, but believe me, they have their own way of doing things. When they set up a plant, they want it run in a certain way; they don't want your input, they don't want you to get creative, they want you to do your job just like they explained it to you. Pretty soon I decided it wasn't for me."

"So, how are things different here? Do you have some kind of input here?" I really didn't see how an electrician could get terribly creative.

"Well, for example, the guy who runs my department is a really smart guy. He always asks me, 'If you were going to do this, how would you do it? Which option would you choose and why?' That's important to me. I know I'm having input here, and so do the other guys on my team. Nobody likes to take orders all the time.

"As for creativity, the best ideas come from the operators. Somebody on the floor says, 'This would be better if it could do this or that,' and then that becomes a challenge for us. If we add some switches here, maybe we can make it run better for the operators. We have to get creative, to figure out the best ways to do something, and then we make it happen."

"And the company lets you do that?"

"As long as what we're suggesting is safe and we run it by the managers first, we can go ahead. Actually, that's the really fun part of the job."

"So you're not moving to another company anytime soon?" I joked.

"Are you serious?" He was laughing, too.

Suddenly his radio crackled. He touched the mike, tilted his head and said, "On my way." Then to us, "Sorry...got to go. Is it okay if—"

Dick nodded and said, "Go!" and I called out a big thank you as Bud took off down the hall. In a few seconds, we were standing alone once again. I looked at Dick.

"Wow," I said, my voice echoing slightly in the empty hall. "That was unusual."

"No, no it wasn't. I think you're going to hear pretty much the same thing from anyone you talk to."

There's a confident manager, I thought. I was anxious to see if his confidence was justified or not.

"Okay," Dick turned and started walking again. "I promised you a crash course in making soy sauce. Let's go." He subtly shifted into lecture mode.

"Basically, *shoyu* starts with soybeans and wheat. We buy the highest quality of both, then select the best of what we've bought for processing. We heat both the soybeans and wheat in special high-pressure, high-temperature cookers. The heat acts in a certain way on the proteins in the soy and on the carbohydrates in the wheat; I'll spare you the chemistry, but let's just say it makes them easier to process, to get the fermentation going. So right from the beginning, controlling the temperature and pressure is vital."

"Got it. So, what is *koji*?"

"*Koji* is what we call it after we have added a special, living culture, actually mold spores, to the mix. That's why we say we *brew* shoyu. It's a bit like making beer or wine; it's ultimately a fermentation process, only instead of brewer's yeast we use a proprietary mold. And this special mold is the key to the whole process. It's like our secret ingredient. Kikkoman patented it long ago, so technically it's Kikkoman Aspergillus."

"But it isn't really a secret, is it?" I asked as we walked. "I mean, people make soy sauce all over the world."

"They do... but not exactly like this they don't. There are parts of our process that are distinctive, and that's what makes Kikkoman *shoyu* different." He was smiling again. We stopped in front of a long, low window at about chest-height that revealed a dark, spacious room entirely occupied by a giant, circular metal dish that looked to be about a meter deep. To an untrained eye like mine, this big, shallow vat was full of dry oatmeal or some other kind of rough, chunky cereal, and a giant mechanical arm was slowly stirring the mixture.

"This combination of processed soybeans and wheat plus the special mold is what we call the *koji*. It sits here for a few days, under very precisely controlled temperature and humidity conditions, and gets ready to perform its magic. We stir the mixture, in part by injecting air from the bottom of the vat, what we call puffing."

We walked on, and eventually he opened another huge steel door and we stepped inside. The room was filled with a double row of tall, cylindrical tanks. I looked up at one of these enormous tanks and asked Dick how much it held.

"Several thousand gallons in each one," he said.

"The *koji* is still a relatively dry mixture. We move it into these tanks and mix it with brine — salt water. When the *koji* is combined with the salt water, we call it *moromi*. Hey, I can get you the Japanese characters for all these words if you want…?"

I assured him that wouldn't be necessary. "So, the *koji* mixture is combined with salt water and it becomes something called *moromi*. And these are the *moromi* tanks we're looking at?"

He nodded.

"So what do you do with the *moromi*?" I asked.

"Very little. The Aspergillus mold does all the hard work. Our job is to carefully control the temperature so the fermentation process can proceed as it should. It takes beer anywhere from a couple of weeks to a couple of months to ferment, but soy sauce — at least the way we do it — takes several months. Think half a year to make a bottle of *shoyu*.

"During this time, the mixture of soybeans and wheat are transformed into a semi-liquid, reddish-brown mash. During this slow fermentation process, more than 300 distinct flavor and fragrance compounds begin to develop. Those dozens of subtle flavors are what gives naturally brewed soy sauce such a complex taste."

"So the *moromi* yields soy sauce?" I asked, scribbling frantically in my small notebook.

"Not so quickly. First, the mash is part liquid — that's the raw soy sauce — and also part solid — the residues of the soybeans and wheat. We have to separate the liquid from the solids, which we do by pressing."

Now he opened another door and we stepped into a huge room with a three-story-high ceiling. Machinery was everywhere. There were some unusual devices, one of which looked like a two-story-tall blanket-folding machine. It was being belt-fed with a meter-wide cloth from a gigantic spool down below, the cloth being transported upwards via rollers, then fed into the top of the machine, where it was layered by mechanical arms gently folding it back on itself again and again. But instead of stacking up higher and higher, the pile at the bottom kept compressing, making room for new folds to be layered on top. Only then did I notice that the cloth wasn't dry. It was soaked with some dark liquid, which was leaking out the bottom of the pile. Aha!

Dick motioned for me to follow him up a metal stairway next to one of the machines. I did so and found myself up close to the cloth, which I now saw was some strong synthetic fiber capable of being folded, pressed, stretched, dried, rolled up again and then used for the same operation again and again. From up there I could actually see the top of the giant folding machine and look down inside as the liquid-soaked material was neatly folded in layers and stacked its tall frame.

"Here you can see how the filter material, which is soaked with raw soy mash, is then folded and stacked by these machines. In this first step, we let gravity compress the material so that the liquid is naturally squeezed out. We also have big mechanical presses to finish the job, which takes about half a day or more, but the first stage is done like this, just an automated version of a very traditional process going back centuries."

We went back downstairs and walked back the way we had come. As we left the room and started down another empty hallway, Dick explained that even the liquid that was collected from this separation and filtering process is not yet finished. This is the "raw" soy sauce, and it accounts for a lot of the fragrance I noticed inside the plant. The raw *shoyu* is left in a clarifier tank for a few days to allow its various components to separate: the oil floats to the top and whatever sediment remains then settles to the bottom. (Later I learned that the oil, sediment and "soy cake" are recycled: Soy cake, for example, becomes livestock feed.)

"The clarified soy sauce is then run through a steam pipe to heat it. This heating process also stops the activity of the enzymes and stabilizes the quality, and in addition, helps to adjust the color, flavor, and aroma. This heated soy sauce is then sent to the filling room to be bottled and packed and made ready for shipping."

As he said that, he opened another large door and we were standing in a room full of conveyor belts delivering various sizes of bottles to filling machines like high-speed carousels. The carousels whirled the open bottles around in a circle, filled them with a reddish brown liquid, capped them, then spun them out to another line where they were packed into cardboard boxes, which moved quickly down another line, where computer-driven ink-jet sprayers affixed bar codes and other labeling information. Then they moved to a final loading station where each case was stacked neatly on a pallet. The whole operation was moving at a speed that seemed sure to break down at any second, yet the few workers I saw in here looked quite satisfied with the steady march of empty bottles to be filled, sealed, packed and stacked.

"These are just the standard retail-size bottles," Dick said. "We also prepare much larger containers for restaurant and commercial use." He took me to another room, where I saw forklifts moving pallets stacked high with white plastic drums.

"Five-gallon drums," he explained, waving to one of the men driving a fork lift. "Very popular with restaurants." We walked on a bit and he pointed to other, much larger plastic containers. "Those are fifty-five gallons, and there are bigger ones, too. We also fill 270-gallon drums and even big tanker trucks."

"It looks very interesting," I said, trying to sound more interested than I felt. "But so much seems to depend on a natural process — fermentation — that you can't control precisely. How do you know that the end product is just the way you want it to be? How do you know it all tastes the same? Because it *is* a natural process, there could be lots of variation in the results, right?"

"You're absolutely right," he replied, nodding his head. "Which is why we conduct quality inspections at every stage of the process. Inspectors analyze the ingredients, and check the color, flavor, and aroma of the soy sauce. Samples of the final product after pasteurization are sent to the lab right away for analysis. Periodically, we send samples back to Japan for comparison testing. So does every other Kikkoman plant around the world. Quality control is the name of the game around here."

I asked several more questions and he fielded them one after another, and then I said I'd seen enough manufacturing equipment for one day. He looked at his watch and suggested we head back to the conference room where we had first begun to talk. I suddenly realized that I hadn't eaten today other than a quick bite of fast food breakfast at O'Hare, and now it was well past lunchtime. Dick said not to worry, Barbara was getting sandwiches. He didn't explain further, so I assumed I would meet this secretary, personal assistant or fast food delivery person shortly.

A few minutes later we were back in the conference room, minus our white coats, shoe covers, hairnets and helmets. There were two Japanese men already seated there, both wearing company jackets. They introduced themselves immediately: Kenji Tanaka ("Call me Ken," he said in perfect English), the president of KFI, and Takeru Kato, the Vice President of Manufacturing.

"Why don't we sit down? You must be hungry," Ken said, gesturing for me to make myself comfortable. I had barely sat down when a bubbly middle-aged woman with a 150-watt smile came in carrying a tray loaded with generously sized sandwiches of various types, and then returned a minute later with another tray covered with bottles of soda, mineral water, and assorted soft drinks.

"Gee, I don't know. Do you think this will be enough?" she said to no one in particular.

"Dave, this is Barbara," Dick said by way of introduction. She set the trays down on the table and shook my hand.

"Hi, I'm so pleased to meet you," she said, turning the smile up to 200 watts.

"I think Dave might enjoy chatting with you after lunch, if that's all right," Dick said.

"Oh, sure! No problem! What time shall I come back?"

"How about in an hour?" Ken interjected.

"Great. See you in an hour." And she was gone.

"What does she do?" I asked.

"Everything," Dick and Ken said in unison, not even laughing at their unexpected chorus. I took that to mean that this answer was obvious when discussing Barbara. Dick added, "You'll get the idea as soon as you talk to her."

We all turned our attention to the sandwiches and drinks that she had kindly provided, and for a while there wasn't much conversation. Then Ken — it was already hard for me to think of him as President Tanaka — asked me about my visit.

I told him a brief version of my encounter with Ron Yates, our discussions about Kikkoman, and my growing interest in the company. I said that I had basically come to research the factory and its products, and that, if possible, I wanted to talk to some employees and some former employees and some people in the community who were knowledgeable about the company. Simply put, I didn't want to get all my information from the PR Dept.

"That's okay, we don't have a PR Dept.," Dick said with a grin.

"Yes, I remember that. My point is that I want to make my own opinions by talking to all sorts of people in and around the company, like the way we just bumped into Bud the electrician today and I got a chance to chat with him. I really want to do that without bothering you people any more than necessary and not get in the way of your work."

"It's not a problem," Ken assured me. "I've already talked to someone at our head office in Tokyo. Your friend, Mr. Yates obviously knows people there, and his mail was well received. We were asked to cooperate by showing you around. I wasn't here back in the nineties when he wrote his book, but I understand that he did pretty much what you're doing now, so Tokyo has asked us to help you in any way we can."

I was delighted to hear that. Ron had told me that things would be okay, but I wasn't really as confident as I wanted to be when I set out. I also didn't want to belabor the point with Ken and Dick and the others, but Ron Yates' book had been done with the full support of the Kikkoman head office, while I was just a writer poking around, talking to anyone I could find, and hoping to discover an interesting story. The Kikkoman people had good reason to be nice to him, but much less incentive in my case. Or so I had assumed until today.

"Would you like to go check into your hotel now?" Ken asked thoughtfully.

I said no, that would come later. Right now I was at the plant, it was only early afternoon, and I wanted to meet a few more people.

"Sounds good," he said. "Where shall we start?" He looked at Dick for a suggestion.

"How about Barbara? She expects to pop back in and chat anyway." Dick looked at me knowingly. "And even if you didn't ask to talk to her, she'd probably catch you in the hall somewhere and talk your ear off anyway." At that, everyone laughed.

"Okay," I said, "let's make her our next victim." We'd finished our sandwiches and I was ready to get back to work. I knew I would start to feel a little tired later on — travel never used to bother me, but the years have slowed me down a bit, and any plane ride that involves changing time zones tends to mess with my sleep system. But that would come later. For now, I pulled out my little IC recorder and my trusty note pad.

"Let's see if Barbara is as anxious to meet me as I am to meet her."

Ken and Kato-san excused themselves so they could get back to work. Dick found Barbara and asked her to come chat with me for a few minutes while he got back to his office. I already felt bad distracting people from their work, but there was no way I could move around a factory like this or talk to the people I needed to talk to without cooperation from the local managers. That meant bothering them to some extent, and I would try my best to minimize the burden of my visit. Of course, everyone at Kikkoman was already being so nice (just as Ron had warned me they would) that I felt like a special guest instead of an intruder.

5

The Family Feeling

*B*arbara Hermann came in, smiling nonstop, and took a seat in front of me across the table. I told her I just wanted to chat for a few minutes about her job and her experiences, and I assured her that everything we said was private and would not get back to anyone at the company. I have interviewed a lot of people around the world, and I always find that preserving confidence pays off many times over. Sometimes I hear a really wonderful story, good or bad, about a company or a manager, and I know right away that I want to use it in an upcoming article. That means I need to rewrite the story, move it a couple of continents away from where I heard it, and put it in someone else's mouth. A good story is a good story; the reader doesn't care much who said it as long as it's true, and my job is to collect revealing stories without getting any of the people who told them to me into trouble. So I guaranteed Barbara that our conversation was private.

"Oh, that doesn't matter," she said, waving as if brushing away my offer. "Anything I would say to you I would say in front of Dick or anyone else. We're a family here. We don't have a lot of secrets from each other."

"Okay, great. Let's get started. What exactly do you do here?"

"I'm an administration supervisor and I've been here twenty years. I was with another company, a very well-known firm, for about eleven years, and I was ready for a change. Now, you have to understand two things. First, in this community Kikkoman Foods has a very, very high reputation. I mean, even employees' kids brag that their mom or dad works here. The kids may not know what we do, but they're proud that we work here. It's that kind of place.

"And second, KFI doesn't hire a lot of people. Back then they hired almost no one. People would apply for a job here and wait seven years without even getting called for an interview. And if anyone did get hired, they knew they had a job for life. By and large, no one gets fired and no one quits, so people hold onto this job for dear life. That means there aren't a lot of openings.

"One day — and I now think of it as my luckiest day — I came in here just to put in an application, and I was talking to someone at the front switchboard. Just by chance I ran into someone working here who knew my kids. It turned out she lived right next door to where my kids went for day care. We chatted, she asked me what I was doing, I said I was looking for a new job, she asked me a few questions, and we said goodbye. I didn't think anything of it, because as I say, when you hand in an application here you're prepared to wait a few years just to get a response. So I thanked everybody and left and forgot all about it.

"Not even two hours later I got a call from the head of HR. Apparently the woman I'd chatted with in the lobby had gone directly to him to tell him all about me. He asked if I could come in for an interview, and I said, 'Sure!' So I went for the interview, and it was nothing like what I expected. It wasn't at all about my skill set or my experience or anything like that. It was all about me: What kind of person am I? Where did I come from? What's my family like? What do I want out of life? What are my goals? Things like that. So of course, when I went home I was thinking, 'That didn't go well at all. He didn't even ask me about my skills! I must have made a bad impression right from the start and he was just too nice to end the interview on the spot.'

"So the next day he calls me again. He asks if I would come to the plant again. He said he wanted to show me the job and let me see if it was something I wanted to do, would it interest me, would it challenge me? It turned out the job was in the warehouse, mostly order entry, keypunching data, which is basically the same kind of work I was doing before, so that was a no-brainer. And then he said, 'Would you be interested in this job?'

"Now, even before I went for my first interview I'd already decided what my attitude was even if they offered me some really dull job: 'This is Kikkoman Foods; if there is *any* way I can get in the door here, I want the job.' So I said yes and that was that. It was the best thing that's ever happened to me."

She continued without pausing for a breath.

"So I worked in the warehouse for four years, and then I heard that a woman who was working in HR was retiring. Now remember, there isn't a lot of hiring here. About the only way a job opens up is when someone retires. Of course, I didn't know beans about HR, but I went to Dick and I asked for the job. I don't know why, but he gave me the opportunity to move in here, which was a really good change for me, and I will be forever grateful. I think he saw things in me that even I wasn't aware of. Whatever, Dick has promoted me a few times, and now my job responsibility is taking care of HR. It's been wonderful.

"Kikkoman even paid for me to take courses at a nearby university, and I learned a lot about HR functions and responsibilities. I met a lot of great people and made a lot of friends there, and I really enjoyed it. And one of the really interesting things is that it opened up my eyes to the other world."

That caught my attention: "Sorry, the 'other world'?"

She continued, "When you've been here for a while, you learn the Kikkoman way of doing things, and that is definitely *not* the way that other companies do things in the regular world. I used to frustrate my HR teachers, because they'd ask basic policy questions with textbook answers, and I'd say, 'Well, that depends.' And they'd say, 'What does it depend on? Policy is policy.' And I'd tell them that at my workplace policy often depends on individual cases and circumstances. We look at each situation separately. Things aren't black and white here, not like at other companies.

"For example, I learned that many companies count up negative points against employees. If you get a certain number of points against you, you're out the door. No discussion, no appeal. KFI is different. We look at each situation individually and always try to do what's best, both for the employee and for the company. A lot of what's written in those HR textbooks doesn't apply to us."

I wanted to know more. "Such as?"

"A lot of HR policies are designed to manage disgruntled employees, trying to keep them from affecting everyone else and starting trouble. We don't have any of that. Oh, sure, people sometimes have bad days or personal problems; everyone does. In that case, we sit down with them in the break room and talk it out as friends. A lot of those problems either go away or turn out to be a lot smaller than they thought. It's all about communication. Lots of problems really start at home, and talking about it makes it better.

"We talk to them as friends and co-workers. I tell them, 'If you have concerns, let me know. I'll take your issues directly to upper management and you know they'll listen. Maybe you'll like their answer and maybe you won't, but I guarantee that they'll listen.' And that's what's so important. People need to know that their feelings are really being heard. They may not always understand *why* we have to do certain things or make certain changes in the plant, but talking about it makes things a lot better. The employee really matters here. We don't just *say* we're a family, we really believe it!"

Even my IC recorder was starting to melt, trying hard to keep up with Barbara's rapid-fire discourse, and I was scribbling notes as fast as I could write. I asked her to give me a couple of concrete examples to illustrate her last statement.

"Lemme see... There are so many... Well, for instance, a while ago one of our employees lost a child. His son passed away one night, and he was terribly upset and he needed someone to talk to. I was at home, working on my iPad, sitting there in my pajamas, and suddenly there's somebody knocking on my kitchen window. I let him in and we talked. He told me what the situation was and said, "What do I do? I don't know what to do." I told him to go home and wait. I would rally everyone right away.

"Then I got dressed and went over to his senior manager's house — the manager was Japanese, by the way — and I told him what was going on, then I called his foreman and his operators, and we all went around to his house to sit with this guy and his family, to make sure they knew that they're not alone and anything they need, they can call on us. Lots of companies talk about an open door policy, well, our open door policy extends right into our living rooms.

"People in the plant all know us and they know they can call us anytime. No one hesitates to call me or Dick when they have a problem; they know we're there. They have my cell phone number, they have Dick's number, they know they can call us day or night if they need to talk about something, professional or personal. Nobody has to wait until we get into the office to talk to us. Or they can come to our homes — like I say, I've had more than a few people show up at my home when they had problems.

"Last year the husband of one of our employees called and told us their child had been in a car accident. I went right over to their house, and when I left I knew exactly what I had to do. We immediately ordered all sorts of food and other stuff for them, because these are things that you shouldn't have to worry about at a time like that. Mostly, we were just there for them. I think that's what's really important. But you know, it's no big deal. We do these things because we're a family, and that means not just for our employees, but their own families are part of our family, too. Like I said, we don't just say that; we really believe it."

I was still writing notes as fast as I could scribble.

She continued: "In a big corporation, you don't just waltz into the vice-president's office unannounced and start chatting about your hobbies and such. Those doors are usually closed and guarded by his personal secretary. Not here. And this is a big company. But I've seen one of the guys show up early in the morning with a big fish and say, "Look, I just caught this big walleye." Where do you think he's going with that trophy? Straight into Dick's office to show him! He knows Dick's a fisherman, too, and Dick will appreciate what the guy has caught. Nobody's thinking, 'Hey, you can't go in there. He's the Vice President of Administration.' That's just not the way we do things here. It works because everyone in management, not just Dick, takes the time to talk to our workers. We all care. That's part of what makes Kikkoman special."

I told her that Dick didn't strike me as any kind of stuck-up corporate executive, nor for that matter did anyone else. She nodded vigorously.

"Titles don't mean a lot around here. We all have different responsibilities, but everybody is part of this family. If anybody isn't working right for whatever reason, it affects all of us. We don't care much about job titles."

I pointed out that, with twenty years of experience and academic HR training on her resume, Barbara (just like Bud) could go on the job market any time and probably get a nice salary bump at a prestigious American company.

"What for?" She looked genuinely perplexed. "Money isn't the only thing in life, and besides, I'm happy with my situation right now. I used to be one of the youngest ones here, now I'm one of the older ones. People always ask me when I'm going to retire. I say, 'What? Are you kidding? Retire?' I don't know what I would do. This is my home."

We chatted a little more, and I thanked her for spending so much time with me. She opened the door and called Dick, who reappeared in a few moments. The three of us stood there, drinking fresh coffee and talking about the research project I had just started. They thought it sounded interesting — neither of them had been to Kikkoman factories in the Netherlands or Singapore, much less Japan, and they sounded envious that I might get to see so many different plants and compare them.

Eventually we came back to talking about my story and the kind of people I wanted to interview. Suddenly Barbara looked at Dick and said, "You know who he should talk to?" Big smile. Dick looked blank. "The Art of Shoyu!" Even bigger smile.

Now Dick's face lit up, too. "You're right. He'd be perfect." Then to me, "Would you like to meet one of the real old timers, someone who was here right from the beginning, long before I got here?"

I said of course, that's just the kind of person I'm looking for.

"His name's Art Gunderson, but he was one of the very first hires here, so people got to calling him The Art of Shoyu. He's not a young guy, and maybe he's a little rough around the edges, but he's as good as they come. He helped to build this plant and make it a success right from Day One. I think you'll like him."

While he was saying this, Barbara was on her cell phone. I could hear her taking to someone. "Art. Hi, it's Barbara! How you doin'? Great. Yup, me, too. Say, we got a fella here who's doin' a story about Kikkoman and he'd really like to come talk to you. You did? Well where are you? Okay, can we stop over? Great, see you soon."

She looked at her boss, "He's at Sammy's having a late lunch. He says we're welcome to come over and talk to him there."

"Okay. I'll take him," Dick said.

"No, you're busy. I'll take him," Barbara argued.

Dick's brow furrowed. Not angry, not upset, just stating a clear, indisputable fact. "You've been bending Dave's ear for most of an hour. And I know you've got things to do. I'll take him." End of discussion.

We went out to the parking lot and jumped in Dick's black Sierra. It had been a while since I'd been in one of these things. People in foreign countries (like New York City) don't realize that pick-ups are by far the most popular vehicles in America, or that a Ford 150 has been the No. 1 selling vehicle in America for close to 40 years. But here in Wisconsin you didn't need to tell anybody. People who live in the country need dependable transportation, and sometimes they need to carry a lot more than a couple of bags of groceries, so pick-ups make sense. I reminded Dick that Toyota and Nissan both made pick-up trucks right here in the USA, and after all, he did work for a Japanese company.

"Very good point," he said. "And I know those Japanese trucks are good machines, but you know what, I like mine." He tapped the steering wheel gently with one hand. "Not ready to give this up just yet."

We drove for about fifteen minutes and pulled up at a small roadside diner. Dick parked the truck and we went inside. It was mid-afternoon and there were only a couple of people in the place. It wasn't hard to spot Art, an elderly guy of indeterminate years occupying a table all by himself, eating an omelette. There was a small, red-capped glass bottle of Kikkoman on the table and a few drops of telltale dark liquid on the main dish.

Dick called his name as we approached and he looked up with a big grin. Dick introduced me, and Art stood up to shake my hand. I immediately felt as if we were old friends just getting together for a beer. I pointed to the dark smudge on the omelette and asked the Art of Shoyu about his taste in seasonings.

"You know, they used to have that Chinese soy sauce here, but I tasted it once and told them to get rid of it. That stuff tastes awful. It's made with chemicals. It isn't brewed like real soy sauce." He pointed at the little bottle on the table. "Besides, this is brewed right here in Wisconsin. I persuaded the owner to change to the real thing. Now I know his customers are happier, and I'll tell ya, so am I!"

I discovered that Art was eighty-six when I met him, and he still sounded ready to compete in a tractor pull... without a tractor. His hair was snow white, although he noted there wasn't as much of it as there used to be. He was wearing glasses because his eyes "aren't as sharp as they used to be either," and he was quick to point out that there are three stents in his heart, but he also noted that no machine runs eighty-plus years on original parts.

In just five minutes of chatting with Art, I could tell that there were dozens of stories just waiting to come out. I began by asking him when he joined the company. Fortunately, that's one date that seems seared into his brain.

"February 5th, 1973. I was 42. Back then there was eight of us that started at the new plant, and four of us are still alive today. We were all from farming backgrounds."

"Yes, I've heard that Kikkoman hired a lot of farmers," I said. "And I've heard various stories about why they did that."

"I *know* why," Art bellowed. "It's 'cause farmers gotta work hard; they work every day, they never take sick days. Look at me. From the age of 13 on, I got up at 4:30 every morning of my life to milk our cows. Seven days a week, summer winter, every day, year in and year out. It doesn't matter if you don' feel good, you go out there and milk those cows. Cows don't take a day off. That's why companies like to hire farmers. Guys like us, we don't call in sick, we just come to work every day." He paused and smiled a big, friendly smile. "And we take orders pretty good, too."

So, was it a good job?

"No way! It was a **great** job. Coming here was the best move I ever made. I never had a boss before, so this was a new thing. I didn't know anything about *shoyu* either, but I learned. I was in *koji* right up until I retired. And there were great people, too. The Japanese technical instructors were great, you couldn't beat 'em." He proceeded to rattle off the names of at least a dozen Japanese managers he worked with. He remembers each person in detail and knows all their names.

"Oh, yeah, when we started, the Japanese instructors used to invite my wife and me over to their homes, and they'd cook us *sukiyaki* and *tempura* and all that good stuff. So, we'd invite them over to our place, just an old farm, y'know, and we'd grill hot dogs or bratwurst or something, and serve a little beer. We were friends!"

One of my big questions about Kikkoman and about the experiment at Walworth was how this clash of cultures worked. Japanese from a 1970s-era environment and Wisconsin farm boys — two groups who knew nothing about each other and had no reason to feel bonds of friendship. Didn't the Japanese worry that these rural guys who had no factory experience and no reason to like foreigners might be unreliable or even untrustworthy? How did things come together in that first year or so of start-up operations? How did the Japanese learn to trust the Americans?

Art explained it by telling stories of his early years at the plant: "One winter we had a terrible big snowstorm. All the roads were closed, and the plant manager calls to tell me that they're shutting the plant down 'cause no one can get to work today. I knew that meant the *koji* would spoil, and I sure wasn't gonna let that happen. I told him not to worry, we'd get there somehow; we might be a little late, but we'd get there. So I got on my old tractor and I drove over and picked up a couple of the other guys, and another fellow I know, he got to the plant on foot. And when we all got there I said to them, 'One way or another, we're going to get this done, just the handful of us.' And we did it. We all pitched in, and we saved the *koji*.

"Come to think of it, I came to work three times on my tractor, and we had a guy who used to come to work sometimes on his snowmobile."

I know I shouldn't have been surprised — this is exactly the kind of hard-working spirit that rural America used to be famous for. But I was looking at that era through a historical lens. I remembered that just a decade after the Kikkoman plant opened, some politicians back in Japan were saying that American workers were lazy, unproductive, and not loyal to their companies. I couldn't imagine anyone at KFI even thinking that. People like Art must have convinced them that setting up in Wisconsin and hiring local farmers was a brilliant strategic move, whether it looked like that to the head office or not.

Art continued, "Every summer, vacation time would roll around, and because we were the first ones hired, they told us we could take vacation just about anytime we wanted. But I never took mine. Never. The Japanese could never figure out why I wouldn't take my vacation. And I told them, 'You give it to the workers in our department who have children. Let them take vacation when their kids are out of school and I'll... well, I'll take mine later, when their vacations are over. Who wants to go away in the hot summer anyway?'

"I remember, sometimes I'd be on my way home at the end of a day and I'd hear that some guy had hurt his back or something and couldn't come to work, and I'd say 'Okay, I'll cover for him,' and I'd turn around and work another shift. It was real tiring, but it felt good. We all liked to help each other out."

Did these farmers really like working in a plant, making soy sauce?

"I remember one time some guys from the brewers' union drove up from Milwaukee and parked out front of our plant. They were passing out union literature to our guys. They told us, 'You guys qualify as brewers, too. We're going to set up a union here.'

"I told 'em, 'No you're not! What do we need a damn union for? We got everything we need right here.' And eventually they went away and we never did get a union."

I thanked Art and closed my notebook. Dick shook his hand with deep respect, friend to friend, and thanked him for talking to us. I thanked him again, and Art looked back at me.

"You know, those Kikkoman people treated me right, and I sure hope I did a good job for them. It was a good place to work. No, that's not right. It was a *great* place to work!"

We left Art to finish his omelette in peace and drove back to the plant in silence. There wasn't anything more to say.

6

Mick and the Governor

The day was getting on, but I was sure I had another appointment. Dick looked at his watch and told me the most important guy was probably waiting for me right now.

"Mick Neshek," he said. "He was one of the original lawyers who helped Mr. Mogi to find this site and get permission from the town to build here. He became general counsel to KFI and has probably advised on every important decision this company ever made."

He could see that I was writing notes as best I could in the cab of a moving truck.

"By the way, his real name is Milton, but don't ever call him that. He's Mick to everybody. And a nicer guy you probably won't meet in Wisconsin."

I was starting to wonder if everybody in Wisconsin had come down with the same super-nice bug that made them all so friendly and easy to get along with. Maybe there was something in the water here, too.

We got back to the plant and I found Mr. Neshek sitting in the conference room, casually dressed in a white sport jacket and polo shirt, and halfway through a cup of coffee. Ken Tanaka was keeping him company. Earlier, Dick had told me that Mick was in his eighties, but I would never know it, because he didn't look or act anywhere near that. And I had to admit that Dick was right on target. Mick was full of energy and his voice was firm and clear. He and Ken looked up when we walked in, and he came over to shake my hand. I told him it was an honor to meet him. Why did I say that, I wondered. I didn't know much about him except what was in my sketchy background notes and what Dick had just told me. Still, I instinctively felt that anyone Mr. Mogi had trusted way-back-when to help him build this business and had kept on trusting all these years must be a pretty special person.

Mick looked at his watch and said, "Hey, we'd better get going. We have a little drive ahead of us."

I assumed he was talking to me, but I had no idea what he was talking about. I thought I was supposed to interview Mick right here.

"You and I can talk in the car," he said energetically. "We have to get over to Madison. There's somebody there you need to meet."

"An old employee? A retired manager?" I guessed.

He laughed. "No, a retired governor."

I didn't know if he was joking, but he sure sounded serious. I grabbed my sport jacket off the rack and followed Mick outside. We got in his car, a small, stylish 4WD, he backed out quickly, and headed out to the main road.

Once on the highway, he began talking about himself.

"I grew up in a small town here in Wisconsin. My dad couldn't read, my mom had a sixth grade education. I went to a one-room schoolhouse that had one teacher. I was what you would call a highly motivated student. The one thing I knew for sure was that anything resembling social mobility was going to come through education. So I studied hard.

"One year I played a lawyer in a class play. It was fun, but the image stuck with me. Well, to make a long story short, I went to University of Wisconsin, then to UW Law School, and in 1955 I became a lawyer. I was a partner in a local law firm until 1997. I never got over my commitment to higher education, though. I served as vice president on the State University Board of Regents and also on the Board of Regents for the University of Wisconsin System, and I've been involved in all sorts of advisory capacities for universities, school systems, and community colleges, both here and in California."

I found all this interesting, but I was pretty sure I could get it on a bio sheet from Kikkoman or find it on the Internet somewhere. So I asked him directly about his connection to the company.

"Well, I'm coming to that..." more than a hint of a Midwestern drawl creeping in now. "Back around 1970 I was working in my firm... I was doing a lot of estate planning back then... and this Japanese fellow comes into our office, introduces himself, and says he wants us to represent Kikkoman Corporation in the U.S. I was speechless. I'd never heard of Kikkoman Corporation and I can tell you we didn't have a lot of Japanese clients in those days! Of course, that was Yuzaburo Mogi, and I was so impressed with him. The guts it must have taken for a Japanese fellow to come all the way out here, to what must be the middle-of-nowhere for him, and just go up to an American law firm and ask them to represent his company... that's something, I'll tell you."

The road was speeding by now, we were heading farther away from Chicago and the Illinois state line, and soon I saw the first signs for Madison. I knew that Milwaukee was the most famous city in Wisconsin — it had a baseball team, breweries, and some national media attention — but what little remained from my junior high school education told me that Madison, not its more famous cousin on Lake Michigan, was the state capitol. A little bell rang upstairs: Political capital. Former governor. Natural habitat.

Neshek talked a lot about the friendship he developed with Mogi, a relationship that I gathered was still very close, and how the focus of his work and much of his life came to be on Kikkoman. When his company helped to form the legal entity now known as KFI, Neshek was asked to be on the Board of Directors, a post he still cherishes.

"Walworth was not just the first plant outside Japan. It was the beginning of internationalization for Kikkoman," he said. "It created the model, the template. In fact, we used the Wisconsin template all over the world. That means not just selling soy sauce to Japanese and Chinese restaurants, but getting ordinary people to use Kikkoman on their local foods wherever we are. We realized it's foolish to try to change people's eating habits. Instead, we change their cooking habits!" He was smiling now.

In 1997, the year he officially retired from his legal practice, he became a special consultant to Kikkoman Corporation in Tokyo. That made me take notice, because even today it is quite rare for non-Japanese to achieve that status in a major Japanese company.

"Well, enough about me," he said jovially. "You're going to meet a lot of interesting people, here and in Folsom and maybe beyond." I wasn't sure what he meant by that. "I'm kind of jealous that you're going on this tour and getting to talk to so many people inside and outside the Kikkoman organization. It's a fascinating story, you know. And there's lots of people to tell different bits of it. But it always comes back to the same things. The things that make Kikkoman what it is are the same wherever you go. You'll find that out soon enough. And the people you meet, they're all part of the Kikkoman family. As you go along, you'll see what I mean."

We drove for a bit, then Mick looked over at me and said, "Let me tell you a little story that goes back to the early days of the Walworth plant. I think it may help you to get the idea.

"Way back then, a Milwaukee TV station decided to come do a story about the plant. You know TV news — they wanted a story with some edge to it, maybe an exposé about Japanese management abusing American labor or I don't know what... That makes for sensational TV, and that's good for ratings, right? Anyway, these folks already had a negative image of our operation when they arrived. I met the TV crew and I took them around and I tried to explain that things were not the way they imagined, but I could see they weren't buying it. So I said to them, 'Look, you don't want to interview me. I'm part of the management. Go out on the floor, talk to the workers.' And that's just what they did — they went up to the first guy in a hard hat and overalls they saw, shoved a mike in his face, turned on the camera, and asked him, 'How do you feel about working here?' And he said, 'I love it.'"

Mick was chuckling now as he drove, remembering the incident.

"Well, that wasn't what they wanted to hear. The reporter asked him, 'Why? Are they paying you a lot of money?' And the guy said, 'Not really. I like working here because they actually *care* about me. They respect me and they care about my opinion. I been working as an engineer on this line for about six months. And I noticed something that could be done better, so I told my idea to my supervisor and he took it up with senior management and one day they came down, looked at the line where I was working and asked me to explain it. I showed them how we could tweak something, make it a little more efficient, and save a bit of money in the process. They wanted to be sure that any change would have absolutely no impact on the quality. Once they were sure of that, they said, *'Great. Go right ahead.'* Now, you think that's going to happen at a lot of American companies? Especially manufacturing companies? I doubt it. That's why I like working here.'

"Well, that just wasn't what the TV people wanted to hear at all. They talked to a couple of other workers and they got pretty much the same story from everybody, so they shut down the whole interview and went away."

The highway rolled on by and so did the stores. Mick turned out to be an ideal source of information. He had started out as a complete outsider and soon become a key part of Kikkoman's work in America, and he obviously loved that. He talked about all sorts of things that I would probably not have discovered from chatting with employees and managers. One of the interesting tidbits concerned a private foundation sponsored by KFI.

"The Kikkoman Foods Foundation was established back in 1993 to commemorate the twentieth anniversary of the opening of our plant in Wisconsin. KFF is not a charity; it's not about 'giving back' to the community because we have so much profit. That's not it at all. Kikkoman doesn't work like that. They do things because that is the only way they know how to operate, and what we think of as philanthropy is just common business sense to Kikkoman. Without access to clean water, they can't do business, and without the support of the local community, they can't succeed. They learned that hundreds of years ago in Noda. The local communities are an essential part of keeping the business sustainable."

I learned that the Kikkoman Foods Foundation has donated millions of dollars to charitable causes over the years, mostly in the areas of education and community development, and generally without much fanfare. This is in addition to all the charitable and civic activities that KFI undertakes every year anyway. I was beginning to get a glimpse of what makes this company tick.

In a short while, we turned off the highway and headed downtown. Sure enough, there was the state capitol building in the distance. I realized that I was about to go into an interview with someone whose name I didn't even know, much less why I was supposed to talk to him. I asked Mick to fill me in.

"Tommy? Oh, Tommy Thompson is a good man. He was governor of Wisconsin from '87 to, let me think, around 2000 or so. A Republican governor, by the way, good man. In 2001, President Bush appointed him Secretary of Health and Human Services, so he went to Washington for four years. He was also Chairman of the AMTRAK passenger railroad and a bunch of other things. You'll like him."

As a rule, politicians are not my absolute favorite people to spend time with, but this sounded important, and if Mick said he was a good guy, why should I doubt it?

We drove up to a nice building downtown, not far from the capitol building, and parked in the back. We went in a side entrance that Mick seemed to know well, down a narrow hallway and got into an elevator. We emerged a few floors upstairs in the middle of a wood-paneled private club. The light-colored walls seemed steeped in history, the floors were richly carpeted in deep burgundy, and uniformed staff hurried back and forth. I asked Mick where we were.

"The Madison Club, of course," he said with a smile. "This place has been here for over a hundred years, and believe me, in the old days it was probably the most important building in the state. It's a safe bet more political deals were worked out in one of the rooms here over whiskey and cigars than ever got done over there." He pointed his thumb in the direction of the State Capitol.

"Tommy and I used to come here a lot, and I'm sure he still spends a lot of time here. Wait! I think I hear him now."

Indeed, I could hear a deep, powerful baritone that carried right through the very solid walls of the Club. Mick went up to the door closest to where the sound was emanating from, tapped twice and opened it. But he didn't step in, just stuck his head in and said, "Hi, Tommy, sorry to interrupt. We still on for 2:00? Okay, just checking."

Returning to me, he said, "Tommy's got someone in there with him, but they'll be finished in a minute. We'll just sit out here and wait."

We sat on heavily upholstered antique-styled chairs in the hallway, and in a few moments the door we were waiting for opened. A well-dressed man in his forties backed out, still talking to the unseen occupant inside. "Whatever you could do, Governor, I'd appreciate it," he said, waved, and departed. Old politicians never die, I thought, they just keep getting asked for favors until the sun burns out. We both got up and Mick led the way into the inner sanctum.

My first impression, shaking hands with Governor Thompson (yes, everyone still calls him by his old title), was that he looked and sounded a bit like Robert Mitchum in his later years. Big guy, friendly, with a deep, strong voice that could easily fill a large room with little effort. He was sitting at a desk, wearing a shirt and tie, his suit jacket slung over the back of his armchair.

"Good to see you," he bellowed to Mick. "Why has it been so long?" Then, casting a quick glance at me, and in mock serious-ness, "What can I do for you gentlemen, today?"

Mick greeted him as an old friend and they talked about people they knew, who was doing what, and so on, and then Mick introduced me and my research project.

"Well, I don't know what I can tell you that others can't," the big man said.

I told him that I just wanted to talk to people who knew different parts of the Kikkoman story and could give me an interesting perspective. Since he had been a politician in Madison, not in Walworth, and since he was in office long after Kikkoman first came to Wisconsin, I assumed he knew the company as a more mature enterprise and could speak about its later activities and influence in the state. I should have known that every good politician has a few dozen speeches stored in long-term memory, and you only need to push the right button to start one playing. My questions seemed to have that effect, but after all, it was exactly what I wanted to hear, and I sensed that Thompson believed what he was telling me.

"Kikkoman has had a tremendous impact on the State of Wisconsin," he began slowly, then gradually picked up both speed and volume. "I'm talking about economics, trade, publicity, jobs, tourism, culture — all of these things directly relate to what Kikkoman has brought to the State of Wisconsin.

"You have to realize that until recently this was a 'flyover' state, a place you passed over on the way from the East Coast to the West Coast or vice versa. Most people didn't even know where we were on a map of the U.S.

"But one young man had the audacity to talk to his father and the board of directors of a big company in Tokyo and tell them that the entire future of their company depended on expanding into the United States. That man was Yuzaburo Mogi, and his vision built that company into what it is today and left an imprint on Wisconsin that is second to none.

"Of course, what young Mogi proposed at that time was very risky, and if things didn't go well for him in the U.S., it would have meant a lot more than a black mark on his record back home. He might not have had a company to return to. But his biggest challenge wasn't over here, it was back home: He had to convince his father, who was president of Kikkoman, that this was a good idea. His father was an old-school Japanese who had lived through the war, and I'm sure there was still a lot of distrust of America, and lots of concerns about setting up a company in America. And then for his son to say they should locate this new plant somewhere in the Midwest? That must have sounded crazy. His father probably had to get out a map and say, 'Show me where Wisconsin is.'

"But Yuzaburo is a visionary, and he always was. He knew what had to be done. So he and a friend of his from Columbia University—"

Mick interjected for my benefit, "That was Malcolm Pennington."

"—Right, Pennington." Thompson continued: "He and Mogi went looking for the right place to put this new factory. They started looking in the Midwest because they needed soy and wheat and a good transportation infrastructure. Luckily for them and for us, Mogi hired Mick Neshek's law firm to help him find the right place. Mick's partner—"

"Tom Godfrey," Mick added quietly.

"Right. Tom and Mick became the point men helping to bring this thing to Wisconsin. Mick here convinced our then-governor to open the doors and welcome a Japanese company. Remember, there were no Japanese companies in America back then. This was a whole new thing. Wisconsin is fairly conservative, and to have a foreign company say they're going to build a factory here and have Japanese people come over to manage it and live among the locals, that was a pretty radical thing.

"To tell you the truth, it was Mick who made that possible. He developed a fantastic friendship with Yuzaburo Mogi. They built a plant in Walworth County and made that plant Kikkoman's flagship plant. I believe it's the biggest single *shoyu* plant in the world, and from what I hear, the *shoyu* they make there is the best in the world!

"Yuzaburo and his father both came to the Grand Opening in '73. It was a bad winter, too, several degrees below zero that day, right Mick?"

Neshek nodded, looking more like he wanted to forget the weather that day.

"And Yuzaburo has visited here many, many times. The Mogis have planted roots here in Walworth County, and they made all sorts of contributions to the area. I can tell you, they became a part of Wisconsin, and they've done a tremendous job not just for us, but for the whole Midwest. They brought a whole new culture into our state, and they built a highly automated plant that exports all over the world and is a showpiece for us as well as for them. They also made Kikkoman the top-selling soy sauce in America because people like the company and the taste of the product. All these things add up to a great partnership.

"It has been very profitable for the company and for Wisconsin. It also showed many other Asian companies that they should look seriously at the Midwest as a place to locate their businesses. And we have tourism here that we never had before. They provided a great tax base for the state as well as the town, and they pay good salaries to their workers, and those workers also pay taxes, so it's been real good for us economically.

"I even appointed Mr. Mogi as Wisconsin's honorary ambassador to Japan. Well, he took that title and raised it to a whole new level, inviting all sorts of businesses to visit Wisconsin, and he has become very influential with many governors all across the Midwest, both Democrat and Republican. He transcends both political and business boundaries. He's been a terrific chairman of the Midwest-U.S. Japan Association, and governors all over the Midwest know him and respect him. He is the heart and soul and conscience of that organization."

He paused for just a moment, perhaps needing air, perhaps just looking for the last page of the speech in his memory.

"Every five years the factory there in Walworth has a big anniversary party. And Mogi brings over lots of people from Japan and all sorts of people from around the U.S. It's a tremendous opportunity for people to get to know Japanese culture and understand Japanese business better. They have a big dinner, and we all put on traditional Japanese *happi* coats, and we break open those casks of sake. It's a great time."

I had one awkward question to ask.

"Governor, I've heard stories that not everyone welcomed Kikkoman with open arms when they first came here. You just said that there were no Japanese companies anywhere around and Wisconsin is pretty conservative. Didn't that cause problems?"

"You can ask Mick here about the details, but I'll tell you right now, people *love* Kikkoman. I would defy you to find one person in Walworth County, or even in the whole State of Wisconsin today, who would not agree that Kikkoman is a great neighbor and has been a very good thing for this community. It's a great company. I'm very proud that we have such a first-class company in our community. We're all proud to have Kikkoman here."

We talked a little more, then Mick and Tommy spent several minutes discussing business matters of mutual interest, and then it was time to go. I thanked the governor for making time to see us and for giving me so much good background.

He shook my hand for a long time and showed me to the door.

"It's always my pleasure to talk about Kikkoman and Mogi-san. They have left a lasting mark on Wisconsin. And a lot of it is due to this guy." He pointed at Mick. "Get him to tell you about his role in all of this."

I noticed someone else was waiting outside the door, just as we had been half an hour earlier. Thompson waved goodbye to us, looked at his watch, and showed the next visitor into the room. "Good to see you," I could hear him bellow to his guest. "Why has it been so long?"

Mick and I retraced our route to the elevator, out to the car, and back on the highway to Walworth. Once we were up to speed again, Mick looked over at me.

"Well, was that worthwhile?"

"Yes. For sure. He's quite a character."

"Yes he is," Mick agreed. "But he's a good guy. We're still friends after all this time."

I got the impression that Mick had a lot of friends, not just here in Wisconsin, and maybe not just here in the United States. We chatted a lot and had an interesting ride back to the plant, during which I decided to stop being a journalist, talk to him like a friend, and put away my notepad.

7

Folsom

olsom. Millions of people around the world know the name of the city. Unfortunately, the connection is not the one that the Folsom Chamber of Commerce would most like to promote. In 1955, Elvis Presley's legendary producer, Sam Phillips recorded a then-unknown country singer by the name of Johnny Cash at his now-famous Sun Studio in Memphis. One song, *Folsom Prison Blues,* became a No. 1 hit for Cash and one of the signature songs that identified him throughout his career, and it spawned dozens of cover versions by both country and rock musicians. With that background, it is hard for anyone in North America (this writer included) to hear the name "Folsom" and not think of the song and the prison.

Fortunately, the town has much more to recommend it than the century-old maximum security facility that bears its name. A dam built just one year after Cash recorded his famous song created a picturesque lake, home to the Folsom Lake Recreational Area, which is studded with scenic bike and hiking trails (and yes, there's a Johnny Cash Trail and even a Johnny Cash Bridge, proving that the resourceful locals are adept at turning a curse into a blessing). Today, Folsom is a pretty town of about 75,000 people, known as a quiet residential area with attractive natural scenery and also as one end of the American River Bike Trail. It is also quite business-friendly, as evidenced by a large Intel R&D facility with several thousand employees.

However, there is another institution that is gradually changing the image of Folsom, though without either world-changing technology or a huge payroll. Just as it did for the town Walworth, Kikkoman has become a model citizen in Folsom, and the products made here, at its second U.S. plant, are shipped all over the West Coast and far beyond.

I arrived on a sunny afternoon (that seems to be the only kind they have in Folsom), having driven a rental car all the way from San Francisco International Airport. I drove up to Glenn Drive, the home of Kikkoman's expansive facility, where once again I had to stop at the perimeter gate and announce myself to the security system. They seemed to recognize my name, and the gate swung open. As I pulled into the parking lot, I immediately noticed something different from its Wisconsin sibling: An awning of solar panels was mounted over the parking lot. Smart move, I thought. This part of the world is bathed in sunlight, so the shade is welcome, and from a PR standpoint, it's smart to put your support for the environment out front where people can see it. After Walworth, I had a much better idea of how much electric power Kikkoman consumes monthly, so I knew that any movement toward alternative energy made a lot of sense. What's good for the planet is also good for the bottom line — that's what most CEOs mean by "sustainability."

Before going inside, I walked around the front of the plant. There were acres of grass, some green and a lot brown (I did mention the Sahara-like sunlight, yes?), a bike trail that my research said Kikkoman had donated, and of course, the massive airplane hangar-like structures and silos that made up the plant. Anyone looking at this large structure would naturally assume that at least 500-1,000 people worked inside. After my experience in Walworth, though, I knew that automation was the name of the game and the actual workforce must be a fraction of that. I took some snapshots and looked up at the hot sun, then walked over to the office building, where I knew there would be air conditioning.

I discovered the Plant Manager, Takuma Morita, waiting for me. Like his counterpart in Walworth, he wore a beige company jacket, but otherwise looked the part of a Japanese "salaryman" (company employee), not a haughty manager. Switching my brain to Japanese mode, I quickly apologized for wandering around outside, taking pictures and sightseeing, and thus keeping him waiting.

"No, not at all," he said politely, as he extended his business card to me. "Please call me Tak. Would you like to see the plant first?"

I told him yes, I was eager to see how this plant compared to its "big brother" in Wisconsin. But first, my impressions from the outside view had made me curious about the work force. How many people operated this plant, I asked? 150? 100?

"Altogether?" He thought for a moment. "Around thirty."

Incredible, I thought. This was a very large plant, perhaps not as large as the one in Walworth, but still quite big, and yet a handful of people ran the whole thing. And of those thirty, some were administrators, secretaries, and so on. The actual number of line workers must be very small.

"Two things to remember about *shoyu* production," Tak reminded me. "One, the whole process is now highly automated, so it doesn't need hundreds of people, and two, the *koji* mold does all the hard work, the fermentation process. It's working hard even while we are all asleep." He gave me a big smile.

As before, we changed into white coats, hairnets, and blue shoe coverings. Then we proceeded into the production area.

Once again, the first thing that struck me was the warm, moist air and the indescribable, musty smell of *shoyu* being made. I imagine big beer breweries must be something akin to this. Anywhere that yeasts are at work has a special aroma, one you get accustomed to very quickly.

Tak walked me around, just like my previous tour with Dick. The Folsom plant had the same long, empty, cinder block corridors without a single motivational poster, note even a "Safety is No. 1" sign. One difference was that here, at the intersections to these 100-yard corridors there were "street signs": Wheat Way and Soy Street and so on. The halls were painted a pastel yellow and were wide and tall enough to drive a large fork lift through. The long expanse was broken only by an occasional set of large, steel double-doors, with signs to identify each room. Opening any of the doors usually led to a cavernous room filled with some kind of machinery.

Just as I'd expected, the basic manufacturing process here was exactly the same as in Wisconsin, and as we walked I tested my memory. I knew the big silos I saw from outside held large supplies of wheat and soy beans, and I mentally ran through all the steps in the production process before Tak showed them to me. I mentally ticked off each step as we walked along.

At the end of the tour Tak pointed to a sign for the Laboratory and said, "Did you see that in Walworth?" I shook my head. "Well, as you probably know already, we sample the product and send the samples to our lab for analysis."

I said that I assumed the company tested its finished products occasionally.

"Oh no," he looked surprised. "We take samples at every stage — when it is raw, pasteurized, refined, heated, and so on. And, of course we constantly sample the finished products that get bottled or packaged. Oh, and in case no one mentioned it before, we regularly send samples back to the big lab in Japan for testing. They want to verify our results and also monitor for even tiny changes in quality. You've probably seen already that at Kikkoman, quality control is like our religion."

We both laughed at that, because it is obviously true. If auto-makers were as meticulous with their production, there would be no such things as recalls. Tak paused for a moment, thinking, then said, "You should meet Elena. She's in charge of the labo-ratory. I'll make sure she has some time to talk to you...if you're interested, that is."

Just as I was saying that I was very interested, he opened another big door and we stepped into yet another big room. Before I could even ask what all this equipment was for, Tak called one of the guys over, a big, friendly-looking fellow, and introduced him.

"David, this is DK."

We shook hands and he grinned.

"Darren King, but everyone calls me DK."

By way of introduction, Tak said, "I was just showing David our production process and telling him about sampling..." Then, turning to me, "DK is our brewing supervisor. He knows this stuff inside-out."

I asked if I could steal five minutes of DK's time. Tak nodded, and we went over to one side of the room and found something to sit on. I asked DK how he came to know this business so well. Was he involved with brewing or something like it before?

"No way. I worked in a sausage company before this. Of course, I knew the Kikkoman name, and I was getting ready to change jobs, so I decided to try my luck. I had to go through four interviews, and I was real nervous, believe me. I had to admit that I didn't know anything about making soy sauce, but they said that's okay, nobody else does either. I was real lucky they hired me."

"And how long ago was that?" I asked automatically, my nose buried in my notes.

"Let me see. How long has the plant been here? I guess that was eighteen years ago. Time goes fast."

Even as I wrote that down, a little bell was ringing somewhere in my head. One more person had somehow found his way into the Kikkoman family and never left.

"So what happened?" I asked. "You got hired but you didn't know anything about making *shoyu*. How did you learn?" I wondered if California boys were being shipped to Japan to study at the Noda plant. But I had forgotten the obvious.

"They sent us all out to Walworth for three months of training. I studied hard and worked hard and took lots of notes. I came back here and started working in pressing and refining, which I liked. They sent me back to Wisconsin for another month of training. I actually enjoyed it. Pretty soon I was the foreman here, and eventually they made me the Brewing Supervisor."

Training at the Walworth plant made a lot of sense. But packing these guys off to Wisconsin, maybe in the dead of winter, for three months sounded a little rough. I remembered that Japanese companies routinely send their staff overseas for long periods, often without their families, and I knew many an office worker who had returned from a five-year posting in Africa or Southeast Asia to discover that his kids were grown up and in high school now. Meanwhile, he had missed some of the most important years in their development and they had essentially grown up without a father. No one in Japan thinks this is strange. Making sacrifices for the good of the company is normal and expected, and I had already noted that a few of the Kikkoman staff in America were here solo (*tanshin funin*) without their families. Nobody likes it, but the men accept it, and so do their wives and kids. The practice is gradually fading in Japan, but it is not likely to disappear, because the head office always wants to send men it trusts to work in key overseas posts, and it also wants to give them international experience, which is becoming more and more important in climbing the executive ladder these days.

Still, this was not Japan. And these were brand new hires, not men who had already made a lifelong commitment to the company. I had to ask him about it.

"DK, I'm sure all that training was necessary, but wasn't it hard on you and the other guys, you know, to be away from home for three months so you could study *shoyu*-making in Wisconsin? What if your wife was having a baby or something?"

"No, no. It was nothing like that. They flew us home *every weekend* so we could be with our families. It wasn't hard for us at all."

Okay, that was a new one. I had never heard of a company taking American workers halfway across the country for training, then flying them home weekly to spend time with their families. Even to me it seemed an extravagant expense, and yet, on reflection I could see how important it was for gaining the trust and loyalty of their new hires. The proof was standing right in front of me. Eighteen years with the company and still going strong.

I asked DK about what Tak had just told me about sampling.

"Yes. After pressing, we let the sauce settle for a few days. Then we filter it again and let it sit in heating tanks for a few days to acquire more flavor and color. And we take samples constantly, at every stage."

Tak was subtly tapping his watch, and I knew I should let DK get back to his job. We shook hands again as we stood up and I thanked him for taking time to talk to me.

"You going to stick around here a few more years?" I asked half in jest.

"At least a few more." He smiled again, "I like it here. This is a really good job and a really good company. I still give samples of Kikkoman products to my friends — I'm proud of what we do here."

He waved as he walked away and I looked at Tak. Once again I was impressed by the kind of person I had met in a Japanese-owned food plant in rural America.

"Where do you *find* these people?" I asked rhetorically.

"There are many good people wherever you go," he said. "We are just lucky to find so many to work for us."

Right, I thought, just lucky. After spending several years searching for just the "right" locations, with the quality of the local labor force being a key factor in what constitutes "just right," and then interviewing people four times to be sure you've found candidates with just the right character, the right work ethic, and the right personality, I was supposed to believe that everything is a result of luck? I didn't think so.

I realized that Kikkoman's attitude towards its employees was not really necessary in order to run a manufacturing plant, but it was very important if the company expected its employees to bond with the company and become members of a large community that they would never leave, and one that was ready to drop everything to come to the aid of any employee if someone was ever in need.

I realized that I was beginning to understand Kikkoman's "corporate DNA," the core values that make it what it is. Every good company has that essential DNA, but it's not always easy to see. I didn't see it when I first began looking at this company, but I was starting to get it now.

Tak and I chatted some more as we continued walking around the plant. I asked to see the bottling operation, something I had only glimpsed in Walworth. He took me to the bottling room, where I saw an endless flow of bottles being filled, packed into cartons, labeled, and stacked. I noticed a bright yellow Fanuc robot arm with a very sophisticated-looking computerized control panel. The robot picked up each carton of *shoyu* coming down the conveyor line and stacked it neatly on the pallet. Not just stacked them in a single tower, but placed each one in proper order in a 4 x 4 grid, with only a few millimeters between the stacks. Of course, cartons were coming along at a fast clip, so the robot arm had to move rapidly to pick and stack properly. I was impressed.

Tak also showed me a giant storeroom holding not only cartons of retail-size bottles such as I'd just seen, but also four different sizes of big, commercial-use containers. The main one was a white plastic bucket that held five gallons. These were crammed onto pallets and the pallets were stacked up high.

"These buckets are very popular with restaurants," he explained. "They can buy one bucket and refill a whole roomful of small bottles to set out on tables."

Then he pointed to what looked like large, blue plastic kegs, also stacked up.

"Those each hold eleven buckets' worth, or fifty-five gallons. Also popular with big restaurants or other commercial kitchens. And over there," pointing to even larger containers, "Those hold 270 gallons. Those go to special commercial customers."

I was impressed at the size of these things. I never imagined anyone, even a big commercial kitchen, would order a 270-gallon drum of *shoyu*. But Tak surprised me again, saying they had a 4,700-gallon tanker. Back at Walworth, someone had hinted that *shoyu* was such a good flavor enhancer that it was regularly used as an ingredient in all sorts of commercial sauces, stews, soups, and so on. I'd heard it was one of the secret ingredients that a giant, globally famous hamburger chain used for one of their dipping sauces and other famous food chains used in similar products. I found it hard to believe that only a couple of weeks ago I was in New York, where Barb Stuckey had surprised me by calling *shoyu* a "magic seasoning" that sparked up everything, not just sushi, and now here I was in California, finally beginning to understand how ubiquitous this magic seasoning was in the American diet.

I asked Tak if the rumors about the big hamburger chain and other popular food companies using Kikkoman *shoyu* were true. He smiled and said, "Between you and me, yes they're true. But you can't write about that. Those companies don't want to advertise what goes into their recipes." He thought a moment, then added, "Besides, *shoyu* is never the star on the stage of a great meal. It always plays a supporting role, helping the star to look better. We are happy to be in that role."

He mentioned a few famous-brand spaghetti sauces, pizza sauces, and other popular canned goods you would find on the shelves of any food store anywhere in America. Apparently, they all used Kikkoman sauce in their mix, although their labels list only soybeans and wheat as ingredients. It was beginning to sound as if an average housewife's shopping cart in any U.S. supermarket would have at least a couple of items made with *shoyu* (often labelled only as "natural seasonings" or some such vague term). I was also beginning to understand why Kikkoman needed 4,700-gallon trucks to make deliveries to certain customers.

We wandered back to the office area, and Tak showed me to a conference room similar to the one in Walworth. While I relaxed and had a cup of coffee, he said he would check with the lab to see if Elena could take a few moments to talk to me. I was barely halfway through my coffee when he popped back in, saying, "She's pretty busy today, but she said she would make a little time. If you could keep it brief, she would appreciate it."

He showed me to the laboratory and quickly introduced me to a pleasant-looking middle-aged woman in a genuine lab coat. Elena shook my hand a bit tentatively and motioned for me to sit down. I pulled out a chair for Tak, but he said he had work to do and begged to be excused. I understood. He didn't want to sit in on employee interviews. If we were walking through the plant and he spotted someone to introduce me to, that was different. But in this kind of situation, where I was talking to someone who had a private office or workspace, it would feel more relaxed if the boss were elsewhere.

I told Elena that I hadn't had a chance to see the lab at Walworth and I was interested in her work.

"Actually, I don't normally work in the lab," she said. "I sit at a desk. My responsibilities are not just the food safety program, but also the company's environmental program and more."

"Tell me about the environmental program. That's another thing I forgot to ask about at Walworth."

"I'm sure you saw the solar panels in the parking lot..."

I nodded.

"Well, Kikkoman is basically a very environmentally friendly group. Long before we had an official environmental program, they were already very forward-thinking in that area. They recycled almost everything. Now we pay careful attention to things like natural resources, preventing pollution, sustainability, reducing waste, encouraging green practices, and more. This plant has won many, many environmental awards year after year, so many that I think they stopped including us in the competition. Like California's state-wide waste-reduction award program, which we won every year, and the Sacramento sustainable business award that we won several times. The Business Environmental Resource Center gave us an award, and a whole lot more.

"As you can imagine, this is a pretty clean operation to begin with, not like a chemical plant or anything like that. The main byproducts we produce are soy cake, which gets recycled as animal feed, and soy oil, which goes into biodiesel. Of course, we have air pollution controls, and we pay a lot of attention to waste water. But on the whole, it's a pretty clean operation from the start. Still, it's my job to see that we monitor everything all the time, just to be sure."

So far, everyone I'd met at Kikkoman was a lifer — people who joined and never wanted to leave. The only person I'd met who had retired was the "Art of Shoyu," who told me he regretted it. So, was Elena a lifer from the beginning?

"Not at the beginning, no. Like a lot of Americans, I was expecting to work a number of different jobs, pick up some knowledge and experience at each one, and work my way up to increasingly responsible positions. So in the beginning I came here mostly to gain more experience. Everything that I did, I thought of as one more line on my resume. My attitude was:

Give me more experience, help me build my skills, and then maybe I'll go elsewhere."

What happened?

"I never even sent out my resume."

Why not?

"From the time I first started here, I felt very lucky. I felt I was contributing a lot and they were giving me a chance to learn so much. I realized that a lot of the things I was getting to do were things that other people pay money to learn. Here, they were paying me and giving me more and more opportunities for learning and growth. After a while, I began to feel that the company needs me and I don't need to be working on my resume.

"More than anything, I would say there have always been learning opportunities here, and that's important to me. There's always something to do, always more to learn, not just for me but for everybody. That's a really good environment to be working in."

—§—

After my interesting chat with Elena, I met Tak coming down the hall to get me. He said Mick Neshek was waiting for me in the conference room. That was a surprise. I had just left Mick back in Wisconsin after our chat with the ex-governor. No one had told me he was coming to Folsom, but Tak informed me that Mick is constantly in motion. And sure enough, there he was at the conference table, again in a lightweight summer sport jacket and a classy polo shirt, looking as bored and impatient as a man thirty years his junior. He jumped up when he saw me coming and shook my hand quickly.

"All done? We have another meeting. I want you to get a little more background and history about the situation here in Folsom. I hope you've got an appetite, because we're going to have a good meal."

Two minutes later, we were speeding down the road, heading to some restaurant that he was talking about and I wasn't paying much attention to. My brain was still stuck in the, "What is Mick from Wisconsin doing in California?" mode. Much later I learned that, from long ago Mick had been traveling the globe for Kikkoman, acting as a permanent ambassador for the company. He was, as one of the guys in Walworth said, "a force of Nature."

After a short drive, we pulled up to a big, fancy-looking restaurant. Mick was still going on about something and I was nodding but not taking any of it in. Sensory overload from driving around California for the first time in years. We walked into the restaurant and almost immediately I spied a good-looking fellow with wavy white hair sitting alone in a private dining room. Blue sport jacket, button down shirt, striped tie — way too formal for California in the warm weather, I thought. He must be waiting for someone. He had a tall glass of beer in front of him and seemed not at all impatient for his guest to arrive.

"Bob!" Neshek called out to him, in a voice that carried across most of the restaurant. The well-dressed gentleman looked up, saw us coming in, and rose to greet us. He and Mick shook hands like old friends, then Mick introduced me to Bob Holderness, who pumped my hand vigorously and motioned for us all to sit down. Mick ordered a bottle of wine, and he and Bob exchanged "What have you been up to?" chit-chat for a few minutes. Just listening to their conversation, I could tell that Bob was a smart, modest guy with a good sense of humor. We were going to get along.

After a bottle of good Napa Chardonnay arrived, I interrupted their friendly catching up and asked Holderness about his connection with Kikkoman.

"Well, I was the mayor of Folsom at the time Folsom had the opportunity to court Kikkoman and convince them to come to Folsom."

That was interesting. I remembered Governor Thompson's comments about Kikkoman trying hard to persuade Walworth to let them in. This sounded like just the opposite.

"So you had to court them? They didn't try to sell themselves to you?"

"No. We wanted them. Actually, Kikkoman was not the first company of its kind to arrive. Gekkeikan, a famous Japanese sake maker, opened a factory here. They came here for the same reason Kikkoman did — for the water. They said the chemical composition of the water here was perfect, just the same as what they were used to in Japan. Gekkeikan was a good addition to our community, but it was a bit small to have any major impact on our economy. When Kikkoman first started looking at Folsom, I was very excited. Kikkoman was a whole different thing for us, and I was determined that they should settle here.

"Ultimately, this guy—" he slapped Mick on the shoulder, "— and I managed to convince Kikkoman that this was a good place for them."

At this point, Neshek added his own perspective.

"For a while we were looking seriously at Corvalis, Oregon. It's a nice town, and we saw a site up there that we liked a lot, but Bob made us such a good deal that we couldn't say no. And we're delighted with that decision. Folsom has been very good for Kikkoman."

Got that. But how good has Kikkoman been for Folsom, I wondered. I put the question to the former mayor.

"It's been wonderful. Kikkoman's contribution to the community has been just tremendous. They're a very low-profile, high-impact contributor, which is a combination you don't see a lot these days. They don't draw attention to themselves; they're not all about getting media attention or press clippings, they just pitch in and help. My feeling while I was mayor was that if Folsom needed something, I would go talk to Kikkoman. I'm a private citizen now and I still feel that way. They're more than just good neighbors."

Could he give me a specific example of Kikkoman's contribution?

"Look at their work with our local community college. They have been fantastic in contributing to Folsom Lake College. For me, it's very inspirational to see how Kikkoman recognizes places and projects that really need help, and then focuses on those. They don't contribute to causes that don't matter just to gain some publicity. Our community college really needs help to grow and develop, and Kikkoman has been very influential. What kind of impact has Kikkoman had on this community? In a word, tremendous."

Before we left, Bob told me something in passing that seemed a minor footnote to the whole Folsom discussion, but which resonated with me very strongly later on. Thinking about it helped me to get a better understanding of the big picture, of what really makes Kikkoman tick.

"After the decision was made to build in Folsom, the company made a generous donation to the town of Corvallis. It was just a kind of thank-you from Kikkoman to the town that had almost become their new home. How many companies have you ever heard of do something like that? 'Sorry we weren't able to become part of your community, but we'd like to show our gratitude for you being such nice hosts.' It's hard to believe!"

I looked at Mick for confirmation. He waved his hand, looking a bit embarrassed.

"Yes, it's true. But that's just the way Kikkoman is. You should understand that by now. Not everything is a business transaction with this company; they're not trying to buy goodwill from anyone. They do things that don't make much sense from a textbook perspective, but make perfectly good sense from their perspective. Our contribution to Corvallis was no big deal; we weren't looking to get anything, just to give something, because we wanted to. It was just a friendly gesture. And what's wrong with that?"

I shook my head. Nothing's wrong with that. But now I was beginning to see that occasionally Kikkoman operates more like an individual than a giant business. It had that kind of "personality." And where did that personality come from? Whose DNA was imprinted on the company's DNA? I was pretty sure I already knew the answer to that.

—§—

After we left the restaurant, Mick and I talked a bit about Bob Holderness and some of the things he mentioned. I was especially interested in the college he mentioned.

"Folsom Lake?" Mick asked, a bit surprised. "Would you like to see it? Or better yet, see the jewel in the crown? How about tomorrow you and I drive over to the Harris Center and get President Rosenthal to show us around?"

I instinctively told him that sounded like a good idea, although I had no idea what he was talking about. I assumed the Harris Center was the main administration building, and having a meeting with the president of the college (another aging Robert Mitchum, no doubt) sounded like the best way to get information. Odds were good that Mick already knew the guy and they'd be into a second round of martinis over lunch before I was able to ask a question.

Mick drove me back to the hotel where I was staying, and we agreed to meet the next day. I spent the following morning writing at my desk, had a bite to eat downstairs at the hotel restaurant, and then Mick came to pick me up. Folsom isn't all that big, and it wasn't a long drive to the college. But instead of driving into the front of the campus, Mick entered from the rear and drove us up to a large, very modern complex. A big sign high on the wall said, "Harris Center" and in smaller letters, "Three Stages." Above the entranceway big, cut-out metal letters spelled out, "Harris Center for the Arts." Okay, I thought, so it isn't the Administration building.

We stepped inside the cool, high-ceilinged lobby of some kind of performing arts center. There were posters and flyers and card stock advertising upcoming events. I took a quick peek — Broadway shows, dance recitals, contemporary music, solo artists, orchestras, classical, jazz... several of these were nationally famous acts and a couple were international. This was quite a place, and I'd never even heard of it. Mick spoke to a young woman nearby, perhaps one of the staff, perhaps a student, and asked where we could find Rachel. Hello? I thought. Who is Rachel?

We were directed to a small room nearby, where we found two women deep in a discussion about the planning for some upcoming show. The one doing most of the talking looked rather young to be a professor, perhaps an actress here. I had to remind myself that college faculty these days look more like their grad students than like the chalk-grey, walking-dead professors of my college days (full disclosure: the Pony Express was like the Internet when I was a student).

When the discussion was finished and the other woman left, Mick stepped up to the woman I had noticed right away said a bright, "Hi, Rachel. Good of you to meet us like this."

The well-dressed executive turned around to look at me. Okay, she was definitely older than her students, but not like — how would my son describe it? — "college-president *old*."

"Dave, I'd like you to meet Rachel Rosenthal, the president of Folsom Lake College," Mick said, almost formally.

Rachel and I shook hands, and she invited us to sit down.

"What do you think of the facility?" she asked.

I told her I had just arrived, but the little I had seen was impressive. She insisted we take a tour later on, which sounded good to me, but first I needed to get some quick background. She picked up the cue and I picked up my notebook.

"This is the Harris Center for the Arts, which is many different things," she said. "It's the home for Folsom Lake College's visual and performing arts classes, but it's also used for other learning programs to benefit the community. It's probably best known as a special performance event space open to the public, acting as a virtual home for our local artists and arts organizations, and also presenting outstanding artists from around the world.

"In a nutshell, Harris is a $50 million performing arts center, the only one of its kind in the State of California. As you'll see in a moment, it's a stunningly beautiful theater. We bring Broadway shows in here, plus all sorts of music and dance from around the world. Of course, the college uses it, too, but much of the activity here is more for the community. We bring in all sorts of performances that we think will interest people in the local or regional community and present them at reasonable prices."

"It all looks brand new," I said, looking around.

"It is," she stated simply. "The building opened five years ago, so it still feels very new."

"How big is the whole facility?"

"About 80,000 square feet, which is a *lot* of space for a community-oriented performing arts center like this."

I looked at Mick and asked, "I assume Kikkoman is involved with this somehow?"

He simply pointed back at Rachel.

"To build this unique structure there was a capital campaign. Kikkoman was instrumental in helping to raise funds for that campaign. In fact, the green room is named for Kikkoman. And Kikkoman has sponsored several of our annual galas at Harris. To put it simply, this place probably wouldn't exist without Kikkoman."

I got the feeling that Rachel was getting tired of being interviewed. "Come on," she said, standing up. "I'll show you around. We can walk and talk."

She opened the doors to Stage One, the largest hall, which I had to admit was absolutely gorgeous. It was a brightly colored, well-lit, comfortably-sized theater for about 800 guests, with a balcony and a few private boxes. Rachel went on in detail about Stage One, even showing us around back stage. Then she took us to Stage Two, which was much smaller, though also attractive, and Stage Three, an intimate recital hall for solo acts.

"As you can see, we have excellent venues for everything from a full symphony to a student play or a solo recital. All the acoustics are superb and artists tell us they love it here."

Interesting as this all was, I had come to learn about the college, the president, and what a Japanese soy sauce company was doing here. Rachel took us to the mezzanine area, where we could relax and chat. I asked her for a quick, thumbnail sketch of the school. She told me it was a normal two-year community college spread over three campuses and serving over 8,000 students. Because it was a community college, it didn't offer the same BS or BA degree as a four-year college, but it did offer sixty-five different associate degrees and certificates. Most of the students were college-age and most transfered directly into traditional four-year schools after graduating from FLC.

Fine. Now, what about the president?

"I grew up in Oklahoma," she explained, unconsciously showing off how completely she had lost her Okie drawl. "I came to Folsom Lake in 2012, just after Harris opened. And right away I encountered Kikkoman... and this guy." She squeezed Mick's arm affectionately. "He's a founding member of the Folsom Lake College Foundation Board. That foundation has raised, and continues to raise funds to help students. There is also a special President's Circle funded through the foundation that allows me discretionary funds to use for whatever special initiatives I choose, without state or local control. That is truly a luxury for a college executive. The only criteria are that the funds are to be used by the president to support any individual or event of cultural or educational merit."

"And Kikkoman—" I began.

"—was the first to donate to the President's Circle," she finished. "I should add that the college has only three endowed scholarships, and one of them is provided by Kikkoman. They endowed a scholarship in 2012 that will provide tuition assistance for one student and will operate forever. It's a very significant contribution to our mission."

Once again, I had discovered how deeply the company wanted to sink roots into the communities where it operates.

"Kikkoman is very active here," she continued. "The thing everybody loves most is the sushi events. Every year we have a big sushi event, which brings in over a hundred people from the community. It doesn't sound like a big deal, but it is one of the best-received social events of the season. Kikkoman brings in a top-notch sushi chef and throws a big bash. You'd be amazed at how popular that is!"

Years ago, I researched another Japanese company, and while I was traveling around the world talking to people, someone said something that suddenly came to mind as I was sitting here in the Harris Center, listening to an American college president talk about a soy sauce company:

"There's a big difference between doing PR because you think it's good for your company image or it's the smart thing to do, and actively engaging with people because it's what you *want* to do. It's rare, but occasionally you see cases where companies aren't doing it all for show; it's actually the way they think, it's part of their corporate character. That's where you see what a company is made of. That's when you see their DNA."

8

San Francisco

I was still getting my things together in Folsom, deciding how to structure my itinerary from here on, when Tak Morita asked me what my plans were. I said I wasn't quite sure yet, but it certainly seemed like I should get out of the U.S. and go see what the company was doing in Europe.

"That's a good idea," he agreed. "But can you wait a couple of days? You haven't been to KSU in San Francisco yet, have you? That was our first company in the U.S. You should really go there. Of course, we've got a research outfit near Chicago and JFC down in LA and other locations here and there, but before you go see what's happening in Europe, you should definitely check out KSU. You've seen two production plants. Now go see what the sales and marketing side looks like. I can make a call and tell them you're coming down."

He gave me an address in downtown San Francisco and wished me well. Okay, why not, I thought. I still had my rental car, and I'd pass right by San Francisco on my way to the airport anyway, so I decided to take Tak's advice and head back toward the Bay.

I'm an East Coast boy, born and bred, but I have to confess that San Francisco is one of my favorite cities. Not too big, not too small, full of energy, art, music, culture of all kinds, lots of boutique hotels in every price range, and arguably, the largest number of great restaurants per capita of any city in the U.S. A few days in San Francisco are never a burden, and besides, why shouldn't I enjoy myself a little?

I booked a room at the Fairmont Hotel downtown, left the rental car with the valet, dropped my bags in my room, and stepped out into the sunshine. I'd chosen this hotel in part because it adjoins California Street, one of the major avenues running roughly East-West towards the Bay, and California St. features a cable car line down the middle of the street. Many European cities still have trams, but most American cities do not. San Francisco is special in maintaining its old cable car system, which not only entertains millions of tourists each year, but actually serves as a useful means of transportation for many of the local residents. I planned to use this century-old transport to take me directly from my hotel to Kikkoman Sales USA, which is located in the Financial District, close to the end of the cable car line.

I found the right office building, took the elevator to the top floor and announced myself at the glassed-in security entrance. In an instant, a charming young Japanese woman appeared to escort me to the president's office. Her English was pitch perfect, so I figured she was either born here or came over at an early age. She promptly introduced me to her boss, Mr. Nakajima, who was waiting in the doorway of his office to greet me. He was medium height, balding, and wore glasses — probably just what I'll look like a few years down the road, I thought. His time in San Francisco had obviously had an effect — his blue-and-white striped, button-down shirt was open at the collar, and I was sure the blue blazer he was wearing was usually hanging on a hook in the office, kept just for unexpected occasions such as this when some client or visitor came to call.

The first thing I noticed about Nakajima's office was that it had windows on two sides and a spectacular view of San Francisco Bay, Alcatraz, the Golden Gate Bridge and more. I nodded hello to the president and went straight past him to the window. "How do you get any work done here?" was the first thing I said, which might be a humorous greeting to an American executive but was downright rude to a Japanese company president.

"You eventually get used to the view," he said nonchalantly. I looked back at him in total disbelief. "Well," he looked a little embarrassed, "you never really get used to it. It is pretty amazing, isn't it?"

The second thing I noticed, when I turned to face him again, was Derek Jeter. There was a framed photo of Jeter's final game at Yankee Stadium, with a large Kikkoman sign prominently displayed in the stands far above Jeter's head. The photo was obviously official New York Yankees issue — there was a title card in the center, below the picture, saying "Farewell Captain," with the Yankees logo on one side and the Kikkoman logo on the other.

"What, no San Francisco Giants souvenirs?" I joked. Nakajima shook his head. "Wrong Giants," he said and pointed to the shelf below the Jeter photo. There was a bobble-head doll of Hideki

Matsui, the former Yomiuri Giants slugger, in his Yankees uniform and three signed Rawlings Official MLB baseballs, one of them Matsui's. Next to them, for what possible connection I could not grasp, was a bottle of Kikkoman Triple Ginger Teriyaki Sauce. East meets West, I thought.

"We were an active sponsor of the Yankees games," he explained, but I had already figured that out. On the bottom shelf of another bookcase I saw a brass bell like the one my dad attached to the back of our house so my mom could call my brother and me to dinner when we were out playing. This one was slightly bigger, maybe nine inches tall, and it was mounted on a wooden plaque. I looked at the inscription, which was too small to read, but the large letters said "San Francisco Cable Cars." I asked Nakajima what this non-baseball souvenir was all about.

"That's before my time," he said. "A cable car was destroyed in a fire or something, and Kikkoman donated a fair sum of money to restore the car or help buy a new one, I don't remember the story too clearly. But yes, Kikkoman is a supporter of the cable cars of San Francisco.

"Now, Mr. Russell, what can I do for you?"

I told him that I had just visited the factory at Folsom and met a lot of people, so I did not come to interview him. (He looked relieved.) But I would appreciate it if he could introduce me to some of his American staff and point me towards things that I might not have seen yet in Walworth or Folsom. He understood what I wanted, but also that I had not yet grasped the enormous difference between where I was and where I had just come from.

"We are not a factory. We do not make anything. We are a sales office, charged with marketing, advertising, distributing and selling Kikkoman products all over America," he said. "That's how we come to be involved with things like this." He pointed to the photo of Jeter. "We work together with Kikkoman Marketing and Planning outside of Chicago and other Group companies, but selling the products is our main responsibility."

We sat down, me still hypnotized by the panoramic view of the Bay but trying to pay attention to what he was telling me. I had the presence of mind to ask about the name of the company on his business card. I remembered that Kikkoman's first office in the U.S. was here in San Francisco, and that it was established long ago, before Mogi even went to the U.S. for graduate school. But the name was different.

"Yes, that was KII — Kikkoman International, Inc. — and it, too, was a sales office. This company is called Kikkoman Sales USA, Inc. (KSU), and it is a direct descendent of that company."

We had been speaking in English, of course, and I suddenly noticed that I hadn't had the slightest bit of difficulty understanding a word he said. His English was excellent, and once again I was impressed by the quality and training of the Japanese staff who managed these operations overseas. I noticed a well-worn *New Concise English-Japanese Dictionary* on his desk, old enough and frayed enough that it had probably been carried with him from one posting to another for decades. Nakajima confessed that he had lived abroad for most of his working career, first at several posts in the U.S., then in Europe, then back to the U.S. When I commented that few Japanese executives spend so much time away from home, he shrugged and said his kids actually grew up overseas, not in Japan. That, too, was quite unusual.

We talked about market strategy, how in the old days Kikkoman had been forced to contend with what was viewed as Chinese-style soy sauce, most of it produced by America's two biggest names in Oriental foods, Chun King and La Choy. Most of the so-called Chinese versions were chemically produced "instant" soy sauce, what is known in the industry as HVP because it starts with hydrolyzed vegetable protein, which is then combined with corn syrup, salt water, and artificial coloring, among other chemicals. HVP soy sauce is inexpensive to make because it can be produced in as little as a day, whereas naturally fermented *shoyu* requires half a year or more to develop. HVP was the standard type of soy sauce on American restaurant tables for years, but once the Walworth plant opened, everything changed. American consumers coast to coast quickly recognized the difference between Kikkoman-style *shoyu* and HVP soy sauce. Kikkoman's market share soared, eventually surpassing that of both Chun King and La Choy (both of which were later absorbed into ConAgra, the Chicago-based packaged food giant).

Nakajima pointed out that KSU handled all sorts of products, not just *shoyu*, and that demand for Oriental foods in general was rising steadily. He sounded quite confident that business, at least in the U.S. market, would continue to grow.

"Did you know that some predictions say that in just one generation from now, around 2050, roughly half of the U.S. population will be Asian? That includes Indians, Vietnamese, Chinese, Koreans, Japanese and many others, of course. But the chances that a variety of Oriental foods will continue to sell well are pretty good." He seemed happy in the thought that his company would be around for a while.

While he was speaking I finally turned away from the dazzling view and looked around the office. Aside from the trophy-laden bookshelves, I saw that one wall was mostly covered with what looked like Excel-generated sales charts. I saw market share pie charts and rows of colored blocks denoting sales results of various product lines in cities across the country: Los Angeles, Dallas, Atlanta, San Francisco, and even Canada. There was also a framed award from a few years back, thanking Kikkoman International for its outstanding efforts to promote friendly relations between the U.S. and Japan. It was signed by the then-Foreign Minister of Japan.

We talked for a few minutes more, and then were interrupted by his secretary standing in the door. "Joan is here," she said. "Should I send her in?"

"Yes, please," he replied, and in just a few seconds a large, dark-haired woman who radiated positive energy came into the room. She shook my hand and introduced herself. "I'm in charge of the food service business," she said.

"What does that mean?" I asked.

"Basically, I get to eat at all the good restaurants in the Bay area!" She laughed out loud. "No, seriously, I'm in charge of marketing to all sorts of food businesses, from single restaurants to restaurant chains to giant commercial kitchens and huge fast food businesses. I work with the R&D people, I look at trends in the industry, I talk to gourmet chefs and industrial chefs developing menus for schools and gigantic industrial organizations. Hey, why don't you come down to my office and we'll talk?"

I liked Joan right away and nodded to Nakajima as if to say, "Thank you. This is just the kind of person I wanted to meet." He got the message and pretended to shoo us both out of his office so he could get back to work. But I knew what he was going to do: sit back in his armchair and stare out at the Bay all afternoon — at least, that's what I would have done.

Joan and I adjourned to her office down the hall and sat down to talk. She told me she started working in the food service business from an early age ("I was waitressing when I was fourteen"), had travelled around Asia with her family, had earned an MBA and had spent years working for various companies in the food service business — customer liaison, marketing manager, consultant, and so on. She was happy to be recruited by KSU: "I'd been using Kikkoman products forever. I knew it would be easy to talk to people about Kikkoman because everyone knows the brand. When you're introducing some new product, it's so much easier if you've got strong brand recognition and years of trust built up in that brand working for you. People in the food business know that Kikkoman stands for consistent quality above all else, and they know how much the company values that identity. Doing marketing for a company like that, well, it doesn't get much better!"

I asked what kind of food programs she had developed. She explained that KSU sponsored events with the famous Culinary Institute of America to teach people about the flavors of umami, and also ran programs to show chefs how they could use soy sauce instead of salt in many dishes to actually lower the sodium content of prepared foods. I asked if she was just kidding about dining out at the best restaurants in San Francisco, a fantasy that was already gnawing at the back of my mind. As I said before, I am neither a foodie nor a gourmet, but I do appreciate the finer things in life if they happen to come my way, and Joan shocked me with her response.

"In fact, I do get to talk to some of the top chefs in San Francisco, and yes, I do get to sample those restaurants occasionally. When I heard that you might be coming, I set up a quickie interview for today and dinners at killer restaurants for both tonight and tomorrow night. Is that okay?"

Was that a trick question? Who needed to think about work? I asked her where were we going?

"Well, the toughest reservation in town for the past several years — if you can believe that — has been a place called Restaurant Gary Danko over near Ghirardelli Square. People book two months in advance just to have a chance of sitting down. I've managed to get us a table there for tonight and a chance for you to interview the owner/chef today. Then there's another awesome place right on the water called The Slanted Door, also super-popular. The owner there is Vietnamese-American, and he's also one of t

he most famous chefs in the city. I'm expecting him to join us for dinner tomorrow night. How's that?"

I could tell that Joan and I were going to get along fine. A moment later her phone rang. She said, "Great. Show him to the conference room when he arrives." Then, turning to me, asked, "Want to meet Chef Gary Danko in person?" The question was rhetorical, I knew. "He'll be here in about fifteen minutes and we'll both have a chance to talk to him. Before he comes, I have a few things I have to take care of..."

She was already getting to her feet. I waved off the thought that she should worry about me at all. "Go do whatever you have to do and call me when Mr. Danko arrives," I said. "I'll wander around and talk to people."

She was already heading out the door. I got the feeling that Joan's days were pretty busy even when famous chefs were not stopping by to visit. In any case, I was happy for the few minutes I would have to chat with people in the office at random. I stepped out into the hall and went in the opposite direction from the president's office. There were quite a number of small, semi-private offices, something you would never find in a big company in Japan, and even the larger rooms were bright and attractive and seemed to have lots of space. The staff all seemed totally focused on their work, not looking up at the strange visitor. I went over to one woman who was busily entering data into her computer screen, piles of papers on her otherwise neat desk. I excused myself for interrupting her; she stopped her work and looked up at me.

"What can I do for you?" she said pleasantly with a trace of a Southeast Asian accent.

I told her what my mission was, and that I'd just spoken to the president and he had said it was okay to talk to the staff. She nodded and said she probably wouldn't be a very interesting person to interview. I asked how long she had been with the company.

"I don't know... twenty-something years."

I did a double-take. Another twenty-year vet, but this time in an office job, not a factory?

"It's no big deal. You should talk to her." She pointed at a slightly older woman sitting in a small office a few feet away. "She's been here over thirty years."

I asked her why people stay so long.

"This is a good company. It's like a family, not like a corporate office. I worked in a bank before I came here; believe me, this is much better."

Of course, this just added one more voice to a chorus I had been hearing since I began my research in Walworth. I looked at my watch, thanked her for her time, and stepped next door to talk to the woman she had pointed to. As usual, I introduced myself, apologized for interrupting her, and explained my mission. Then I asked how long she had actually been with this company.

"Let's see..." She had to think about it. "I guess it's thirty-four years, maybe thirty-five. I don't keep count. I started here as a receptionist a long time ago, and now I'm the Senior Accounting Manager."

I congratulated her on her promotions, but I had to ask: Why so long in the same place?

"I don't like job-hopping," she said, showing the typical modesty that I found with so many employees of this company. "And I'm not very ambitious. I could have left, but I like it here. This is a good, stable company, and they treat people really well."

So, was she planning to stay longer at Kikkoman?

"I'm certainly not planning to go anywhere else. This job is good, and sometimes it's fun. And when you've done a really good job one day, you go home that evening feeling good. And this place is like your family. Maybe you like some people and not others, but they're all still your family. That's normal."

It sure seemed to be normal at this company, I thought, as I scribbled down what she'd just told me.

Suddenly I heard my name being called. The president's secretary was standing in the hallway, waving for me to come. I thanked the woman I had been speaking with and hurried down the hall to the conference room. Joan was seated on the window side of the big table, and I gratefully took a seat next to her so I wouldn't be tempted to gaze out at the view when I should be paying attention to our guest. Joan set a laptop computer on the table in front of me and Googled "Gary Danko," then went back down the hall to her office, leaving me to learn something about the man and his restaurant. After a few minutes, I wanted to skip the interview and go straight over to the restaurant...

First, I noted the photos of Mr. Danko — the classic chef's whites with the name tastefully embroidered on the chest and also a more tongue-in-cheek shot of him with a large fish tossed over one shoulder. Obviously a man who could be poised and polished when the occasion demanded, but who also had a lighter side that put everything he did into perspective. If his cooking was the same, we were in for a treat tonight.

I looked over Gary's impressive bio — just a string of awards for him and the restaurant, including Best New Restaurant in San Francisco; Best Service; Top Restaurant; Chef of the Year; Best Chef in California; Outstanding Chef, etc., etc. Every year his humble establishment garnered a Five Diamond rating from

AAA, a star from the Michelin Guide, and a Grand Award from *Wine Spectator* magazine. Okay, I thought, not your run-of-the-mill burger joint.

Suddenly Joan appeared in the doorway, leading the guest of honor into the room. If I'd been expecting my New York image of a famous celebrity chef in a starched white jacket with an even more starched attitude, I would have been badly disappointed. San Francisco's reigning top chef looked completely relaxed in a dark grey hoodie over a stylish black T-shirt. It set off his greying hair and gave him the appearance of an aging artist. His face was strong and intelligent, with a hint of a mustache. Joan introduced us, and he lit up as soon as I mentioned that I was researching a book about Japanese soy sauce and Kikkoman in particular.

"Oh, I catered the dinner at the opening ceremony for the Folsom plant in 1998. Kikkoman and I go way back." He was laughing and I wasn't sure exactly what he meant.

"Actually, I love Japan," he said. "I was there in the late '80s, running the kitchen at the Swan Court at the Palace Hotel. I had fun doing California cuisine in Tokyo."

Even after skimming his bio, this caught me by surprise. The Palace is one of the premier hotels in Tokyo, if not all Japan, and the Swan Court is equally famous. I remembered dining there a few times on business outings. I asked how he ended up cooking in Japan.

"It was basically from my Napa experience. Back in the mid-1980s, when California cuisine was becoming a big deal, I was the executive chef at Beringer Vineyards." From my quick reading, I knew he had also been executive chef at Chateau

Souverain in nearby Sonoma. I simply nodded and he went on. "I was helping to develop their culinary program. Around that time, I started reading more about food and wine pairings, and I got interested in umami — I discovered the term in some technical book on food and food processing — and I tried experimenting with it. Soon umami became a very big deal, not only at Beringer, but everywhere else. All the food people were talking about it. I was glad that I'd gotten a little head start there.

"Anyway, I was sent to Japan, mainly to promote California wine to the Japanese market. It gave me a chance to try out some new dishes, study Japanese ingredients, and learn all about Japanese cuisine."

I asked Gary if that trip was his first encounter with *shoyu*.

"No, don't be silly! I think I started using tamari sauce back in the 1970s — back then you could buy it at health food stores. Then Kikkoman soy sauce came along, and I knew right away that it was the real thing — you know, not that cheap stuff I'd seen in Chinese restaurants when I was young. So I wanted to use *shoyu* right away. I started out just brushing it on meat before cooking it. Even now at the restaurant we sometimes do a soy-glazed beef, where the *shoyu* becomes the marinade for the fillet. We basically mix some mustard and soy, which blend very well together, and maybe add a little ginger garlic, and then brush it on the meat and cook it. It brings out flavors very nicely.

"Honestly, I use Kikkoman soy sauce quite a bit, and Kikkoman tamari sauce and Kikkoman panko bread crumbs, which I use in vegetable gratins and all sorts of other things. But the main one is the soy sauce, which I think of as a very clean, standard product that we rely on in the kitchen."

The president's secretary appeared with a tray of coffee, and we all accepted them gratefully. Before Gary could even enjoy his coffee, I asked him for some more specific examples of how he used soy sauce. I wanted to be sure that he was serious about all the nice things he was saying about Kikkoman.

"One of my signature dishes is seared rare ahi tuna with avocado. It's a wonderful dish, shaped like a butterfly. We use soy sauce, lemon juice, herbs, and extra virgin olive oil; I think the soy sauce helps to *blend* the flavors. In general, it also helps to *clean up* flavors and underline them, and it takes the bite off of sugars. The saltiness in soy sauce is very different from table salt, and I like that flavor.

"When you're pairing food and wine, you can put a drop or two of *shoyu* on almost anything. Especially with red wine, you need something substantial to pair with, and not all dishes have enough body for that. I like adding a couple of drops of soy sauce to enhance things... We use it wherever we can. You can use it in desserts, you can use it on ice cream... We're talking about drops, mind you, not splashing it on. Basically, it helps to enhance and unify flavors."

Okay, here was somebody whom a professional in the food industry (the woman sitting next to me) had reliably informed me was one of the top chefs, if not *the* top chef in America's most food-crazed city, and he sounded almost like a spokesman for Kikkoman. That in itself was remarkable. Looking at the collection of awards he had won, and the standards that his restaurant had set, and his incredibly long run as a "top" restaurant in a city where that honor seldom lasts six months, I knew that no company could pay him enough to use anything in his kitchen that he didn't personally approve of. So these comments about soy sauce and the other Kikkoman products were for real. He used them because he liked them, and he was sitting here, in Kikkoman's offices, because Joan had invited him to come chat.

I had to confess that I had not been to Gary's restaurant. What was it like? Could he define his style?

"Well, it's a combination of my personal tastes and what I've learned over the course of my career. I like food that has bold flavors, food that is well prepared, and food that people can understand. You know, sometimes when I go to restaurants, I read menus and I can't get past the names; I'm already turned off. Also, as I get older I like to eat simpler, so this is becoming my style.

"Basically, I stick to what I believe in. I really don't think I have to change what I do to follow trends. There are enough people doing the trendy thing right now. In a sense I have a style, a product if you will, that I do, and I'm going to keep doing it until nobody wants it any more. Maybe it will be remembered and maybe it won't."

Joan rolled her eyes and, looking at me, silently mouthed the word, "Awesome."

Gary smiled and added something interesting about running a restaurant, something that shattered my old assumption that a celebrity chef accounts for 90 percent of the success of any famous restaurant.

"I'm a bit unusual in that I have worked in the front of the house greeting guests, as well as in the kitchen. Most chefs have only kitchen experience, so they're all about their ego and what they want to do. I look at a restaurant from a 360-degree viewpoint, because the front of the house is just as important as the kitchen and the dishwashers and the reservations desk — they all come together to make the thing work."

I scribbled my notes and thanked Gary for taking the time to stop by and chat. I told him that I had just skimmed a few dozen reviews on the Internet, and everyone seemed to think Restaurant Gary Danko was, in the parlance of New York City, "to die for."

He looked slightly embarrassed and waved away the compliments with one hand. "Don't believe everything you read on the Internet," he said with a grin, shaking my hand and then hugging Joan. "I hope you'll have a chance to find out for yourselves tonight. I'm very sorry to say that I won't be able to be there — I promised to cook for a charity dinner party at my home tonight."

I was disappointed; Joan was imagining what a private dinner at Gary Danko's home must taste like; and both of us were starting to feel the anticipation of dining at his restaurant later that evening. We chatted for another few minutes and then he had to go. Judging by the number of messages that arrived on his phone while he was talking to us, he was as much in demand in the daytime as when he was working at night.

After he departed and I finished up my notes, Joan checked the schedule and informed me that we were on for dinner at 6:00. She said she would meet me at the restaurant, so I could go back to my hotel and clean up. I thanked her, said goodbye to Mr. Nakajima, and wandered out into the San Francisco sunlight. I walked a few blocks aimlessly, then took a taxi back to the Fairmont, stretched out on the very comfortable bed, and promptly fell asleep. I had been up writing late into the night last night and I guess my body was trying to tell me something. About thirty seconds later the phone was ringing — the front desk with the wake-up call I had requested. I angrily reprimanded the cheery voice on the other end of the line that my call was for 5 PM.

"The current time is 5:01, sir," came the upbeat reply.

Not possible. Had I actually slept for a couple of hours? It felt like a couple of minutes. Ah, the wonders of travel.

I showered quickly and got dressed, not too formal, not too casual. I remembered Gary saying about his restaurant, "We're not pretentious. We want people to be comfortable." In SF, a sport jacket with no tie was about as formal as anyone was likely to get, and that worked just fine for me. I headed downstairs to catch a cab and, on a hunch, mentioned to the doorman that I was on my way to Gary Danko's restaurant.

"Excellent choice, sir," he said, beaming. "There are plenty of trendy spots, but I can guarantee you won't find a better meal anywhere in San Francisco."

I got into the taxi, and as soon as I mentioned Gary Danko, the cabbie nodded his head and off we went. That's a sign of success.

Five minutes later, we pulled up in front of RGD, an attractive but not at all ostentatious corner entrance in a totally unprepossessing three-story grey building. No crowds of party-goers, no rope line of tourists fighting to get in, nothing to indicate that this had been the hottest ticket in San Francisco since some of the city's restaurant critics were in high school. Inside, the small bar was packed — optimistic diners without reservations routinely camped out at the bar, hoping to inherit an open seat at a table if someone left early, but no one ever left early. The interior was all muted dark colors, and yet the feeling was not at all dark, and there were large displays of flowers everywhere. So far, so good. I spotted Joan and Mr. Nakajima seated in an elegant semi-circular booth. For someone in the food business, she looked like a giddy schoolgirl. I greeted them both and expressed my surprise at finding Nakajima-san there.

"You don't think I'd miss this, do you?" he said with a warm smile. "We don't get to dine at Gary Danko every night."

Almost as soon as I sat down, a uniformed waiter appeared with a bottle of good Champagne in his hands. I looked at Joan and Nakajima. Did they splurge on this before I arrived? Both shook their heads. I politely told the waiter that he must have the wrong table.

"Compliments of Chef Danko," he said softly. He magically produced three Champagne glasses from thin air and began pouring. A few seconds later, the three of us toasted our very good fortune to be here tonight.

Joan was already enjoying the menu so much that I doubted she would actually order anything. I finally turned away from my Champagne and decided to see what all the fuss was about. It didn't take long.

I remembered what Gary had said earlier about his standard menu: "Basically, we offer our guests a choice of three or four or five courses, whatever they feel like. We let the customer choose freely from the different categories on the menu. You can pick whatever you want in any order that pleases you with no surcharges. And I try to keep it as affordable as possible, which is not easy here in San Francisco."

Since I was expecting to treat Joan and Nakajima-san tonight, this last point was more of a concern than it would normally have been. None of the entrees had prices, which is usually a danger sign. At the bottom of the menu there were single prices for a three-course, four-course, or five-course dinner. I was almost afraid to look, expecting to shell out at least $250 per person just for food, bringing the with-wine total for three people to well over $1,000. When I discovered that I could have a four-course meal at one of the best restaurants in the city for $100, I was sure this was a misprint. I began to relax and enjoy myself. Somebody bring me the wine list!

A different waiter appeared, also in full livery, and introduced himself. He mentioned a few specials that sounded so good I was ready to throw away the menu, but I held fast. I remembered a review on the Internet that said something like, "You can order the prix-fixe menu and then substitute for any item from the a la carte menu at no charge. If you want to have a five-course meal that starts with three desserts and finishes with a pair of salads, that's your privilege. At RGD, the customer is always right."

While we were contemplating how best to orchestrate the evening's procession of flavors, another waiter arrived and helped us to decide on our orders. Then the three of us talked about the restaurant scene in San Francisco, and Joan gave us some interesting insights about trends in the food service business.

I wanted to get Nakajima talking about business, because that's what Japanese businessmen like to talk about most, so I asked him about Kikkoman sales outside of retail and the obvious restaurant-oriented commercial sales, the only difference being the size of the bottles ("We sell a *lot* of five-gallon drums of soy sauce to Chinese restaurants," he said). He surprised me by mentioning that one of KSU's biggest businesses was selling very large quantities of products, often in powder form, to the nation's largest food chains. "I cannot tell you the clients' names," he confided, repeating what managers at two factories had told me. "But trust me when I say that if you eat at some of the largest food chains in America, you are eating things flavored with Kikkoman ingredients. If you buy almost any packaged sauces, soups, pastes, and so on, you are tasting flavors enhanced by Kikkoman. Our products, both powdered and liquid, find their way into all sorts of packaged meat and poultry dishes, beef jerky, salad dressings, stir-fry vegetables, and lots of other foods."

Joan nodded her head vigorously. Nakajima noted that giant tanker trucks holding thousands of gallons of *shoyu* made regular deliveries to the industrial kitchens where their largest clients produced their food. I jokingly suggested that Kikkoman launch a marketing program like Intel's famous branding campaign, so all "enhanced" foods would come with a brightly colored logo sticker that said "Kikkoman in it!" He didn't crack a smile and replied that some makers of packaged foods were already doing just that, putting Kikkoman's name and/or logo on their packaging to inform customers that natural Kikkoman flavoring was part of the mix. The brand was that well respected in the marketplace.

I was going to delve into this further, but just then my ahi tuna arrived. It was every bit as delicious as I'd expected, which put an end to all conversation. I then doubled down with the lobster risotto. Of course, I should have been paying attention to what my dining companions were eating, and if I'd been smart I would have been stealing tastes from both of their plates, but I was enjoying my own dinner too much. I do remember Nakajima and Joan occasionally remarking to each other which dishes might have used *shoyu* or some other Kikkoman ingredient to enhance the flavor, but I wasn't really listening (I can't work *all* the time), just enjoying the food and the wonderful atmosphere of the restaurant.

At some point a sommelier approached and introduced himself. I had already perused the star-studded wine list, and quickly discovered that I was out of my depth. Rather than stay inside my comfort zone and choose something I knew well, I decided to get adventurous. I let the sommelier recommend both a red and a white to accompany our meal. Nakajima-san nodded his approval to both selections, so off we went.

I'm not a food writer and could never do justice to our meal in any case. Besides, I don't want to bore readers with all the details of our dining experience. Suffice it to say that we all enjoyed every mouthful and had to be forcibly removed from the restaurant by six burly San Francisco cops. Well, not really, but it felt that way. Nobody wanted to go home. Both the food and the service were superb, and not only at our table, because I kept an eye on how things flowed at tables nearby, and the wait staff were flawless. I never thought I'd say that in an American restaurant.

When we were finally ready to leave, I reached for my credit card and saw Nakajima also going for his wallet. There is an old saying in Tokyo that you only see real physical violence when two people both insist that they should pay the dinner bill. Just as I was preparing to go several rounds with the president, another waiter appeared, bowed ever so slightly in our direction, and informed us that the dinner came with the chef's compliments. I was stunned. I began to fantasize about ordering at least twelve courses and a couple of '97 Barolos to wash it all down.

Of course, both Nakajima and I protested, but to no use. We thanked everyone in sight and stepped outside to hail our taxis. Nakajima-san turned to me and said, "I think you'll find tomorrow's dinner a bit different."

What? Oh, right, Joan had said something about going to another restaurant. At the moment I was full and happy and hoped that tomorrow's menu would be nothing more exciting than plain soba noodles and cold green tea, because I didn't think I could handle more haute cuisine within a 24-hour period.

But I was wrong.

The next day I had planned to do more interviews, although I had only one person definitely on my list — a PR writer who knew Kikkoman well — and it was pouring rain outside. I was feeling a little under the weather (perhaps too much Champagne and wine?), so I opened one eye and called the

KSU office to see if they needed me to be anywhere or meet anyone that day. Both Nakajima and Joan said they had no one in mind to introduce me to except the Vietnamese chef whom we were scheduled to meet in the evening. I mentioned the PR guy I wanted to talk to, and Joan suggested that we invite him to join us for dinner. I could interview him while we were eating.

I told her that was an excellent idea. It would give me a chance to slow down for a day and use the time productively to get some work done on my laptop. She wished me good luck on my writing and hung up. Then I immediately went back to sleep.

That evening Joan came to my hotel in a taxi to pick me up for dinner. "I usually ride a cable car to work every morning," she said. "I go right past this hotel, so it's no problem to swing by in a cab to get you. And we're not going very far."

We headed down towards the Bay, not far from the world-famous tourist mecca called Fisherman's Wharf. Just to the east is a stretch of piers called The Embarcadero, a long, curving wharf with ferry terminals, warehouses, a few offices, and more recently, a bunch of interesting restaurants and bars. Our cab pulled up at one of the Ferry Buildings and Joan jumped out. We walked out onto a nearby pier, and there, on our right was a stylish, glassed-in restaurant already overflowing with customers even though it was only about six o'clock. Nakajima was waiting for us inside the entrance, where I saw a tall, black slab of metal with "The Slanted Door" in cut-out letters. We were shown to a table in the middle of the room, which was a very different scene from the night before. The place was modern, but quite attractive, and also noisy, a much livelier atmosphere than RGD and undoubtedly more to the liking of the younger crowd that makes restaurant reputations in San Francisco. The waterfront location was very nice, especially as the evening lights all around began to come on.

We sat down and ordered a round of drinks. Joan handed me a bio sheet on the chef so I would know a little more about the man and his cooking than I did when I met Gary Danko. Tonight's master of the kitchen was Charles Phan, born in Vietnam in the early 1960s, escaped along with his family after the war, essentially as a family of refugees who eventually ended up in Guam, then moved to San Francisco. Charles grew up cooking for his family of ten relatives, learning the subtleties of Vietnamese cooking from his mother. After trying his hand at other businesses, he decided to open his own restaurant, and in time The Slanted Door was born. Like Danko, he had won James Beard Awards, including one for Best Restaurant in California. His two cookbooks had also won awards, and from what Joan was telling me, this was not only one of the best kitchens in town, but also one of the most fashionable, a place to see and be seen. Now that I was awake, I only wanted to see some appetizers.

Fortunately, Joan seemed to know her way around the extensive menu. Nakajima-san told her to order for the table, and she did so confidently, starting with a big plate of the house signature spring rolls. She also ordered a bottle of German Riesling wine and passed me the drink menu so I could see the extensive list of Belgian, Austrian, German and French beers and ales. If I didn't already have a large glass of white wine in my hand, I would have ordered several of the brews to see what they tasted like. I mentally gave Charles extra points for adding variety to the beer menu.

While our first dishes arrived, so did our first guest. A tall, slim, good-looking guy in his forties came over to our table, dressed all in black. At first I thought it was the waiter, but Joan and Nakajima welcomed him with big smiles and warm greetings. He pulled up a chair at the end of the table with me on his left side and Joan on his right. They started the usual "What've you been up to?" chit-chat right away, then Joan turned and introduced us.

"David, this is Scott Salinger, one of our main PR writers."

We shook hands and swapped cards. This was the guy I was supposed to interview this afternoon but Joan had kindly suggested we merge into the dinner. Scott's card was colorfully designed but had no company name. I asked if he worked independently for Kikkoman.

"Actually, I'm with Ketchum, the PR, marketing, and advertising agency. I've been working on the Kikkoman account since the very first day that I joined Ketchum back in 1990, and I've never stopped. They're my longest-running project."

"So, what exactly do you do, Scott?" I asked.

"I'm a writer. I love food — I helped start a restaurant in Berkeley right out of college and I've written lots of cookbooks, scripts for food-related TV shows, tons of PR copy, all sorts of stuff. I'm interested in cooking trends, restaurant trends, food trends, what chefs are doing, that kind of thing. My specialty is ghost-writing; I really enjoy doing books for chefs."

As with my meeting with Ron Yates, I immediately enjoyed talking to another professional writer, especially one not lacking in self-confidence. I could see we had a lot in common. I, too, had ghost-written half a dozen books and never missed an opportunity to tell people that I was good at it.

"But what about Kikkoman?" I said, trying to steer the conversation before it got side-tracked. "I assume you are involved in positioning and helping to develop the brand in the U.S.? Isn't that pretty much over with? I mean, Kikkoman has been actively selling products here for over half a century, right?"

He smiled, running a hand through his dark hair, and answered quickly and precisely, sounding more like someone who grew up in Manhattan than Berkeley, CA: "You're right about the history, but not the results. Yes, Kikkoman has been selling here for decades, but no, the brand is not finished developing, not by a long shot. There is so much more to do and new strategies are constantly being discussed, both here and in Tokyo."

Such as?

"First, recognition. At Ketchum, we believe that Kikkoman is the only real Asian food brand that anyone in America could name. There are lots and lots of Asian brands, but no one knows them. The only two names people knew in the past were La Choy and Chun King, and neither of them is really Asian. So Kikkoman is de facto the leading Asian food brand in America.

"Second, brand identity. When Kikkoman started in the U.S., it did not emphasize its Japanese background or its Asian heritage or anything like that. In fact, they downplayed it. All their advertising was focused on American dishes, and with good reason. There were still mixed feelings about Japan at that time. But decades went by and everything changed. Then the umami story broke, and we decided to do a big umami campaign before someone else did it. But it still wasn't about Oriental food. It was mostly American and European chefs showing how they used soy sauce in their everyday dishes.

"Now we have a whole new generation that is fascinated by Asian food and very comfortable ordering or even cooking it. We're seeing Asian-style fast food chains expanding now. And Chinese restaurants are no longer assumed to be cheap, badly flavored take-out joints. So, to be the No. 1 brand in this rapidly evolving new Asian food market, the brand that everyone knows and respects, is a huge, huge opportunity. The question is: What are we going to do with that opportunity?"

He paused at that point and consumed one of the delicious spring rolls that Joan had put on his plate. More dishes arrived — papaya salads, Hanoi-style Seabass, Grilled Lemongrass Pork Over Rice Noodles, Tea-smoked Duck Breast, Stir-fried Organic Chicken, Seared Ahi Tuna, Stir-fried Wild Gulf Shrimp, with side orders of organic tofu and snap peas, baby spinach and summer squash. We all took a short food-and-wine break before we came back to discussing Kikkoman's marketing strategy.

I turned to Scott once again. "From what I can see, the whole thrust of Kikkoman's message regarding soy sauce is that it's an 'all-purpose seasoning,' not a condiment to be used on Japanese food and definitely not something limited to Asian cuisines. Do you think Kikkoman should position itself as more Asian and try to take advantage of the increasing interest in Asian food?"

"That's a more difficult question than you know," he said thoughtfully. "First, what *is* Asian food? Today, if you order a teriyaki steak, many people would not see that as Asian at all. And what about a noodle salad with lots of grilled vegetables and pieces of steak? You could say it's Asian, but it's also everyday, normal American cooking. American food culture is changing so quickly.

"The marketing quandary is whether to emphasize Kikkoman's Asian origins or emphasize that Kikkoman is global and its sauces work well on everything. And I don't have a simple answer for that. The more complicated answer is that I think Kikkoman could brand a whole range of products, even products that it did not prepare itself. It could do co-packaging with other companies or it could open a chain of restaurants. It could do all sorts of things if it wanted to. It could easily leverage the trust that consumers have in that brand to expand in multiple directions."

At this point Nakajima signaled that he wanted to join the conversation. He leaned both elbows on the table, his hands loosely clasped in front of him, like a professor in a pale blue blazer, and spoke slowly to be sure his words were heard clearly in this noisy room.

"Kikkoman's main product is, was, and always will be *shoyu*. The company is committed to positioning what we call naturally brewed *shoyu* as an all-purpose, goes-with-anything global seasoning. That strategy began half a century ago, and it may continue for another half-century — as long as there is steady sales growth, we are not in a hurry to change course. I feel confident in saying that there is no scenario in which Kikkoman will consider changing its global strategy with respect to that fundamental brand identity. We want to be seen as *the* global seasoning.

"So, in sum, no, I do not think the company will move towards a much more Japanese or more Asian stance in its marketing. As for some of the other ventures you just mentioned, we have tried our hand at running restaurants and discovered how difficult that business is. We have tried co-packaging products, also with mixed results. We have already created sub-brands, such as Pearl organic soy milk, that have been successful, and we have thought a great deal about how to use our brand name to maximum advantage. There are many nuances to the answer, but the fundamental thinking inside Kikkoman is that we should probably stick to what we do best — making *shoyu* and other sauces the very best way we know how."

He paused a moment while everyone took in what he was saying, then continued.

"On the other hand, we are *very* much aware of the rising interest in Oriental foods, not only in America, but in Europe as well. This is something we have seen growing for many years and have been paying close attention to." He was looking at Joan now, and then, a moment later, over at me. "As you know, KSU is a sales office for a wide range of Kikkoman products, not just soy sauce. But down in LA there is another Group company, called JFC International, which handles a much wider range of Oriental food products. That is also part of Kikkoman's business, and it is doing very well — they have branches in ten U.S. cities, three more in Canada and another in Mexico, plus eleven sales offices in the U.S. And that's just in North America; they are already a global group. In other words, Mr. Salinger, we are doing both. We are marketing soy sauce worldwide as an all-purpose seasoning, **not** as a Japanese condiment, and at the same time we are riding the growing wave of interest in Asian foods by selling more than 10,000 Oriental food products through JFC International."

I had paused in my exploration of Nouvelle Vietnamese cuisine and was scribbling notes in my little notebook. Scott was nodding, taking this all in. I got the feeling that none of this was news to him; he already struck me as a very bright guy who was way ahead of the curve on what his clients wanted.

He faced Nakajima-san, leaning a bit forward and also speaking slowly. "I understand what you are saying, and I agree with it completely. I am certainly not advising you to do away with a marketing strategy that has proven increasingly successful for many years. I only want to point out that because of that success, the brand equity in Kikkoman soy sauce is tremendous. I would be serving your company badly if I did not think about what else that brand could offer your customers and how else it could add to your revenues."

There was a brief silence, then Nakajima smiled broadly and raised his glass. "Thank you, Scott. I sincerely appreciate your comments. We are all working towards the same goals. We are all on the same team, and I am very happy to have such an excellent team here in San Francisco."

We all toasted to that and emptied our glasses.

"Another bottle of wine?" Joan said rhetorically, looking at the drinks list again.

Meanwhile, the food kept coming. The service was good, although I had to admit I'd been spoiled by Gary Danko's place. Maybe I really was an Old School type after all. I was certainly enjoying this food, the flavors were wonderful and the restaurant, though crowded and noisy, was also attractive and fun. Still, the taste and ambience of last night's dinner was not something I would soon forget.

Thinking of great chefs, I suddenly remembered that our guest of honor was not present. I asked Joan if Charles Phan was in the kitchen and if he would be joining us soon. She looked concerned, said it was not like him to be late, and called his cell phone. A few seconds later she was laughing and chatting with him as if they were old friends. She looked at all of us and announced, "Charles apologized profusely for not being here early to greet us. He has a new restaurant, actually a high-class bourbon bar, just a few hundred yards from here, and he's been over there, dealing with start-up issues. He'll be back over here shortly."

We probably should have waited for the chef to arrive, but everyone was hungry and the food was very good — the chef's own fault, I say — so we finished our entrees and dove into the desserts. There was a very nice selection of teas, so we all chose teas to sip after dinner rather than exploring the dessert wine selections. I'd had a few glasses of wine already and didn't really need any more alcohol tonight.

Suddenly there was a hand on my shoulder and a cheery voice saying, "Sorry to have kept you all waiting. That was very rude of me. I see you've already finished dinner. Well? How was it?" I looked up, and there was Charles Phan standing right behind me, looking in total command. People at nearby tables were starting to whisper and point discreetly with their heads. I gathered Charles was a local celebrity.

Joan spoke for all of us when she said, "The food was wonderful, the wine was excellent, the service was attentive, and the ambience was stimulating. Other than that, it was just an ordinary meal." She laughed, Charles laughed, and then we all joined in. It was good to see that this now-famous chef was a down-to-earth guy and had a good sense of humor.

I noticed that Charles' English was as clear and colloquial as anyone you were likely to meet on the street, a result of his years of residence here in San Francisco. If he sat next to you at a ball game, you could probably talk for an hour without even imagining his Asian ancestry.

Before I could ask him any questions, Charles took charge of our group like a tour conductor.

"Well, if you're all finished with dinner, what else can I show you? How about I give you a private tour of the kitchen?"

Without waiting for an answer, he started off, weaving in between tables. Joan was hard on his heels and the rest of us followed. Charles took us back into the depths of a kitchen complex that was much bigger than the simple open kitchen visible to customers. We wandered up and down narrow aisles as he pointed to batches of fresh produce and explained his position as a restauranteur and head chef:

"I am fanatical about using fresh ingredients. So are a lot of other chefs. But I am also fanatical about studying the original ingredients, flavors, and techniques used in each dish I put on the menu. I want to blend Vietnamese cooking techniques and flavors with local ingredients as much as possible. Whatever it is, I first recreate it in my own test kitchen downtown, then I find the best way to make it authentically but using

159

contemporary methods and local ingredients, and then I bring it to the Slanted Door."

As he was saying this he led our little conga line through the various aisles of the kitchen interior. Charles would pause to pat one of his cooks on the back, whisper words of encouragement to another, warn a young assistant cook not to overheat something, and generally make himself a felt presence in the kitchen. As he guided us, he held up a bottle of soy sauce here and there, and pointed to several other bottles of Kikkoman sauces, which I could tell were being used regularly. So this was not an accident; we came here so Charles could show us the kitchen, but also so he could skip the explanation about how he was a serious fan of Kikkoman products: Seeing was believing.

Noting my interest, he turned to me, now walking backwards as he continued to lead us through the culinary labyrinth. "I'm a nut about quality. I don't buy ingredients from farms that I don't know," he said. "All our food comes from known sources, and all of it is as organic or as natural as possible. For me, consistency is essential. I use Kikkoman in my restaurants because it is very consistent, year after year. Regardless of what size I buy or where I buy it, I always get the same exact quality. And it's fresh, made from all-natural ingredients. That's important to me and to our customers. I also find that Kikkoman has a unique flavor profile, which is irreplaceable. Bottom line? I use Kikkoman because I like it and I trust it. End of story."

We finally exited the kitchen and I saw Nakajima-san making for the cashier's station. Although I had not planned to take everyone out tonight, I felt guilty for having dined for free the night before, so I pulled out a credit card and tried to get the cashier to pay attention to me and not him. Since he had the bill in his hand, I would have to wrestle him, Tokyo-style, for the honor of paying. He saw that move coming and evaded my tackle, using the crowd of people flowing into the restaurant to block me off. I would have to move quickly and catch him in mid-stride if I were to wrestle the check from his grasp.

While we were still preparing to do combat, Charles appeared out of nowhere and lightly snatched the bill from Nakajima's hand. "I came late. I kept you waiting. I wasn't even there for dinner. Tonight is my treat." He handed the check to the cashier face-down and smiled. Nakajima and I both protested this unexpected largesse, especially after last night, and did the whole "we insist" dance, but Charles was having none of it.

"I am so pleased that you could come here tonight," he said. "I do hope we will see you again. Now, who likes whiskey?"

We all looked at each other blankly. With a big smile, Charles announced his new American Bourbon specialty bar, Hard Water, was open for business right nearby. He invited us to join him for a nightcap, and after a half-second of contemplation, we all accepted, and a few minutes later were sampling rare, aged bourbons that I didn't even know existed. While that experience was a very enjoyable part of the evening, it offers no insight into Kikkoman's business, so I will not bore my readers with the tedious, absolutely delicious details that carried us into the early hours of the next day.

I will say that with a head full of single-barrel bourbon much older than most malt whiskies I usually imbibe, I was barely able to get a cab back to my hotel, where I made a foolish effort to type up my notes. I realized that in just two nights in San Francisco I was taken to two superb restaurants (and a fabulous bar), ate way too much food, and discovered that the city's top chefs are big fans of Kikkoman products. I soon gave up my pointless attempt at writing coherent sentences and went to bed.

I awoke early the next morning, booked a flight to Europe, and looked over what I had written a few hours earlier. Much to my surprise, the last thing I had written in my notes seemed to sum up everything I had learned from both Gary Danko and Charles Phan: "People who appreciate quality appreciate Kikkoman."

9

Dutch Masters

$\mathcal{A}$msterdam. Just the name quickens my pulse. I have wanted to visit the city for years but was always too busy, scoring near-misses with assignments in Frankfurt and London and Paris. Now at last I had an opportunity to visit.

In fact, Amsterdam was not my real destination. As in the U.S., Kikkoman would not build a factory in or close to a major city. Instead, I would have to travel a few hours to the east to a small, rural area, the Walworth of the Netherlands, in order to visit the home of soy sauce in Europe.

But first there were important things to take care of. Number One on my personal list was to see the old city, explore the canals, and soak up some culture. Yes, I was well aware that the two things the city is most famous for outside of Europe are not the Rijksmuseum and Van Gogh Museum, but the red light district and the hundreds of cannabis coffee shops. Bizarre world traveler that I am, I had no interest in either legal prostitution or legal cannabis. That left me free to focus my attention on more salubrious pursuits.

However, work is work, so before I could enjoy the cultural pleasures of Amsterdam, I needed to take care of business. My ostensible purpose in coming here was to meet a prominent Dutch lawyer about whom I had heard much from Mick Neshek in the U.S. He'd told me that Martin Brink had played an important role in the birth and growth of Kikkoman in the Netherlands. On the flight over here I had done my homework, so I had already skimmed a bio sheet on Martin Brink, Ph.D. of the Van Benthem & Keulen law firm in Amsterdam. According to that sheet, he had been practicing law for more than forty years, advising clients on mergers & acquisitions, strategic alliances, issues involving boards of directors, protection of minority shareholders, conflicts of interest, and more. He was currently serving in a number of judicial posts, the most important one being a substitute magistrate in the Court of Appeals of The Hague.

More interesting to me was Mr. Brink's devotion to mediation activities — he was accredited by the Dutch Mediation Institute, the International Mediation Institute, and the Centre for Effective Dispute Resolution in London — as if too many years of listening to clients fight over who is right and who should win or lose in a court battle had taken their toll, and now he wanted to find a path towards more mutually satisfactory outcomes. I noticed that he had published two books on the subject. A quick search on the Internet turned up dozens of testimonials from corporate and government officials who had benefitted from his fundamental, win-win approach to conflict resolution.

Brink came highly recommended to me as well. When I had asked Mick for an introduction to someone in Europe who knew the company but was neither a current nor former employee, he suggested that I talk to Brink. Someone had contacted him and set up a meeting, not out at the factory in the Dutch countryside, but here in Amsterdam at the Hotel Okura, the local branch of a luxury hotel I knew well from my days in Tokyo. Since I was doing research about a Japanese company, and I now had an appointment to meet Mr. Brink there, I had accepted Mr. Nakajima's suggestion that his office might easily book a room there for the duration of my short stay.

At the beginning of this project, I had explained my "rules" to Kikkoman: I would gratefully accept any introductions to their staff that they could provide and access to any facilities I wished to visit, but they must at no time compensate me with either money or services. Cooperation, not cash, is my standard deal, and Kikkoman agreed. However, they seemed genuinely interested in helping to facilitate my travels, and Nakajima implied that booking with their company name might have intangible benefits. Of course, the *omotenashi* (hospitality) of the Okura was legendary, and I thought I deserved some TLC after my ping-pong flights from New York to California to Chicago and on to Europe, so I accepted.

My taxi from the airport dropped me in front of the Okura, which turned out to be fairly close to the center of the city and right next to a small canal. When I went to check in, the smiling, efficient Japanese woman at the front desk said to me in perfect English, "So nice to see you, Mr. Russell. It seems the Kikkoman people made a reservation for you a few days ago." I was happy to see that things had gone smoothly in that department, but I asked the girl to make sure that the bill was on my credit card. A moment later, she looked up from her computer and said, "Mr. Russell, you must be hungry after a long flight from the U.S." I thought she must have ESP, as my stomach was already complaining about the privations it had endured since leaving San Francisco. She continued, "There's a table reserved for you in the restaurant right over there." She pointed across the lobby.

Intangible benefits! Once again I was both surprised and grateful. I knew Kikkoman was only making the reservations, not picking up the tab, but the effort to make me comfortable did not go unnoticed. I left my luggage at the front desk and asked to have it deposited in my room, then went directly into the restaurant. I was happy to find a small table set just for me in the extended sun room that protruded out onto the hotel's patio overlooking the narrow canal. I sat down and enjoyed a wonderful lunch while watching several working boats move up and down the canal, transporting goods, just as they had for centuries.

Amsterdam is inextricably connected with water traffic (its name derives from a dam on the Amstel River), and it is often compared to Venice, because both are made up of canals and small islands. One big difference is that Amsterdam's canals were planned and most are full of fresh water as opposed to the Italian city's sea water. Although some have been filled in, there are still over 150 canals visible today, and I planned to explore some of them in detail. But first I needed to take care of business. After finishing my lunch, I went upstairs, unpacked my computer, took a shower, and changed into clothes that didn't look like they'd been stuffed into an airplane seat for the past twelve hours. By the time I was ready to face the world, it was almost time to go meet Mr. Brink.

A few days earlier, I had sent him a mail from San Francisco to say that I wanted to meet him, and he had replied courteously, kindly arranging this appointment on short notice. My only problem was that I wasn't quite sure how I would find or even recognize him or where we could sit and talk quietly for an hour or so. At the appointed time, I went downstairs and looked around the lobby, not sure if my special guest might already be sitting somewhere waiting for me. Seeing nothing but tourists and local businessmen in the lobby, I hesitantly inquired at the Front Desk if they knew a Mr. Brink.

The young woman's face fairly lit up. "Mr. Russell? Of course! You will find Mr. Brink waiting for you in the Executive Lounge upstairs. Use the lifts right over there." She motioned towards the nearby elevators, and I soon found my way to the Lounge, which was almost at the top of the hotel. Stepping off the elevator, I took a deep breath. The rooms beyond lay behind multiple sets of wooden doors with inlaid, cut-glass windows, across a sea of thick carpeting, and once inside, the atmosphere proved to be even more luxurious than I had expected. An attractive woman in an Okura uniform greeted me and asked my name, then escorted me to a private room within this private enclave. Sitting inside was a very distinguished-looking gentleman with wavy, white hair, gold-rimmed glasses, a dark blue suit and blue striped shirt with a white collar setting off his blue check tie. I knew that this must be the eminent Mr. Brink.

He stood up immediately and extended a hand in greeting. I liked him instantly as we shook hands. Was it the warmth of his smile, the sincerity in his first words, or the geniality with which he welcomed me to Amsterdam? His voice was soft and precise with only a faint hint of an accent. He spoke impeccable English, with a lawyer's habit of choosing his words carefully, but exuded such a friendly ambience that he put me at ease right from the first. We bantered about his work at The Hague and the many companies and government agencies he had worked with, represented, or encountered in his long and varied career. Of course, I asked about his continuing work in mediation as opposed to litigation, just the opposite of the trends we see in the United States.

"I try to help people resolve their issues outside of the courts. My job is to facilitate communication rather than argument, and to help people to cross bridges in terms of perspective. That is what mediation is all about. Decisions handed down by courts of law or even arbitrators tend to result in black and white outcomes — someone is the winner and someone the loser — which seldom resolves the underlying problem. My work is to help both parties reach workable compromises where their greater interests are met. That is what mediation is all about. It isn't always easy, but when it works well, it is immensely satisfying."

The look on his face told me that he meant every word of it. Just from chatting with him for a few minutes, I realized I was meeting quite an unusual and impressive man, not because of his titles or background, but because of his character. Why was I not the least surprised that he had some strong connection to

168

Kikkoman? I asked him when and how he had first come into contact with the company.

"In 1996, a German law firm in Düsseldorf introduced me to someone, a young Japanese executive who was talking about a factory they were going to build in the Netherlands. I was then very carefully scrutinized by Mr. Milton Neshek, which turned out to be a great pleasure. He and I became very good friends, and I still count him as a good friend today. My early role with the company was mostly as a corporate lawyer, an individual working with a number of attorneys at a respected firm. I helped with intellectual property law, contracts, business structures, and that sort of thing. But soon my role changed. I was asked to join the Executive Committee."

I asked what that was.

"Well, it's really a very smart strategy for any company that is investing abroad, and I would say it's an idea that other Japanese companies should emulate. When you go into a foreign market for the first time, it makes good sense to select a number of local people and ask them to become part of your project in a formal way, not just as friends but as members of an Executive Committee. These people can help you get to know the local culture, they can act as ambassadors or help open doors with local businesses, and they can function as go-betweens in dealing with local politicians and regulators. They have no legal power to decide things, but they can draw on their personal networks, both nationally and internationally, and also on their various types of expertise. Kikkoman selected someone important from academia and someone who knew his way around the government well, and also someone from local

business circles, who in this case was myself. We still meet perhaps two or three times a year. We help to connect the company
with local and regional governments, which has been a big help
to Kikkoman. By the way, there is also a European Executive
Committee, a body covering all of Europe, and Mick Neshek is
a member of that."

"So you were one of those few people who was with
Kikkoman in the Netherlands right from the start?"

"Oh, yes. I still remember the Opening Ceremony: October
10th, 1997. It was wonderful. And all of us who got to know
something about the company in those early days were so
impressed — this beautiful building, a product made from
all-natural ingredients, and a centuries-old process to make
a traditional sauce that was known here centuries ago. We all
felt so proud.

"The opening ceremony was quite an event and many of
us, myself included, assumed that Kikkoman would instantly
become a household name in the Netherlands. In the following
weeks and months we wondered, 'Where are the TV commercials? Where are the billboards along the highways?' We
thought that this is such a great business and a wonderful corporate culture that we wanted to tell people about it, but the
Kikkoman general manager said no, that's not the way they do
things. He said, 'We are going to build our brand here slowly,
step by step, and do it right.' He knew that over time the company would grow and people would come to learn about the
products and the company."

This was all fascinating, but ever since Folsom I was growing
more and more interested in learning about the man who

seemed to be the spark plug for the entire Kikkoman global effort. I had already met Mick Neshek, who was obviously one of the drivers of Kikkoman's growth in the U.S. and beyond, and I had heard about Malcolm Pennington, Mogi's classmate at Columbia and a sharp business consultant who had been instrumental in choosing the Walworth site and involved in most of the company's major decisions over the next few decades. But the man who interested me most was the one who had started the whole "insane" idea of building a *shoyu* plant in North America, and then, as soon as it began to grow, building more — in the U.S., in Europe, and in Asia. I knew that everything that happens in a big Japanese company is a group effort and requires agreement among a large number of people. And yet, the more I learned about Kikkoman, the more I began to see that one man had been the locomotive for the company's incredible global expansion.

Since Martin remembered the opening of the factory in the Netherlands, I knew he must have had many personal encounters with Yuzaburo Mogi. I tentatively asked if he could give me any insight into the man, perhaps things that I hadn't heard before.

"Mogi is a visionary," he said immediately. "I think people recognized that as soon as they met him. He is a most unusual man. He certainly has a lot of charisma, and I think one of his great attributes is that he has a lot of humor. He likes to tell jokes and tell very funny anecdotes. I also find that he has a very special perspective on life. He has that rare ability to go up to the balcony and look down to see how we are all performing on the stage. Not a sense of superiority — Mr. Mogi is not someone who lives above the clouds; he is genuinely comfortable being around ordinary people and he makes them feel comfortable, too. What I mean is that he is able to gain a broad perspective, which I believe is extremely important for the head of a big global group. On a more personal level, he also seems to know everyone, and he pays attention to everyone, and he has a kind word for everyone. Of course, he has a very important position in a large company, but his authority doesn't come from his title; it is part of his person. He is very much a role model for the entire company. He doesn't put on airs and he doesn't pretend to be anyone or anything. He is himself."

This was what I was looking for. I told Mr. Brink that I truly wished that I could have met Mogi decades ago and been able to see him as the young, dynamic, persuasive character that I had heard so much about. I didn't know if I would have a chance to meet him in Tokyo or not, but I was sure that the octogenarian executive in the company headquarters was nothing like the dynamo that had taken Kikkoman to America, overcome all obstacles, and built a hugely successful business there, then pushed the company to open new plants in Europe and Singapore and beyond. Like most Americans, I was vaguely familiar with Akio Morita, the charismatic former head of Sony, and Soichiro Honda, the iconoclastic auto buff who created a successful business against all "sane" advice and stern opposition. Those two are often held up as exemplars of the "new wave" of post-war Japanese business leaders. But until I began this research project, I was unaware of the enormous contribution that Yuzaburo Mogi had made.

Sony and Honda succeeded overseas by refining Western products — radios and TVs, cars and motorcycles — and selling smaller, cheaper versions of those same products back to the cultures that had created them. No one had to tell Americans what a radio was or what a color TV was or a motorcycle or a compact car. Because these products were already well known, the Japanese versions could compete directly on innovation, quality, and price. There was no need to teach people about the product itself. But Kikkoman brought a Japanese food-stuff to the New World and had to start from scratch teaching Americans and Europeans what soy sauce was and how to use it and why it is interesting. That was an enormous challenge, something no other Japanese manufacturer I can think of has faced so successfully.

Little by little, my respect and admiration for Mr. Mogi kept growing. He had done something that none of his rivals had, he had taken huge risks, and he had hit a home run with each successive venture. No one I could think of — including Morita and Honda — had done more to lead Japanese business into the global arena.

Brink put his hands together, making a small teepee with his manicured fingers, and said, "If you had met Mogi years ago, you would have seen what an amazing personality he was. One thing that struck me and many others was his loyalty to his friends. Like his old schoolmate, Pennington, and his pal from Wisconsin, Mick Neshek — Mogi was fiercely loyal to both of them. Do you know that Kikkoman still invites Pennington's widow to all sorts of company events around the world simply out of respect for her late husband? If you work with Mr. Mogi and he comes to trust you, he will never forget you. He is a loyal friend, a loyal partner, and a very loyal person. I feel honored to have known him."

On a hunch, I asked about the Kikkoman culture. Did Brink think that it emanated from Mogi's own personality, as I was beginning to suspect? Was the company's DNA really an offshoot of one man's DNA?

"Oh yes, most certainly," he replied. "Corporate culture is ultimately determined by the tone at the top, and I think this company is very strongly influenced by Mr. Mogi. Not just in Japan, but around the world. The company DNA, as you call it, is truly remarkable. Everyone is very cordial, and they are all nice people. I always enjoy meeting people connected with Kikkoman, not only staff, but people associated with the company. They all turn out to be interesting and very good people to know. Everyone works together; they all have a common goal and common interests, and you all recognize that business can be done in a pleasant, cordial manner. Moreover, there is a very high level of respect inside the organization, not merely respect for the senior management, but mutual respect among everyone in or around the company."

He paused for a moment, looking out over the orange-tiled rooftops below us.

"If you look around and ask around, you will see many things at Kikkoman that are quite different from what you find at other firms. These things demonstrate the culture of Kikkoman very clearly. There is no fuss about it; this behavior is considered normal. All of that, I believe, is the direct result of Mr. Mogi's influence — not his orders or his commands as chief executive, but the influence of his personality as an honorable man."

I could see that Martin Brink was a busy man, and I knew I had taken up way too much of his time, but I really enjoyed talking to him, and as with so many other people I had met on this journey, I felt he was someone unusual, someone I would remember for a long time. Where does Kikkoman find these people? I wondered for the hundredth time.

After Brink and I said goodbye, I suddenly realized that my official work for the day was done. The next stop on my research itinerary was the factory, but I didn't have to be there until tomorrow, so here I was in Amsterdam, with nothing to do. Oh no! I realized I would have to force myself to see the city, taste the food, and sample several types of local beer. Looking over my notes, I found one more Kikkoman connection that would make a nice excuse for visiting one of the city's more interesting cultural assets — the company was a long-time sponsor of Rembrandt House, the refurbished home where the great painter had lived and worked, which was now operated as a "living museum."

The concierge in the lobby recommended that I try one of the city's many trams, and thinking of my cable car ride from just a couple of days earlier, I bought a one-day tram pass and set off. Ten minutes later, I was riding comfortably into the Centrum, the heart of the old city and the area that most foreign tourists want to see.

I took the tram to Rembrandtplein (Rembrandt Square), walked a few blocks, crossed a bridge, and found my way around to the Rembrandt House Museum. My research showed that Kikkoman Foods Europe had provided support for this project since 1997, when the Netherlands plant opened, so I saw an opportunity to see the city, study classical culture, and continue researching Kikkoman all in one place.

The entrance to Rembrandt House is in a more modern building adjoining the original home, which looks like a typical townhouse of four centuries ago. Inside the lobby, I picked up an audio "tour" headset and wandered off to explore the place on my own, which is easy to do with the simple, free-form system they have in place. You enter any room, tag that room's activation panel on the wall, and a prerecorded tour takes you around the room. When you are ready, you can wander to any other room and listen to the "guide" again or just observe it in peace.

The Museum has done an amazing job of tracking down Rembrandt's own possessions (most of which were sold off to pay his creditors), and where those were unavailable, located identical period pieces to make the house as authentic to seventeenth century Amsterdam as possible. From the kitchen to the bedrooms, it is an impressive recreation, so real in places that you would not be shocked to see the old master standing there, gazing out an upper-floor window or admiring various *objets d'art* in his extensive personal collection. The first floor has sitting rooms and other chambers whose walls are lined with his own paintings and etchings as well as many by his students and followers.

The house has many floors, and visitors can easily follow the stairs up to different painting studios and rooms where Rembrandt's paying students worked in what look to us like cubicles. On the third floor is the master's main studio, a high-ceilinged room complete with a row of northern windows to provide the ideal light for painting. There is a large easel placed exactly where Rembrandt is said to have stood. Despite the authentic surroundings and the authoritative voice in my earphones, it was still somehow difficult to imagine that I was standing in the very room where masterpieces such as the expansive, 14 ft. x 12 ft. (4.3 x 6.3 m) canvas we call *The Night Watch* was created. That and many more of the world's most famous paintings were born right here in this room.

After more than an hour wandering around upstairs and down, I felt satisfied. I went back outside and looked up at the building from across the street. I decided that Rembrandt House is too interesting and too well integrated to be called a "museum." It is more of a time machine than a sterile place to hang canvases. My enjoyment of the experience continued to grow long after I left the house itself, and I felt slightly amazed that, of all the many cultural icons in this city, Kikkoman chose this most worthy of projects to sponsor.

One thing I noticed was that neither Kikkoman's name nor logo was prominently displayed when you entered the building, nor were they on any sign visible to visitors. One had to look to find the small Kikkoman room.

I did take the rest of the day to explore the old city of Amsterdam. I walked a lot, took several trams, and walked some more. I took the obligatory canal tour and paused for beers and sandwiches in multiple cafes. One thing I learned was that Amsterdam, like Paris, is a cafe culture — everyone seemed to be sitting outdoors in the afternoon, soaking up sunshine and talking to friends. But where Parisians are drinking coffee all day, the Dutch are quaffing good beer in copious quantities. Everywhere I went, I saw people relaxing in cafes and restaurants and snack shops, always with beer or wine on the table. My kind of town.

While I would gladly have stayed in the city another week or ten, I had lots of work to do. First of all, I needed to visit Kikkoman's only production plant in Europe, which lay a few hours to the east in the small town of Sappemeer. I had planned to rent a car and find my way to the plant in a day or two, but when I returned to my hotel room there was a message from someone at the factory asking when I was expecting to arrive. I sent him a mail to say that I was already preparing to put work before pleasure (a bad habit, I know) and could be there as early as tomorrow morning. Less than twenty minutes later the phone in my room rang.

The caller introduced himself as Satoshi Ando, one of the company managers. "I'm in Amsterdam now on business, but I am planning to return tomorrow. I have my car with me. If you'd like, I can give you a ride to the factory."

Not eager to get back in another rental car, and deciding that a couple of hours together with a Kikkoman executive was a good opportunity to learn about the business in the Netherlands, I gratefully accepted.

The next morning, when I went down to the lobby to check out, I was immediately greeted by Mr. Ando. He turned out to be much younger-looking than I had expected, in his thirties rather than sixties, and very fashionably dressed. Despite his appearance, he looked every bit as serious as all the other Japanese managers I had met. In fact, more so. He reminded me of an accountant I had known in Tokyo years ago, so I wasn't astonished when he handed me his card and I noticed he worked in the accounting department at Kikkoman Foods Europe B.V. in Sappemeer. He drove confidently through Amsterdam and onto the highway, and then settled down to a comfortable 180 km/hr across the Dutch landscape. Even then, most of the traffic was passing us by.

I'd planned to start right off asking questions about the company, but I was so fascinated by the scenery on both sides — mostly farms and fields (no, no windmills) — and with the personal conversation that we developed, that I almost forgot to talk about business.

It is no surprise that in many respects Kikkoman's only European plant is similar to their first U.S. plant. Their usual criteria — a good work force (in this case, the availability of many English speakers), plenty of open land at a reasonable price, proximity to a major city (for air, rail and ship transport), and a central location from which to ship products to every corner of an expanding market area — all came together when the plant opened in 1997. However, as Ando explained to me, the key factor was none of these: "It was the water. We need a good, steady supply of the cleanest water possible. We might compromise on other things, but not on water quality."

And so, after looking at a number of sites, even being courted by other prefectures in the Netherlands (by now, the positive impact Kikkoman would have on a community was no secret), Mogi, Pennington, and their team decided on the little town of Sappemeer (its full name is much longer, but everyone simply calls it Sappemeer). In short order, a Japanese construction company with strong European operations was contracted to build the plant, machinery of all kinds was shipped from Japan, and before they had even opened the factory, they were advertising for staff.

Ando told me many details about setting up the plant, the establishment of KFE as a legal entity in the Netherlands, and the siting and construction of the factory, which opened in October of '97. He rattled off numbers, telling me how the plant had expanded to more than 600 percent of its initial production volume in less than twenty years, that it currently made eighteen types of sauce-based products in fourteen different types of bottles, and shipped to forty-one different countries. I listened half-heartedly to what he was telling me, but as I stared out the window at the passing scenery, I wasn't much interested in statistics or data. I wanted to know the human side of the story, because I was beginning to see that this special quality, not superb soy sauce, is Kikkoman's defining characteristic.

I suddenly realized that Ando couldn't have had any first-hand knowledge of these things. I asked him about his tenure at Sappemeer.

"Oh, I've only been in the Netherlands about two years," he said. "I was lucky to get an international posting and even luckier to be sent here."

"Why was that lucky?"

"Because the Netherlands is a very nice place to live. I'm sorry to say that I haven't picked up much of the Dutch language yet, but you can do business pretty well here in English. More than that, the people are wonderful, the countryside is amazing, the food is good, and the beer is excellent." He smiled as he added that final note. From the little I had seen, I had to agree. The only Dutch I had spoken since arriving in Amsterdam was *Heineken*, *Amstel*, and *Grolsch*, yet I had fared reasonably well.

In what seemed like no time at all we had crossed 200 km of the Netherlands and I saw my first sign for Sappemeer. Ando pulled out his cellphone and called his office. He spoke briefly with someone there and let them know that he had picked up Russell-san and that we were only a few minutes out. Off the highway, the area was green and very rural. My notes from that ride inform me that the plant is located in a kind of a large industrial park, but my photos show something quite different. The area was nothing at all like an industrial park outside a U.S. city, for example. There were miles of homes and farms and then a series of large, corporate buildings, each with plenty of land. The emphasis here seemed to be much more on the "park" and less on the "industrial." It was some distance from the nearest town and farther still from any large town or city.

As Ando drove up to the Kikkoman plant, I noticed the very spacious site and the expanse of green grass around it. There weren't any solar panels shielding the parked cars from the sun, but the grounds looked immaculate and even attractive. I had never thought of a large-scale factory as looking attractive before, but after the two American plants I had visited, I was beginning to appreciate the Kikkoman way of doing things.

I remember thinking incongruously that this European plant could have been a picture postcard: the off-white walls of Lego-like block buildings with a bright orange Kikkoman logo high up on one side, and a lower, red-brick entrance and office building to one side.

Ando pulled up in front of the entrance to let me out. I started to get my bags out of his trunk, but he waved me off. "No sense having a taxi come all the way out here. I'll drive you to your hotel later."

I thanked him for his kindness, and he motioned me to go on inside.

"Mr. Kondo will be waiting for you," he said.

10

Factories and Windmills

I walked through the entrance and into the office area, and sure enough, there was the General Manager of KFE waiting for me. He was middle-aged, well dressed (especially considering that we were in a factory), and looked eager to see me.

"Mr. Russell, welcome to Sappemeeer," said Mr. Kondo in clear English.

As with other plants that I had visited, there was a single nice conference room set aside for important visitors, and today I assumed that meant me. We stepped into the conference room, grateful for the air conditioning, and in Japanese style, immediately exchanged business cards before we sat down.

"I am Kondo, the general manager of this organization," he said formally, and motioned me to take a seat.

Then, much more informally, "You must be hungry. I've taken the liberty of ordering lunch. I hope you don't mind."

I assured him his thoughtfulness was most welcome. I was famished. At this point Ando-san joined us and I had the two Japanese managers to chat with. A woman came in bearing a tray of large, meat-filled sandwiches. My stomach responded with approval, and I greedily helped myself to a pair of good-looking turkey and roast beef sandwiches.

"Please, eat as much as you like," Kondo said. "The Dutch don't eat so much at lunch, but we don't eat much breakfast, so a big lunch is important so that we can work until late at night."

While I was eating, I scanned the room and looked out the windows. I remembered how expansive the property had looked as Ando had driven up to the plant, so I asked Kondo-san about the large plot of land.

"Yes, we bought a lot of land," he said. "We got a very good price, so we bought more than we needed at the time. There is plenty of room for expansion well into this century and perhaps beyond."

I asked him about his company. Ando had told me that KFE shipped to forty-one countries, which, even by my geographically-challenged American education, was far more than there are in Europe.

"Yes, just to give you an idea, our major markets are Germany, the Netherlands, the Russian Federation, France, the UK, Italy, Spain, Sweden, Poland and Austria. In addition, we supply parts of North Africa. We supply both consumer-use and commercial-use products, which means we supply restaurants and commercial food businesses. In addition to *shoyu* in bottles and commercial-size containers, we sell powdered *shoyu* that our clients mix into various products." This was the same story that I'd just heard in the U.S.

I asked about what kinds of new or interesting products were being developed here.

"Well, in the summer of 2015 we began selling gluten-free Tamari sauce, which is already a big product in the U.S. Now we are making a Teriyaki BBQ sauce with honey and another Teriyaki sauce with roasted garlic. Both are new products for us and both are doing well."

We talked at some length about the company, the Netherlands plant, and the products it made. It was all interesting, but it lacked the human touch I was looking for. I asked him if I could meet some of his staff, and he readily agreed. He looked at Ando. "Why don't we call Nicolaas," he said in Japanese. It was not a question

"Nicolaas-san would be good," Ando replied, stood up and left the room.

About two minutes later, a cheery Dutchman in a white Kikkoman uniform appeared at the door and took a seat when I gestured to him. As we had finished lunch, I followed my usual protocol and asked Kondo and Ando to leave the room so that their employee would feel at least a little freer to talk to me.

I asked the fellow now seated across from me to introduce himself.

"My name is Nicolaas Campert, and I am in charge of Operations," he said in clear English.

I asked how long he had been with Kikkoman and how he had come to join the company, already half-expecting the answer.

"For about three years I worked for another food business close to my hometown. I was ready to change jobs and I heard about Kikkoman. At that time the image of a Japanese company was all about state-of-the-art technology, so we knew that the factory would be very clean. It was also interesting to have a chance to go to Japan to study. So I had my first job interview in December 1996 then started working here in February of '97. Actually, my first day of work for Kikkoman was flying to Japan."

My raised eyebrows must have asked the obvious question.

"Like everyone else they hired, I knew nothing about *shoyu* or how to make it. So we all had to go to Japan for training, to Noda City. The people hired before me were already there. We stayed there for two weeks, training at the Noda plant in Chiba Prefecture, learning all the steps to making *shoyu*, then we went to Singapore for another four weeks of training."

We talked for a while about his experiences in the plant and what was different from the place he used to work. As I expected, he had quickly become accustomed to the Kikkoman way of doing business and now taught others.

"Sometimes my younger operators don't understand why we do things a certain way. They have their own ideas about how we could do things better. Young guys are always saying, 'Why don't we do it like this?' I tell them, 'Look, we are Dutch. We know everything there is to know about making cheese. Imagine if you were to go to Japan and set up a factory to make cheese. One day a smart, young Japanese operator comes up to you and says there are better ways to do it. What would you say? Of course, you are Dutch, so you would say, *Hey, we have been doing this for hundreds of years! First, learn the way we do it, and learn it well. And then, if you really think you know a way to improve the process, come talk to me, I will listen.* That is exactly the situation here at Kikkoman. They know this business inside-out. Are there ways to improve the process? Maybe small ones. But are there major improvements that they have never thought about or investigated? I doubt it.'"

I asked Nicolaas about his various roles at KFE. One thing I had observed in Walworth and Folsom is that the best staff were always doing a dozen different things. Job descriptions seemed too confining for these key people, and no single title could explain the real value they brought to the company. I suspected the same was true for Nicolaas.

"Well, I am like the buffer between the two cultures. I don't speak much Japanese, but I have been here a long time and I have a pretty good idea what the Japanese managers mean. Some of our workers ask me to explain what Japanese managers are thinking. For example, an operator may say that his manager doesn't comment on his performance. 'Am I doing something wrong?' he will ask me, and I have to tell them that this is normal. Most Japanese won't volunteer information and they won't just start talking by themselves. They have difficulties with the language, of course, but also they are not big talkers, at least not on the job. If you want to know something, you have to ask. It's just the way they are. But you can ask anything and they will give you a very specific, sometimes amazingly detailed answer."

Another thing he told me was that the Japanese are not by nature micro-managers, but they feel personally responsible for every success or failure, so sometimes they want to be deeply involved in the process. This is something else that he has to explain to his workers. But the biggest thing, he said, is the constant insistence on 100 percent quality in everything

"Kikkoman accepts nothing less than total quality. That is one of the first things I learned. I have to admit that sometimes this is frustrating for us Dutch. Of course, Kikkoman does things their own way. Product quality has to remain at 100 percent all the time. But why insist on 100 percent when 95 percent or even 90 percent would make you the best brand on the market? We ask ourselves again and again, 'Why do we need to make so much effort to achieve this level? Why is it necessary?' The bar is set so high — sometimes it seems a waste of time or effort. But once you achieve the level of quality that Kikkoman demands, you know beyond any doubt that you are miles ahead of any other company. Of course, sometimes it is frustrating, especially for younger workers who are more impatient, and it's my job to explain these things to them. I tell them that once you achieve the Kikkoman level of quality control, it's a very good feeling. You know you're the best by far, and that is very satisfying."

I had an interesting talk with Nicolaas, and he told me all sorts of stories to illustrate the challenges they faced. I knew that Kondo and Ando probably had a list of interviews lined up for me, but I wanted to go off-script as soon as possible and talk to people who were not recommended by management. I asked Nicolaas who in the company would be interesting to talk to. Without hesitation he said, "Willem. You should talk to Willem. You will like his stories."

Okay, done deal. I thanked Nicolaas for his time and went down the hall to Kondo-san's office. He looked up from his desk and picked up a clipboard with a single sheet of names and times printed out.

"Are you ready for the next one?" he asked.

"Actually, I'd like to take a short break and wander around for a bit, if it's okay, and then I'd like to talk to Willem van Gulik." Kondo looked surprised that I already knew the names of some of his key staff. He said of course, I was free to go anywhere in the office area, and he would call Willem for me. I thanked him and set off to stretch my legs.

I took a short walk around the office, and chatted with some of the staff I met (I was surprised that they all spoke English to some degree). Finally, to take my mind off interviewing, I decided to look at the various interesting objects in the display cases in the lobby. I remembered that Kondo-san had pointed these out earlier and explained what each one was.

The ones that most interested me were a pair of ceramic jugs with blue hand-painted lettering, dated 1602. They said, *Japanschzoya*, which I took to mean Japanese shoyu. Back in the early 1600s, the only contact Western countries had with the Shogun's Japan was through a single small island off the coast of Kyushu, and the principal trading partner was Holland. The Dutch had privileged access to the wealth and the knowledge of the Japanese at that time. One of the things they began to export from this hermit kingdom was an early version of what we now call *shoyu*. Over the next century, *shoyu* became a must-have ingredient in many of the royal kitchens of Europe, an early tribute to the sauce's power to enhance any flavor without overwhelming the dishes where it is used. I had read stories about Louis XIV's chef demanding to have *shoyu* in the royal kitchen, and there were similar stories about its use in Austria and other parts of Europe centuries ago.

There was also a gold medal in the cabinet marked, "Exposition Universelle Inernationale 1900." It is from a later period when Japanese *shoyu* (especially Kikkoman) was winning medals at worlds' fairs and international exhibitions in Vienna, Amsterdam, Paris, and elsewhere. By the nineteenth century, a great many European chefs were well aware of the virtues of soy sauce and able to judge which types were most attractive to their palates. From what I had read, the best of the naturally brewed sauces were winners year after year.

I saw Kondo-san motioning me from down the hall, so I made my way back to the conference room. Inside, I found a smiling fellow with short-cropped blonde hair who could have been thirty or fifty or anywhere in between. He was smiling and made me feel as if we were friends before I even sat down. He introduced himself as Willem, and we began talking. I asked him my standard questions.

"I am an area leader in the production side," he said. "I've been here for twenty years, longer than the factory has been open. Before that, I made cartons in a paper factory. One day I saw a newspaper story saying that Kikkoman was going to start producing soy sauce here in the Netherlands. I did a little checking to find out what kind of company it is, and then I went for an interview."

"So you joined Kikkoman before there was even a plant here. What was your first job?" I asked.

"My first job was making the seed mold for the *koji.*"

"And how did you know how to do that? You made cartons before. How did you learn to make seed mold?"

"I went to Japan for training for four weeks, then to Singapore for six weeks." That echoed Nicolaas's story.

"What was it like working at Kikkoman in those days?"

"I came from a manufacturing company that was totally automated. My image of Japanese companies was based on Toyota. We thought it would be super-automated. And when we joined the company, Mr. Pennington told us it was a 'high-skills job.'

"But when we started we had to do everything by hand. We made the seed mold by hand because back then we had no mixer or other equipment. We did everything by hand, all of us sweating and groaning, and we would joke to each other, 'This is a high-skills job.' But to be honest, we learned so much by doing it that way. The people who joined later found a totally automated plant, and the result is that they don't really understand the underlying processes as well as we do. So we were ultimately grateful for this learning experience. We know the hands-on feel of almost everything in this factory. We old-timers still like to joke that this is a 'high-skills job.'"

Willem seemed to have a good perspective on his work and on Kikkoman, and I was prompted to ask him about something I had wondered about. The image of Wisconsin farm boys flying to Japan to study soy sauce production in a small town in the provinces was incongruous enough, but the idea of rural Dutch workers doing the same thing seemed equally improbable. I asked Willem what it was like.

As expected, he said the work went smoothly but the culture gap was palpable. Of course, none of the Japanese could speak a word of Dutch, so all communication had to be done in English. "That was one of the reasons they put the plant in Sappemeer,"

Willem explained. "In that area you can find good, well-edu-cated workers. Lots of people understand enough English to work in a foreign company. I think most of our English was better than most of the people who had to train us. All these guys in Noda carried little electronic dictionaries. For the most part, we could understand them pretty well and they could understand us."

I enjoyed talking to Willem. He was a cheery fellow, good-spirited and obviously proud of his work for Kikkoman. Like so many others I had met, he had joined the company early and stayed for decades, and as far as I could tell he had no plans to retire or go anywhere else. At one point I commented on how easy it was to become part of the Kikkoman family.

"For many people, it takes years," he said with a big smile. "For me it was much faster. You see, I got much more than I bar-gained for when I joined the company."

I felt a good story coming on and I signaled Willem to relax and tell me about it. He looked a little embarrassed at first, but became more animated once he got going:

"As I told you, right after I joined the company I went to Noda for training. I was a single guy back then, and they put me up at a hotel in Noda. I didn't have to work on Saturdays, so I had a little time to explore the local area. But of course I couldn't speak Japanese and I didn't know where to go or what to see. Fortunately, there was a nice girl at the front desk who spoke English. Her name was Kumiko, and she was very friendly and gave me advice about where to go. One day I asked if she would show me around on the weekend, and she agreed. We had a good time and discovered that we liked each other. All too soon, my four weeks in Noda were up and I had to go to Singapore for a month and a half." He laughed, shaking his head at the memory. "I spent a *lot* of money on international phone calls — there was no Internet or text messaging then, of course. Anyway, we got to like each other even more from those calls, and when I got back to the Netherlands I bought a fax so we could communicate without spending all my salary on phone calls. We really got to know each other through the letters we exchanged on that fax, and then Kumi came to the Netherlands for a holiday, and I showed her around the country, from Amsterdam to the countryside. By this point I knew I wanted to marry her, but I also knew the biggest challenge was still ahead.

"I went to Japan for a holiday and I met her family. At first they were not overjoyed at the thought that their daughter might marry a foreigner and move away from Japan. But then they came over here and they saw my house, only one kilometer from the new Kikkoman plant, and they saw that I am a good person and I had a good job.

"Anyway, they finally decided that I was a good fellow, and since I was working for Kikkoman, maybe things would work out okay, so finally her father agreed to the marriage. I flew back to Japan and we got married in the same hotel where we had first met, and we had a big party and lots of people from Kikkoman came. It was a very good time. Because I married a girl from Noda, I feel like I've married into the Kikkoman family." He was smiling broadly.

We chatted a bit more, and then I thanked Willem for his stories and we shook hands. He seemed like the kind of person I would want to know if I lived in the area — honest, diligent, sincere — in other words, what I was beginning to see as the profile of a typical Kikkoman worker.

After a brief rest, Kondo asked who else I might like to talk to. "I have the names of several people you might like to meet. We could keep on going if you're feeling up to it, or we could meet them tomorrow if you are tired," he said.

I assured him I wasn't tired. I just wanted to talk to someone who wasn't on his interview list, perhaps someone who had an unusual perspective on the company. Kondo thought for a moment.

"There is one very interesting fellow, but he is not an employee, so we did not think of inviting him. However, he knows Kikkoman very well, and if you would like to talk to him, I can arrange it. He is supposed to stop by here next week, but I could call him and see if he might visit us today…"

Perhaps a little too eager for a chance to talk to someone outside the factory, I said yes, by all means, please call him.

About twenty minutes later, a car pulled up and a slightly tall, professorial man stepped out. He had short, sandy brown hair, glasses, and wore a blue blazer with a dark blue tie. Very corporate, which means not at all like the Kikkoman employees I had met.

"How are you?" he said, shaking my hand. "I am Pieter de Keyser."

I immediately offered him a seat in the conference room, we exchanged business cards (being around Japanese companies was having a bad effect on me), and we set about talking. His card said he was with some architectural firm.

As it turned out, Pieter had been working with Kikkoman for many years but was not a member of the company.

"Back then I was a project manager for a large Japanese construction firm. They had offices around Europe, and at the time many big Japanese clients were expanding into Europe, so they set up offices to serve these clients. Japanese companies felt more comfortable doing business with other Japanese companies, and there was a great deal of security in having a famous Japanese construction firm building your office or your factory or whatever."

Always one to point out the obvious, I remarked that Pieter was not Japanese.

"No, of course not." He smiled. "The company I worked for was a familiar name to Japanese clients, and they had a few Japanese managers in the office, but the staff were all local people. Just like Kikkoman." He nodded in the direction of the production area.

"All of my career I was managing big projects for large Japanese companies. I gradually got to know things about Japanese people and Japanese companies and the way they do business. Anyway, Kikkoman had a good relationship with this construction company, and wanted them to take charge of building the new plant in the Netherlands. My Japanese directors sent me to be the project manager and to make sure we kept our good relationship with Kikkoman, which was a valued client."

So a Japan-owned construction firm had an office in Amsterdam or somewhere that hired local people to do the work in the Netherlands, but had only a few Japanese faces at the top to make their clients feel comfortable, to provide what they call *anshinkan* (peace of mind). The whole arrangement made perfect sense to me. In many cases even today, Japanese companies expect to be served by other Japanese firms that they know they can trust. It sounds a little silly and provincial, but in many ways American companies did the same thing long ago and so did many of the European nations. Hand-holding clients and providing *anshinkan* as part of your service is not in any way a uniquely Japanese concept.

I asked Pieter how long his stint as project manager lasted.

"Sixteen years."

"What?" I was caught off guard by that. "It doesn't take sixteen years to build a factory!"

No, he explained, it doesn't. But the Kikkoman plant did not simply get built, start operating, and that was that. It grew bit by bit, and there were continual changes and modifications and... I got the idea. Yes, it made sense that small sections of the factory layout would change from year to year, and Kikkoman might rely on a professional contractor to oversee all those modifications, but there was still no need for a "project manager" with expertise at running large-scale construction projects to be available day after day for a decade and a half. Clearly, Pieter's real job, as he had hinted, was to maintain good relations between his company and Kikkoman. And he must have been good at that to stay on as long as he did.

I asked Pieter exactly what he did for the factory.

"When this project began, I was in charge of managing the construction, and gradually that shifted to overseeing machinery and other installations. The building materials were sourced locally, but at first most of the machinery came from Japan. Many production items had to be brought in from Japan, so I had to coordinate our construction work with the constant shipments arriving from overseas."

"What kind of shipments?" I wondered. What were they bringing from Japan?

"For example, all the bottling equipment was shipped from their usual supplier in Japan. That might have made sense in the start-up phase, but even good equipment breaks down sooner or later, and then you need parts and maintenance and repairs, and then everything has to be shipped from Japan. It's expensive and it's time-consuming and sometimes it's just frustrating to have to wait. Not a good situation.

"I understand why it takes a while for Japanese companies to get comfortable with local suppliers. But eventually, they trusted me to buy some of their important equipment locally. Like the bottling equipment. My team located a German firm that supplies the same kind of equipment to a local brewing company here. Kikkoman examined their equipment, liked it, and gave me the okay to purchase and install it. The German firm is very dependable, and the machinery they supplied is first-rate."

Knowing a bit about how fanatical Kikkoman can be about quality, I had to ask, "Was Kikkoman satisfied with this German transplant in the heart of their Japanese production facility?"

"Yes," he said. "They're still using that equipment today."

Many of the people I had interviewed said they were hired before the factory was completed, and I realized that I had sitting before me one of the people who were there right from the beginning and someone who was not sent off to Noda for training. I asked Pieter to tell me a little about the early days here.

"I got to know Mr. Pennington, who lived here for quite a while. He and I became friends and we maintained that friendship for a decade. Thanks to him, I had the opportunity to visit both the Walworth and Folsom factories. He took me over there so that I could see how things were done at the U.S. sites and compare them with what we were doing in Sappemeer. He was very kind and I miss him."

To change the flow of the conversation a bit, I asked Pieter if he had ever tasted soy sauce before he came to Kikkoman. He looked surprised.

"I'm over sixty now, but I still remember the little Kikkoman bottle with the red cap in my mother's kitchen. We went to Chinese restaurants when I was young, and my mother used *shoyu* at home. So I was already familiar with the little bottle from the time I was about seven. Now many Europeans are getting to know the taste of Kikkoman."

I suggested that if the European operation continued to grow and the demand continued to grow, Kikkoman might need to double the size of the plant someday.

"They can double production, yes. But they would not simply build a plant twice as big." This was interesting to me, coming as it did from someone whose company stood to gain from any future construction.

"If you just build a larger-scale version of the plant," he explained, "it means that the product has to move greater distances through pipes. Kikkoman has discovered that moving the soy sauce over longer distances affects quality. Maybe it's only a slight difference, or maybe it's something that you and I wouldn't even notice, but they notice. So if it changes the flavor, it's no good. There is lots of space here to build new storage tanks for raw materials or expand bottling or shipping or storage, but my guess is that they would increase production volume through other, internal changes. Remember that the whole process is highly automated now and they can change a lot of things without adding much floor space."

We talked on and on. Pieter was a very interesting guy, his English was pleasant to listen to, and it was clear that he understood the thinking of Japanese managers very well. He said that he was sixty-two and he had left his employer, and thus his Kikkoman job, about a year or so ago. That change, which would be perfectly normal in the "outside" world, seemed very unusual in the Kikkoman universe. I asked him why he decided to leave the fold.

For the first time in our talk, he looked down and his face took on a pained look. He didn't speak for half a minute or so, and when he started again, his voice was shaky and he seemed to be choosing his words one by one.

"A couple of year ago, we had a... tragedy in my family. My daughter took her own life. I was heart-broken. At the funeral, no one from my company showed up. There was no one from the firm where I had worked for more than twenty years. Not one. But of course, there were many people from Kikkoman.

They surrounded me like good friends do, and that made me feel just a little better. It was then that I understood — *they* were my family, not the people who had been signing my paycheck all that time. Even though I was not an employee of Kikkoman, I was not an outsider. To them, I was family. They were there to support me, and I will never forget that.

"I quit my job soon after the funeral. I have a good job now, and I am very happy." He paused for a moment and looked out the window behind me. "By the way, I heard that not long afterwards Kikkoman severed its business relationship with the big Japanese company I had just quit."

Though I was trying to take notes, my throat felt strangely constricted and my eyes were misting up a bit. Warren Buffet once said, "You can't do good business with bad people," and now I saw that Kikkoman felt the same way. That is not a company policy that you create in a boardroom or have cooked up by a big consulting firm. It's a fundamental part of a company's way of thinking and way of doing business. It's a part of that elusive corporate DNA that defines an organization rather than being defined by it. I suspected, not for the first time, that this was passed on through successive generations of the Mogi family. Whatever the case, Pieter's story was one that I knew I would never forget. His feeling and the simple power of his expression in telling it would linger in my mind. And I suspected that nothing I would hear afterwards on any continent would tell me more about what it means to be part of the Kikkoman family.

I shook his hand and thanked Pieter sincerely for taking the time to come visit and for sharing a very personal story with me. His face brightened once again and his old demeanor returned in an instant.

"No, I am grateful to Kikkoman for inviting me here to talk to you. I am so happy that they remember me. I really enjoyed working here for so long. It is a good company."

We shook hands again and I walked him out to his car. We joked about how foreigners imagine the Netherlands, and at some point I must have said that I was disappointed not to have seen a single windmill. He looked up and pointed off in the distance, just beyond the road that led into the factory, "Why don't you go to the Kikkoman windmill? It is a beautiful area. You will enjoy it. Get outside, enjoy the sunshine and see some of our Dutch countryside."

I thanked him for the advice, although I had no idea what he was talking about. Fortunately, Mr. Kondo appeared in the doorway to join me in seeing Pieter off. After his car pulled away, I turned to the GM and asked him about something called the Kikkoman windmill. Was there such a thing? Was it real? What was it for? Could I see it?

"Absolutely," he said. "It's part of a special area, a nature preserve that Kikkoman is supporting. If you like, you can go there tomorrow.

That evening, I asked Ando-san to drive me to my hotel in Groningen, the only town of any real size in that area. Groningen (the first "G" is pronounced something like a guttural "F," I discovered, and the same is true for the famous Grolsch beer, which explained why my horrendous American pronunciation brought only puzzled looks from local bartenders) isn't a big city by any means, with lots of small streets, quaint little restaurants and lots of bars.

One thing I had noticed in Amsterdam was the profusion of bicycles. I chalked that up to sensible European preference for non-polluting vehicles, but even so, there seemed to be millions of bikes in Amsterdam (a slight exaggeration, but the fact is there are more bicycles than people), and a pedestrian must remain vigilant at all times to prevent accidents. In Groningen I discovered that this phenomenon was common to every city. There were a dozen bikes for every car on the streets, and I swear there were times when the bicyclists seemed to literally run both cars and pedestrians off the road. I reminded myself that no matter how many delicious beers I consumed, I would look both ways before stepping out onto any sidewalk or street.

I got a good night's sleep at my hotel — a compliment either to the establishment's fine bedding or to the effectiveness of my nightcap, I cannot say for sure. In any case, I arose early and refreshed in the morning. I had barely finished an excellent breakfast in a nearby cafe when Ando's Toyota appeared. I gathered my things and jumped into the car.

"Where would you like to go today?" he said brightly.

"To see the windmill," I replied.

"I thought so. Kondo-san said you were interested in visiting our nature preserve. Let's go. It's not far from the plant, and I have already called two of the caretakers to meet us there."

We drove a short while and then pulled onto a small side road, and finally turned off the road altogether. Ando parked and we walked along a path next to a very narrow canal. There was tall grass on our side of the waterway and an expanse of thick vegetation on the far side, stretching off for as far as I could see. When we had walked some distance, we came to a simple gate. There was a small sign welcoming us in Dutch and another, larger sign in both Dutch and English announcing that this area was a nature preserve and explaining why it was supported by Kikkoman (in part, because of the importance of clean water to the company's business).

Two men were waiting for us in front of the gate. Ando introduced them as Jelle and Marco, representatives of the local organization that cared for this area. We exchanged cards, and though theirs were obviously in Dutch, I guessed that their organization looked a lot like "Groningen Landscape." They were both dressed in casual sport jackets and jeans, both of them easy-going and laughing a lot. Neither of was young, but they seemed completely at ease out here, more like a couple of grad students from a nearby university than two men who could easily be professors. And though they were not quite fluent in English, between the two of them they communicated reasonably well.

For the next hour they guided us around this completely wild area, filled with all sorts of plant and animal life, waterways, marshes and such. They explained that the total area of the preserve was about 2,000 hectares (about 5,000 acres). They referred to it as the "project," a conservation effort by local government to preserve and enhance the environment. It was something they both seemed very proud of. If I understood correctly, this was one of many such projects being carried out across the Netherlands to restore the balance disturbed by urbanization.

Marco beamed. "There are over 100 species of animals here. We have many otters and beavers, swans, spoonbills, and even a couple of white-tailed eagles. All this within twenty minutes of Groningen city. We have two small terns here that breed nowhere else in the Netherlands. In fact, there are enough rare birds here that bird watchers come all the way from the UK to sketch and photograph them."

We walked for a while along a clear path but with dense foliage and small ponds on both sides of us, until we came to the landmark I had wanted to see. The Kikkoman windmill is nothing like the Dutch windmills of old that you see on picture postcards. It is a small metal frame perhaps 20-25 meters high atop a brick base. But it is a real, functioning mechanism, designed to raise water, but not to grind grain. I walked around the brick building, finding a black stone plaque embedded in the red brick wall on one side. In large letters, it said: *Molen Kikkoman*, the Kikkoman mill.

Jelle explained that the mill was not just decorative: "Dirty water comes in from the river, then the mill lifts it up into the project area where it gets filtered through the natural environment and passes out much cleaner through little streams and into the lake over there."

I couldn't help but notice the constant background of bird calls in the air. I began to understand what they meant about birdwatchers flocking to this area. We came to a two-story wooden parapet, an observation post that afforded a grand view over the marshes and fields and wetlands around us. We climbed up and looked out. It all seemed so peaceful.

Marco picked up the narrative: "Our organization sends volunteers into the elementary schools to explain about this area, what we are doing, why we are doing it, and why it matters. Several of the schools organize field trips out here. It's good for the kids to see this kind of nature and to understand why it is so important that we all work to protect it."

I originally went to the "project" intending to see the Kikkoman windmill and go home, but I ended up staying for almost three hours, talking to the two energetic Dutch guys about their successes in revitalizing this area, getting animals to return and breed here, and then doing everything possible to preserve and improve the environment. It was much more interesting *in vivo* than it sounds on paper, and it was hard for me to turn to Ando and say it was time to go.

We went back to the Kikkoman plant, but only briefly. I had got what I came for and then some. I thanked Kondo and Ando for their hospitality and asked them please to thank all the people who had taken time to talk to me. But I was already thinking about my next stop — Germany.

Kondo had arranged a rental car for me in Groningen. I picked up my car — appropriately enough, a big Volkswagen sedan — and set the GPS for Düsseldorf. In a few minutes, I was leaving the Netherlands behind me, though I had to admit that it was one of the nicest visits of my entire trip, and I promised myself I would be coming back sooner rather than later.

11

Düsseldorf

*D*üsseldorf is not far from Sappemeer, only a couple of hours at German highway speeds. Not being accustomed to cruising for long stretches at over 200 km/hr (120 mph), I settled back to a more relaxed pace, which probably led everyone on the road to assume I was a centenarian just coming home from a long hospital stay. But 170 km/hr felt fast enough to me. In any case, I was in no hurry.

When I arrived in Düsseldorf it was raining. I easily found the hotel where I was staying, turned in my big VW at a nearby office, and checked in. All very easy. The next thing was to get in touch with the man I had been told to call, Mr. Hasegawa, the general manager of Kikkoman Trading Europe or KTE. I was beginning to get all these acronyms mixed up in my head — KFI, KII, KTE — but the one thing I understood clearly about this upcoming meeting was that there was no production plant in Germany. In fact, Kikkoman's only plant in Europe at this point was the one in the Netherlands that I had just visited (although several people had hinted that if growth continued as it had, a second European plant might become a reality one of these days).

The office I was about to visit next was the European sales and marketing arm, much like the one I had seen in San Francisco. While I had originally expected to focus only on production facilities to try to learn more about the secrets of *shoyu*, I had discovered that the Kikkoman story was more interesting than soy sauce alone, and I was eager to pursue certain themes to see if they played out in Germany as they had so clearly in the U.S. and the Netherlands.

I asked the tall blonde woman at the front desk if she would write down the address of my destination in German to give to the cab driver. She smiled politely at my foolish question and replied politely, "The driver will have no difficulty understanding you. Just speak clearly and tell him where you want to go."

And, somewhat to my amazement, she was right. In slow, clear English, I told him the address on Theodorstrasse, and he replied casually, "Very good. First trip to Germany?"

I told him no, but it was my first visit to Düsseldorf.

"Good," he said. "You will like it... if this rain ever stops."

With that, we drove off, and I got my first real view of the city. Perhaps seeing it on such a dreary day was not the best introduction, but I had no choice. I noticed trams running on the main streets, reminding me of Amsterdam. Somehow they didn't look as plentiful or as convenient as Amsterdam, but they looked solid and they ran fast, more like trains than the charming little trams in Amsterdam, which felt more like San Francisco cable cars.

We approached what looked like a big, domed stadium, the ISS Dome, which is owned by the city of Düsseldorf, part of a collection of venues for everything from business meetings to concerts to large-scale sporting events. We turned just past the dome and drove down a drab access road in front of three large, nondescript buildings. I recognized the names of a few famous Japanese companies and another nondescript building, which housed only German firms. At first I thought the driver had made a mistake, but he pointed to a small sign saying, "Kikkoman," and I breathed a sigh of relief.

The offices here actually house two companies: Kikkoman Trading Europe GmbH and JFC International (Europe) GmbH. From my background reading on the airplane from Chicago to San Francisco, I had learned the interesting history of the latter company, which is also part of the Kikkoman Group. Japan Food Corporation was the modern incarnation of a business that had been operating in the U.S. since the early days of the twentieth century. In an interesting reversal of the scenarios I had been looking at, the American ancestor of JFC actually established a Tokyo office way back in 1916. By the 1960s it was the largest importer and distributor of Oriental foods in the U.S. and a potential rival to Kikkoman's expansion strategy, so in 1969, the soy sauce maker bought JFC. Now the new firm, JFC International, is a potent global force, marketing, selling, and distributing many brands of Oriental food around the world, including Kikkoman products. In that capacity, it sometimes competes with Kikkoman Trading, but the rivalry is familial, as I was about to see.

I asked the cab driver to take me around so I could look at the building. One side was a row of loading docks, with a dozen or so large white trucks parked there, each with a picture of Kikkoman sauces or some other major product on the side, and of course, the JFC logo. I decided I wanted to learn a little more about this operation.

I went upstairs to the office area, a spacious, brightly lit, very modern office with a dozen or more people all absorbed in their computer screens. A few of them were moving about, carrying papers or going from one office to another, but no one paid me much attention.

Suddenly a pleasant female voice behind me reached out in very friendly English. "Can I help you? You look a bit lost." The voice belonged to a middle-aged brunette seated behind a large L-shaped desk slightly less cluttered than the others I saw around me. She was holding her reading glasses in front of her with two hands and smiling up at me like a teacher to a favorite student.

I told her my name and that I had an appointment with Mr. Hasegawa, the General Manager. She brightened even more.

"Oh, you must be the fellow from America who has come to write about us!" She got up and came over to see me up close.

"Well, I've come to investigate Kikkoman and yes, I'm looking at it from an outsider's perspective, and from that I'm trying to understand the company's DNA and—" I realized she was not listening to a word of what I was saying. She had already turned and was leading me towards Hasegawa's office.

The door was open, so she stuck her head in and told Hasegawa that the American writer was here. He stood up and invited me in immediately. We exchanged name cards and then, like GMs at all the other facilities, he escorted me into a well-appointed meeting room where we could talk comfortably. There was a large plate of cookies and small cakes on the table and they were soon joined by cups of coffee.

"I see you've already met Anna," he said, smiling. "She is not only our official greeter, but one of the key people who keeps things running around here. She's been here about twenty years. She loves people and is happy to welcome strangers to our office."

I told him that I already had a hunch that Anna's energy and goodwill extended to staff as well as visitors, and I had already met her counterpart in Walworth. He looked puzzled a moment and then brightened and said, "Oh, you mean Barbara. Yes, she is famous even over here."

Tatsuya Hasegawa seemed to me a perfect example of a Japanese manager stationed overseas. He was average height, slender, and looked about fifty, which meant plus or minus about ten years. His hair was close-cropped and just beginning to show grey in places. He wore a blue pin-stripe suit, white checked shirt and a blue tie with symmetrical white dots, and topped it off with sensible, black-framed glasses, stylish enough not to look out of place in Europe, but designed for business, not fashion. What impressed me most was his quiet, even-toned speech. He spoke clearly and politely and he seldom seemed stuck for a word. I was impressed.

I sat down, gratefully accepted the coffee, and got out my notebook.

Hasegawa told me that he'd been in Europe for about eleven years, that he had worked out of an office in the Czech Republic before moving the office to Germany in 2009 and formally establishing Kikkoman Trading Europe. I asked about the market for his main product, particularly how the market situation for *shoyu* might have changed in the past decade

He looked pleased to answer. "The idea that *shoyu* is originally part of Japanese food culture but is delicious on all types of food is more well established than a decade ago. Of course, compared with America, we have fewer Japanese and fewer Asians in general, so the awareness of *shoyu* is lower, but I would say it has grown considerably in the past few years.

"The result is that, overall, European demand for our products is rising, although not evenly in all markets. Some countries are picking up very quickly, while others are about the same as before, and some are lagging. But on the whole, business is growing steadily and we are optimistic that it will continue to grow for a long time to come."

I asked about the Food Expo held in Milan a while back (Expo Milano 2015). The rumors I'd heard were that Japanese food was one of the stars of the show. Was he there, and were the rumors true?

"Oh, yes, I attended, and yes, Japanese food was very popular. To give you an idea how popular it was, I should say that Italians have a reputation for two things: loving food and hating to wait for anything. Even for a very popular new restaurant, Italians will complain bitterly if they are asked to stand in line for half an hour. At the Japan Pavilion, people were waiting for *three hours* or more to taste authentic Japanese food. Kikkoman was not an official sponsor, but of course our *shoyu* was used in all the little stalls and food courts serving Japanese dishes. For Japan, this was a promotion of *washoku* (Japanese cuisine) in general, not any one particular type of cooking. There was even a place serving *fugu* (poisonous puffer fish) sashimi. It was quite an event."

I had eaten *fugu* when I lived in Tokyo. It is a perfect example of the subtlety of good *shoyu*, because *fugu* has very little taste, and it is sliced so paper-thin that you can easily see right through it to appreciate the design of the plate on which it is served. Used sparingly, *shoyu* can enhance the flavor of the *fugu* and make the dining experience truly memorable. (Yes, a little sake helps, too!)

I asked how Japanese food was doing here, in the German market. He replied that Germans don't make Japanese food at home, so they must visit Japanese restaurants, of which there were more every year.

"Teriyaki sauces are not popular here... yet," he said. "It's very different from America. The teriyaki taste just hasn't caught on here, but we're working on it. Our primary goal is still to increase the recognition of *shoyu*, not just in Germany, but throughout Europe."

I imagined Europe must be a much, much more challenging market than America. The U.S. is one country, with one set of food laws, regulations, and so on. You can sell the same product with the same label on the East Coast and West Coast. But Europe is a jigsaw puzzle of different countries and different markets.

"Exactly right. We sell in roughly thirty countries. That means thirty different sets of regulations, taxes, labels, packaging, and so on. In addition, we make market-specific products like sweet *shoyu* for France, plus we have to do marketing in two dozen or so different languages, and deal with all the different food cultures. It is a challenge, believe me."

Just to be clear, I asked exactly which markets KTE serves. He ticked off on his fingers: "The UK, France, Spain, Germany, Poland, Russia, Italy, the Netherlands, the CIS states, Israel, Lebanon, a few in Africa, and several more. Our big marketing push is in the first six I just mentioned. Each country is at a different stage of marketing, product introduction, and development, so we have to keep tabs on all these different markets all the time."

I wondered how KTE could possibly represent Kikkoman's product line-up to all those countries and all the sub-markets within each individual country. It would take a staff of hundreds.

He smiled. "We invite distributors and 'ambassador chefs' from each country to come here, and we let them taste different products and different recipes." He pointed at the floor, "Downstairs, on the first floor is our test kitchen. We make up all sorts of recipes that will appeal to people from different markets, and we let them taste-test for themselves.

We talked a bit about how Kikkoman carried out its advertising and PR. He said it was mostly done through print media and some online promotions, even a little with social media, but not very much with television because the costs were so high and the markets so diverse — they would need to create different commercials for every market.

"We also use a lot of PR, which is much more cost-effective than advertising. Different markets require different PR approaches. We have very talented people to handle those accounts. For example, our PR strategist in Vienna is amazing. She's practically a secret weapon," he said with a smile. "Gigi is terrific, and she's coming to our office today."

I said I'd like to meet her.

"You will. In about an hour." He looked at his watch and stood up. "Come on. I want to show you around a bit and then take you next door to see JFC. Their warehouse alone will give you an inkling of what our market looks like. And if you're feeling warm, they have just the thing to cool you down."

I wasn't especially warm, but I could see he had something he wanted to show me, so I followed along. First, we went downstairs, where he showed me the test kitchen he had just talked about. It was smaller than I'd expected, but a very usable ultra-modern kitchen. As we arrived, cooks were arranging a series of large pans on the counter. The food looked delicious, and the aromas were almost overpowering.

"We will have some guests here very shortly," Hasegawa explained. "I don't remember what the cuisine is for today, but we are preparing something to show them how Kikkoman sauces can be used in their everyday cooking to enhance the flavors of dishes they know well. Then our chefs will also show them some interesting things that complement those dishes, perhaps things they are not so familiar with. Everyone will get to sample lots of different food and go home with new ideas."

I resisted the temptation to stick my hand out and grab something that looked tasty. We returned to the second floor and did a quick tour of the office, which as I noted before, was a brightly lit, very modern space, in most respects just the same as a hundred offices I had seen in various cities over the past several years.

One thing was different, though: At the far end of the room was a large, imposing metal door, and as we approached, I realized we were going to go through it. Hasegawa paused and grabbed an oversized handle on one side. The door swung open with a *whoosh* like the entrance to a soundproofed recording studio. Only then did I realize that this heavy metal door was almost a foot thick, more like a bank vault than a recording studio. I wondered what could possibly be on the other side.

Surprise! On the other side was a mirror image of what was behind me — another brightly lit, modern office space, with people intently focused on their computers. I gathered we had just passed through the physical "Chinese wall" that separates KTE from JFC, but the two offices could have been twins.

Approaching us from the other side was a tall, well-built guy with a white shirt, black slacks and no jacket. He looked like he might be a rugby coach at one of the better universities in Tokyo. He bowed and offered me his card: Koichi Konoe, General Manager, JFC Deutschland. He turned and we walked at a brisk pace, passed through a series of doors, and were soon standing in a vast, three-story warehouse area, bigger than the ones I remembered seeing in the U.S. or the Netherlands. White walls, light grey cement floor, corrugated metal roof held up by giant I-beams, and endless, towering metal racks (called pallet racks), each piled high with various kinds of foodstuffs. In standard Japanese style, the whole room was brightly lit, and there wasn't so much as a cigarette butt or gum wrapper on the entire expansive floor. The overall impression was something like a big Costco or other "warehouse store," but without any shoppers.

In front of us there was a long open corridor along one wall, a five-meter-wide, wide open space big enough for the large forklifts to drive through. But the passageway was now so clogged with pallets of cartons, cases, or sacks of JFC's products that I doubted any of the fork lifts could move around. The only things moving were a few workers pulling small carts of merchandise through the maze.

Stretching out perpendicular to this aisle, like shelves in a library, were over two dozen rows of reinforced steel pallet racks roughly eight meters (25 ft.) high, each marked with a letter from A to Z, with some letters repeated. The racks were stocked to the ceiling with bags and cartons of rice, oils, sauces, even beer — in the back row were two racks loaded to the ceiling with cases of Japanese beer. And each rack had a hand-written sign with a destination name printed on it — most of the ones I saw nearby were big German cities. I called out to Konoe to tell me what we were looking at.

"We supply restaurants, food retailers, wholesalers, and distributors, hotels, catering services, and different kinds of food service companies all over Europe. We ship direct, so if someone needs something, they just place an order and we send it out." I remembered the line of trucks I had seen outside. "We are famous for our wide range of products, our very strong customer support, and our ability to advise customers about what products and quantities might best suit their needs. We even help clients plan their menus."

I asked if this was the only JFC office in Europe, although I had already guessed the answer. If this were the only warehouse, JFC would spend more on gasoline than it could ever earn in profit.

"Of course not. In addition to this office in Germany, we have branches in London, Paris, and Vienna. From that small network we serve all of Europe."

With what kinds of products? Obviously not just Kikkoman soy sauce.

"Well, of course we sell shoyu, but also half a dozen brands of rice, plus *miso*, rice vinegar, pickled ginger (*gari*), sesame seed oil, dried seaweed, udon noodles, crackers, instant soups, ice cream, green tea, tofu, several brands of sake and beer, and much more. We're like a one-stop shop for Asian food supplies."

"And I thought all you had was sushi," I said jokingly, looking up at the wide range of products on his shelves.

"Ah, yes, sushi..." He suddenly seemed to remember something and turned around, motioning for me to follow him. We walked back the way we had come, stopping in front of another room with a wide, grey door. He pulled open the door and we stepped inside. The door closed behind us and I realized we were in a giant, commercial refrigerator room filled with cartons and boxes of all sizes. Fortunately, I was wearing a sport jacket, but within seconds I was cold. I mean really *cold*! Konoe was smiling, almost laughing as he stood there in his short-sleeve white shirt. He turned to a smaller, squarish door in a side wall of the refrigerator, a door I hadn't even noticed when we came into the room. He pulled the door open, but this time stood to one side, graciously gesturing for me to enter.

"Please…" he said.

I stepped inside and could not believe it. There was no light in this small room, which was a fraction the size of the giant freezer I had just come from. But even by the light streaming in behind me I could see that it was snowing inside. That's right, snowing! The floor was like glass and there were white flakes falling on my face. Instinctively, I held my breath. I could dimly see in the interior some long, white plastic boxes stacked against the back wall. I did not dare touch anything for fear that my flesh would stick to whatever it touched. After what seemed a long ten seconds, I backed out of the room and Konoe shut the door tightly behind me. The big freezer room I had now returned to felt positively warm by comparison. I relaxed and caught my breath.

After a moment, we stepped back outside into the warehouse, and I asked him about these spaces.

"Well, the big one is our main refrigeration room. We have lots of merchandise that needs to be kept cold, so we store it here and ship it in refrigerated trucks to our customers," he explained. "The little room on the side, that's our deep freeze. We use that to store frozen fish so that it will still be fresh when it's delivered to customers."

I suspected that anything stored in that small room would take a week to thaw out at room temperature. How cold was it in there, I wondered.

"It's set at minus 25 degrees Centigrade," he said, and I shuddered involuntarily at the thought that I had just been standing in there in a light summer jacket to protect me. "But I'm sure it's much colder now — around minus 40 or 50."

"Okay," I said, looking to Hasegawa for support. "I think I need to get back to KTE and have a few cups of hot coffee." Konoe laughed and agreed.

Five minutes later I was back in a warm office, passing through the big vault-like door of JFC and back into the arms of Kikkoman. There, in the meeting room, I saw a somewhat short, extremely animated woman who looked as if she enjoyed the desserts that Vienna is justifiably famous for. She jumped up to meet me and we exchanged cards, although I had already guessed who she was. She spoke in a pleasing, hard-to-identify, vaguely English accent, telling me her name was Gigi Schoeller, with a hard "GeeGee" not a soft "JeeJee," and I gathered she was the head of her own company.

I was still trying to get my frozen blood to flow again, and for once I wished they served Irish coffee at Kikkoman. In any case, I was happy to let her do the talking.

"I run a PR agency based in Vienna, Austria. My roots are in the hotel business; I was an F&B [food & beverage] manager for Hilton in Germany for quite a while. Finally, I decided I wanted to go back to Vienna, which is my home. I worked for a PR agency there, taking over all their F&B and lifestyle-related accounts, and in time I took over the agency. That was sixteen years ago, and I have been running my own agency since then.

"Food is my love," she declared, her eyes lighting up. "And I enjoy my work. I learned a lot about food culture by working with Kikkoman. It opened my mind to different influences, different kitchen styles, and so on. I also learned about being proud of your own food culture.

"As I'm sure you know, Austria has a long history and a rich culture. Music, art, and so on, but food was sort of left behind, and that got me to start looking abroad, discovering other food cultures. Kikkoman gave me the opportunity to really explore the meaning of food culture.

"When sushi came to Austria, it was new, yet it settled in very quickly. Austrians are open-minded and curious, and if you give them a good reason for something to be accepted, it will be. But you have to tell a story about it. That's what PR is all about.

"After a while, the Kikkoman brand was very well known, and everyone was aware that they are the market leader, not only the No. 1 maker in Japan, but the maker of the best soy sauce in the world. So the local journalists started to ask me if they could go to Japan to see the main factory. I wasn't sure if that was a good idea, so I decided to go by myself first and check it out.

"I went to Japan, and... what can I say? Kikkoman were the most wonderful hosts; they made sure I had a fabulous time. I splurged on everything, breakfast, lunch, and dinner, for ten days, and at that point I'd eaten so much I could barely walk. I learned a lot about Japanese cooking, not just about *shoyu*, and I also learned a lot about Japanese customs. Of course, I did that by making lots of mistakes in etiquette." She was smiling as she remembered some of her faux pas in Japan.

So, did she take planeloads of journalists to Tokyo?

"No, we decided it was too expensive and there was too much to explain to them. Like me, they would probably be overwhelmed — in a good way — by Japanese culture and not focusing on Kikkoman. But my trip was certainly not wasted.

First, I had a chance to get to know the company on their home ground, so to speak. I learned a lot. And, because I made so many social mistakes, I came to appreciate the huge gap between our cultures.

"One thing I did when I got back home was to take all those things I had learned about the rules in Japanese culture and put them together in a sort of business etiquette book for Austrians going to Japan. I called it *Shukan* (customs), and it did very well. In 2009 we had the Year of Austria and Japan, and lots of corporate and state trips were planned, so my book was the perfect thing to help all those important people avoid making the same mistakes that I did."

I was still writing notes while Gigi was biting her lip and thinking out loud, "What else did we do? There were so many...

"Oh, yes! Very important — I also wrote cookbooks! I showed people how you could incorporate soy sauce into our domestic cuisine. That was fun and it was interesting. I showed people how to use soy sauce instead of salt and bring out new tastes in traditional Austrian cuisine. And we even won a big cookbook award, so you see, it was well done.

"Then we got their iconic little bottle with the red cap into the museum of fine arts. That was a great opportunity for good PR. We got government officials to attend, and we got excellent TV coverage."

I was getting writer's cramp trying to keep up with her fast-paced explanations, and even my little IC recorder was flashing a bright red text message: "*Data Overload. Tell subject to slow down!*"

I smiled weakly and she continued.

"I like to prepare simple, easy content that is readily available to everyone. Of course, sometimes we have to be a bit provocative. We never want to be boring. The main product never changes and the whole product line-up doesn't change very much, so in one sense we have to keep telling the same story, keep talking about the same basic message. But we have to be creative. Because we have a very traditional product, my challenge is to always come up with contemporary approaches to make it interesting."

I pointed out that she didn't have to work from scratch. Certainly her client drove some of the PR messaging.

"To be quite frank," she said, "The company is not very PR-minded. That is a good thing, I think. They do all sorts of wonderful things in the community, sponsoring university programs and arts programs and all, but they are not doing it as part of a PR strategy. They do it because they feel a genuine sense of responsibility. It's sometimes a challenge for people like me to promote the PR potential of these activities because Kikkoman is totally focused on doing these events well and not on the PR aspects."

"In the end, rather than promoting the product directly, I try to get consumers to look at it from a better perspective. I try to help Austrians see that soy sauce is not new or strange or incompatible with our own traditions. After all, our grandmothers did fermentation in their kitchens, with sauerkraut and so on. This is nothing foreign or unknown to us. But the company is a fascinating company, and I am always looking for new ways to talk about it and how it touches people's lives."

My hand was getting sore now. Of course, if I wanted to put a cold pack on it, I knew a nice, cool place to go to recuperate. I decided I should walk down the hall and drink another cup of coffee instead. I thanked Gigi for all her help and wished her well. She excused herself, all smiles and bouncy energy, and I noticed that she stopped in to chat with several of the Kikkoman staff on her way out. She was obviously both popular and well respected.

I took a short break, and when I returned to the meeting room, I discovered a tall, distinguished-looking German waiting for me. Like some of the Japanese I had met on this trip, he was in his late fifties, but could easily have passed for forty. He had sandy blonde hair, black-framed glasses and a winning manner that made him instantly likable. No surprise at all, then, to find that Hans Fuchs was the Senior Manager in charge of Marketing.

Hasegawa-san had asked Hans to come talk to me, and as it turned out, I was glad he did. Hans told me he had been in food marketing most of his life, including sixteen years working with a world-famous packaged food company in neighboring Switzerland.

"I enjoyed my time there," he said. "Europe is a very challenging market, not a country, but a collection of many countries, not a culture but a collection of many different cultures. My approach to marketing in a place like this is to focus on the local area: First you learn the language of the people you want to have as your customers, and you study their culture and you learn what is important to these people, and then you create a marketing plan that makes sense for that group. Then it works.

"I spent sixteen years focusing on the Swiss market for my previous employer, and I managed to bring our market share up to 82 percent. Is that remarkable? No, it is just the result of studying the market and responding."

While Hans was working there, he was contacted by a head-hunter who told him that a Japanese company was coming to Europe to set up a production plant and a sales office, but they did not really understand the European market. They decided to hire someone who really knew the European market well and knew how to approach it.

"I really don't know how they settled on me, but they did," he said with a good-natured laugh. "Then the General Manager asked me how to sell in Europe. It was still the 1990s, but I told him that if he really wanted to grow the market for his products, he should source the healthiest, most natural ingredients he could find, because I felt that was a trend that would build in Europe.

"As it happened, the headquarters in Japan had decided that the new factory in the Netherlands should be the 'greenest' of all the production facilities, and that they would use all-natural ingredients. This was a long time ago, and it became a big story all over Europe."

I asked Hans how business was doing. He replied that Kikkoman in Europe had been turning double-digit growth figures for some time, and that this was likely to continue, although the drivers of that growth might change over the years.

"Well, then, which markets are driving it now?" I asked.

"Russia is a huge consumer of soy sauce. Some people don't use it at all, and others seem to bathe in it, always one of two extremes. So Russian growth has been very strong. And the second biggest is Poland and also the new states of Eastern Europe."

He went on to talk about the challenges of developing new products to serve the needs of these multiple markets better.

"Several years ago I realized that the Nordic countries had serious issues with gluten. It is a problem for many people in those countries. So I pushed the company to develop a gluten-free soy sauce. Now it is selling very well, not just in Scandinavia, but in the U.S., which is a huge market for Kikkoman."

Did he think that soy sauce would become a basic ingredient of European kitchens someday?

"Perhaps. But we cannot be a one-product company. Soy sauce is an excellent product, and Kikkoman is the best, but we must look beyond that one product in order to stimulate growth. For example, the first step beyond liquid soy sauce is the powdered kind, and we are already doing a very good business in powdered soy sauce."

"Powdered?" I asked, although I remembered being told about that business back in San Francisco.

"Yes, several giant food companies use our soy powder. They use it in packaged noodles, sauces, and all sorts of foods, not just Asian foods. We even sell to some of the world's largest, best-known fast food chains. Why? Because the flavor helps their products and because our quality control is the best around. Because of that we have acquired 'trusted supplier' status at some of these companies. Several very large European companies buy from us, some of them in large volumes. They are concerned about quality, not just the purity of the ingredients, but the purity of processing as well.

"However, that is still soy sauce. We must move beyond that, and expand into new fields. Just look at the range of products that our partners in JFC are selling. The market has plenty of demand for high-quality Oriental foods of all kinds. We must be flexible."

I realized that Hans was something of an independent thinker in a business known for cookie-cutter solutions. It was clear that he liked the company and its products and also that he was very good at his job. I asked how long he had been with Kikkoman.

"Twenty years and counting," he said with obvious pride.

"And what's the biggest problem you see here?"

He didn't need to think very long.

"There is not enough flexibility in marketing concepts. They want to do things the way they were doing things before. They are not always ready to respond to a changing market quickly enough. For example, we have data showing that 75 percent of local families are one or two-person households. But we are trying to market recipes to four-person families. I said we have to target the majority of the market, but I was told that the marketing plan was decided long ago and they are not yet ready to change it.

"This isn't just a problem with Kikkoman and it's not only a problem with Japanese companies, believe me. Lots of firms have the same conservative approach to marketing campaigns. But I think Japanese companies are particularly vulnerable to that kind of thinking. Once something has been decided at the headquarters, they want to stick with it. That made sense thirty years ago, but today markets are changing very fast. We need to change our marketing strategies constantly to keep up."

Despite his minor frustrations, I could see he was smiling. Like so many talented people I'd met at Kikkoman, Hans was obviously intelligent and good at his job and could easily find work at another company, perhaps for a higher salary or better position. Why didn't he have his resume in the mail already?"

"Because this is a good company. A *very* good company. I don't want to go someplace else. Is it frustrating sometimes? Of course it is. Show me a job with no frustrations, please!" He laughed again. "Seriously, I enjoy working here and I am happy to do my best for this company. And if sometimes they don't listen to my advice, or if sometimes it takes ten years for them to implement something I suggested, well, that's just the way things are. I am not the CEO. These are not my decisions to make. I do the best job I can do, and I accept whatever decisions are made by the managers. I don't want to fight with anybody."

Here was an echo of things I had heard in Wisconsin and California, the same basic sentiment, only with a strong German accent. The kind of people who were attracted to work at Kikkoman were self-motivated, hard-working achievers. And more than that, they liked the family feeling they found at Kikkoman and they would rather look the other way when small problems or irritations cropped up, because in the bigger scheme of things those issues were insignificant.

Any psychologist would say that Kikkoman had somehow latched onto a group of unusually mature, emotionally well-developed individuals. I remembered Dick Jenkins back in

Walworth telling me, "We're just lucky to find so many good people and we're lucky that they want to stay."

As I traveled around the world and saw more and more of this operation, I was certain that luck had very little to do with it.

Hans asked if I would like to see a Kikkoman-sponsored cooking school downtown. I jumped at the chance. I had seen little of the city, and this was the first I'd heard of a cooking school. I imagined rows of German housewives puzzling over how to roll vinegar rice just the right way to make *temakizushi*. I told Hans I would love to see it, he called for a taxi, and in just a few minutes we were headed downtown.

We drove to a modern office area in a business district of Düsseldorf. The streets were lined with the usual German cars, hardly a Toyota in sight, I thought as we crossed the street. Hans pointed to a couple of Japanese restaurants so that I would see the trend was indeed growing. Then we walked up to what looked like an ordinary office building.

The sign in the window said "Kochschule Düsseldorf" (Düsseldorf Cooking School).[4] There was no class in there at the moment, so the place looked dark and quiet. The front of the room was like a storefront, big display windows looking out onto the street, and in this front area were a long table and a half-dozen chairs on either side. A small bookshelf held several pamphlets about the school and copies of a large cookbook by a chef named Thomas Krause. Stepping further inside, I saw a long dining table, the same clean, heavy wood design as its cousin up front, but this one had almost a dozen chairs on either side. There was a small wine rack loaded with inter-esting-looking bottles of mostly red wine, and a short stairway going up a few steps to the kitchen area.

We proceeded to the kitchen, which was well lit and spa-cious, clearly a good place for teaching. There were acres of counter space and lots of wide, deep drawers, a large center island with more counters and drawers, and large sinks, ovens, refrigerators, and so on. The counters were decorated here and there with wooden knife stands, boxes of spices and flavorings, plates of fruit, rolls of paper towels and potted plants all over. The effect was totally modern, neat, and ready to use.

I had barely entered the teaching kitchen and was looking around when I heard footsteps behind me on the half-stair-case that connected us to the dining room next door. There was a gruff greeting in German that made Hans smile, and then a short, athletic-looking man in a cardigan sweater and blue jeans came over to introduce himself. "Hello. I am Thomas Krause. I am pleased to meet you. Welcome to my school." His gesture took in the whole space, a very attractive establishment, but silent and empty at the moment.

Hans handled the explanations. "David, Thomas is a well-known chef, and we are very fortunate to have him working with us. Kikkoman has been sponsoring this cooking school and several just like it for a couple of years. Thomas is our star chef—" he put his hand on the younger man's shoulder, while Krause looked at the floor, a bit embarrassed, "—and his name value brings in the students." The two men looked at each other and laughed, then Thomas began explaining his program to me:

"The classes are small, usually twelve to fourteen people. I teach them basic cooking skills — not Cordon Bleu, but practical, useful, everyday skills."

"Are German housewives so inept at basic cooking skills?" I asked naively.

"Actually," Hans beat Thomas to the punchline. "The most popular courses are for men, not for women. They are the ones who need to learn how to cook."

Thomas held up a copy of his cookbook so I could see the title: *MÄNNER KOCHSCHULE* (Cooking School for Men).

"Okay, why men?" I asked, not satisfied with looking dumb the first time around.

This time Thomas replied, "Because there are so many young men who go to work in a company and live in an apartment somewhere, and they don't know how to cook anything. So they live on frozen food that they just heat up. It's unhealthy, it's unsatisfying, and it's unnecessary. In a few weeks I can teach these guys how to cook reasonably well for themselves."

I said something about how it must be a bit of a shock for his young students to see a professional kitchen.

"This is not a professional kitchen," Thomas corrected. "It's a good, usable kitchen, but that is all. We don't have professional kitchens in our homes, so why should we use one if we want to learn how to cook at home? In this school people learn real skills that they can use immediately in their own kitchens. The teaching here is done in small groups; it is very personal. The chef is standing right next to you, helping, advising, making sure you are comfortable with what you're doing."

Hans chimed in again, "And this is good for us, because a teaching chef is the person closest to the consumer. Marketing agencies know nothing about real consumer tastes. These chefs talk to real consumers every time they teach, and they get real feedback about what people like and don't like."

"I see. So Kikkoman's goal is to get feedback from average consumers?" I asked.

"Well, that's part of it," Hans said, pointing to the different bottles of Kikkoman sauces scattered around the kitchen. "The other thing is to train people to cook their favorite dishes — German dishes — with a touch of soy sauce. Once they learn, they never want to give it up. And they tell their friends. We nudge the market forward by planting these seeds."

I asked how many schools were currently in operation, and Thomas told me there were eight as of now. How many cooking courses was he running?

"I don't really know, but a lot, maybe twenty-something. We have courses in fish, beef, wok-style, Italian-style, and many others."

And German men are interested enough to go to these schools to learn to cook?

"Yes, they are. And they bring their friends." Thomas looked quite pleased. "We enjoy preparing food together. We experiment, we have fun, and everyone enjoys the classes. That is important."

I thanked Thomas, and then Hans and I headed back to the office.

On the ride back, I couldn't help but think once again: Everywhere I traveled, no matter who I met in the Kikkoman universe, whether employees, managers, consultants, legal advisors, suppliers, wholesalers, tradespeople or whomever, they all turned out to be exceptionally decent human beings, the kind of good people you would be happy to meet, talk to, have dinner with, or go out for a drink with. At first, back in Walworth, I thought perhaps Kikkoman is like a magnet that attracts these good people, but in short order I realized that it is much more than that. Kikkoman not only brings the best people in to join its family, it also brings out the best in the people it touches. How often do you find a company like that?

I had to catch myself, because now I was starting to sound like a company PR flack. This is not the story I signed up to research, I thought, but then again, no good story is ever what it appears to be when you start. Good stories develop and unfold in their own way and let you in. A perceptive writer just needs to be open to what is happening and realize that there is more to the story than you first imagined. Sometimes it is disappointing to learn that the great tale you planned to tell is not going to happen, but then you discover that some other, perhaps more interesting story is beginning to unfold. I was having that feeling again with Kikkoman.

More than an exploration of soy sauce, this was turning into a case study in international management, a study of an unusual, perhaps unique, approach to building a successful business across all cultural boundaries. It wasn't about the purity of the water or the fermentation time in the tanks or the quality control or any of the details that made Kikkoman products what they are. In the end, it was all about people. And more than that, it was about a corporate culture that valued people in an extraordinary way, that demanded its own staff live among the locals from Day 1 when they set up a facility overseas. It was about attracting good people right from the beginning and then creating an environment where they felt at home and never wanted to leave. An American company attempting the same thing, particularly a company in the financial business, would use money as the chain to bind its employees. Kikkoman used something else that was far more effective and long-lasting: respect.

12

Köln (Cathedrals & Teppanyaki)

*B*ack at KTE, Hasegawa had promised me a special dinner, and I was eager to discover what it was. I was actually beginning to think I would like to dive into some solid German cuisine, lots of wurst and potatoes, perhaps in some noisy beer hall, with singing and dancing in traditional costumes? Or was that only for the tourists? And what delights did Düsseldorf offer? As it turned out, I was not to find out.

"I'm sorry I have another appointment this evening," he said. "I've asked Mr. Sato to drive you to the restaurant tonight," Hasegawa explained, referring to his Deputy General Manager.

I assured him that he needn't go to the trouble of arranging a car — I could easily take a taxi from my hotel to anywhere in town.

"But it's not in Düsseldorf," he said with a smile. "You're going to Köln. To one of the best Japanese restaurants in all of Germany." And so it began.

Twenty minutes later, Sato took me to my hotel so I could change into clean clothes, then we drove to Köln. As it turns out, it wasn't much of a drive — less than 50 km in total. On the way, Sato educated me about my surroundings: first, that Düsseldorf and Köln are bitter rivals and have been for ages, fighting about everything from soccer to beer to street fairs. I told Sato that the only thing I knew about the city was that its name in English is Cologne and that name is far better known than the German original (just try looking up Köln in Wikipedia, and see where you end up).

He also informed me that it is the fourth-largest city in Germany behind better-known giants such as Berlin, Hamburg, and Munich, and it boasts a long, storied history. The original inhabitants were relocated by Julius Caesar, and in short order the Romans began to build a real city there, which subsequently became a Roman colony (*colonia*, the source for the city's Anglicized name). Though it was the seat of the Roman military in this area, ownership of the city repeatedly changed hands as the strength of the Roman Empire ebbed and subsided. The Rhine River flows through the middle of the city, and in 310 Emperor Constantine built a famous bridge across the river at Cologne. However, what the city is best known for is its awe-inspiring cathedral, known as the Kölnner Domand or Cologne Cathedral."

That rang a bell. I had heard of Cologne Cathedral, but had no idea why it was so famous.

"We have lots of time," my guide said, looking at his watch. "Let's go visit the church first, and then I'll take you to another real German landmark before we go to dinner." Was that a smile I detected after the last remark?

He parked the car in an open lot somewhere downtown and we walked through several back streets, many with cobblestones from centuries past. The city might have several new, modern-looking office towers, I thought, but it still had its share of old brick buildings and much older-looking streets.

We turned a corner and walked down another cobblestone street, and as we rounded another corner I noticed the cathedral. Well, not the whole thing, just the twin spires reaching up higher than any of the buildings in the vicinity. The two spires are over 500 feet (150 m) tall, which looks very, very tall for something built by hand centuries ago.

Cologne Cathedral is supposed to have the largest facade of any church in the world, and I can attest that it is an enormously impressive structure. Construction took over 600 years, and it is still breathtaking, even to someone like me who is seldom interested in old churches. Amazingly, it is the most-visited tourist site in all of Germany, drawing as many visitors annually as the world-famous Oktoberfest in Munich, and in 1996 was declared a World Heritage Site. Part of the Cathedral's attraction is its gorgeous architecture as well as the multiple levels of stained-glass windows, but its place in Christian tradition is also one of the big draws: this church holds the remains of the Three Wise Men of biblical lore, and the gilded Shrine of the Three Kings is a major draw.

We spent almost an hour wandering around inside and outside the cathedral. It is truly a massive structure, imposing, awe-inspiring, and uplifting all at the same time. But we had other things to attend to, and so we made our way back up the cobblestone streets the way we had come. We got back to the car and drove a short distance. Sato parked again and we walked through what looked like a medieval town square.

To one side was a stone building much like all the others, but with heavy wooden doors propped open, and stairs leading down into a murky interior. He led the way inside, and immediately I recognized the friendly atmosphere of a neighborhood pub — the smells, the noises, the ambience being roughly the same in any language. We walked through hallways that seemed like tunnels and found ourselves in a larger room connected to several others just like it. Big, heavy tables and chairs that would not tip over, and a waiter who looked like a professional wrestler, only larger.

Sato said a few words in German, and short glasses of beer began to arrive at our table. I was thirsty, and drained mine almost instantly. Sato did the same, and within a few seconds they had been replaced by full glasses.

"You don't re-order here," he explained, raising his glass in a toast. "They just keep bringing more until you ask them to stop."

"Seems like heaven for college students," I said, draining my second glass and mentally counting the seconds until the next one arrived.

"Yes, this place is very popular with the university crowd. And with workers of all kinds, men and women. It has good food — not a very extensive menu, as you might expect, but good food — and the beer is cheap and good. What more could you want?"

We drank and chatted for about thirty minutes. Finishing off a small sausage, I suddenly realized that I had completely forgotten about our purpose in coming to Köln: We were supposed to visit some famous Japanese restaurant. But Sato hadn't forgotten. He looked at his watch and made a "time to go" sign, and in just a few minutes we had found our way out of the cata-combs and were walking at a brisk pace back across the square. Several blocks away we came to an area that looked like old bank buildings — rough-hewn blocks of cut stone on the first two floors and smooth blocks of a different color above.

We turned down one of these streets and almost immedi-ately I saw a big, vertical sign on another building farther down the block. In large, black letters that were meant to look like cal-ligraphy from centuries earlier, I made out the name: DAITOKAI, which means a big city in Japanese.

Sato guided me toward the restaurant, which was not yet open, but he didn't hesitate to pull open the heavy front door and motioned me to step inside the semi-dark room.

"This is where we will be dining tonight. Unquestionably one of the best Japanese restaurants in all of Germany," he said with a dramatic flourish. Then he, too, stepped into the lobby and called out something in Japanese. In a moment there were footsteps, a couple of lights came on, and people began to emerge from within. My eyes were still getting accustomed to being indoors, and I noticed that the lights had little effect. The place was designed to look dark: all the furniture, the vertical posts, the room partitions, and the ceiling beams all seemed to be made of the same dark wood. The whole place had what I initially assumed was a European-style Middle Ages look. And yet, as my eyes adjusted and I was able to see the inte-rior better, I noticed that there were Japanese paintings on the walls and other decorations here and there that were unmis-takably Japanesque. This cognitive dissonance in the interior was a bit much for my beer-soaked brain, and I was just about to sit down at one of the big tables when a woman who I took to be our waitress came over. She was a bit tall for a Japanese, wearing a black business suit with a white shirt and blue tie, and had her hair pinned up. Her name tag said, "Takeda."

Sato introduced us immediately. "Mr. Russell, this is Takeda-san. She is the manager here. She can tell you all about the challenges of introducing Germans to Japanese food."

I mentally apologized to her for my sexist assumption that she was not the manager, and she, noticing my vaguely bibulous condition, motioned us to sit down at a nearby table. I was grateful that we could exchange cards after we sat, not a very Japanese way to do things, but considering the circumstances, perfect for today.

Digging in my jacket pocket for my little notebook, I began by complimenting her on the appearance of the restaurant, which was spotlessly clean and — now that I could see it more clearly — nicely decorated. The heavy furniture and dark ceiling looked more like a steak house than a sushi bar, and a quick look at some of the adjoining tables showed they were mostly covered with metal cooking surfaces. My fogged brain finally broke through the "Japanese food = fish" stereotype and began to function normally again.

"*Yakiniku*," I said at first, then corrected myself. *Yakiniku* was Korean-style grilling, very popular in Japan, but with small charcoal braziers at each table. Here more than 80 percent of each tabletop was a steel cooking surface, and one side of the table was curved so that a cook could stand on the inside edge and prepare food for half a dozen guests. That meant it was… "*Teppanyaki!*" I said almost in triumph, glad that the effects of the good German beer were fading and the memory was functioning again.

"*So desu,*" she replied calmly with a wan smile, as if to say, "What did the honorable customer expect? A fast-food burger joint?"

I asked about the restaurant and the Japanese food business in general, and Takeda-san quickly filled me in on the situation. Indeed, there was an ongoing "sushi boom" here in Germany, just as everywhere else in the world, but here it was a relatively small thing.

"I would say that roughly half of the German population doesn't like fish and doesn't eat much fish," she explained. "Young people are more adventurous, and they are the ones trying sushi, enjoying it, and sometimes exposing their parents to it."

But the bottom line, she said, is that someone hoping to open a successful restaurant chain in Germany would not choose sushi as their first option. Germans all like meat, she noted, so *teppanyaki* (which consists primarily of sliced meat with perhaps a side order of vegetables, all cooked on an open grill in front of the customer) was the perfect choice.

I noticed that the restaurant was quite spacious. A quick count of just the tables I could see looked like there was seating for eighty or ninety patrons.

"Over 110," she said. "It gets quite busy in here, especially on weekends. We are not a typical family restaurant, but we have no problem if customers want to bring their families, and that has helped to build our reputation. There are not many restaurants in Germany where people are comfortable taking their children, especially young children. We are happy to serve them as long as the families enjoy the food."

I asked about the history of the restaurant. It looked as if it had been operating for twenty years or more, which is a long time for a Japanese restaurant overseas. Again, I was totally off base. The Daitokai chain had been in business in Germany for over forty years. The first one was in Düsseldorf, and then it expanded. Today only two of the original six are still in operation — this one and the one in Berlin.

Takeda explained that, "Düsseldorf and Frankfurt both have significant populations of Japanese businessmen. So those branches were immediately popular with Japanese customers, who enjoyed eating there themselves and used them for *settai* [entertaining clients]. At first they did very well, but they didn't make enough effort to attract German customers. Here in Köln things were difficult. When we first opened, the place was empty. People were initially worried about the quality of our ingredients, so we had to show them how fresh everything is. That has always been our policy: we use only the very best of everything. Very gradually we began to attract a few people, and over time they told their friends, and slowly we built a business. It took several years. We know we can't make a business serving only Japanese patrons. We have always catered to German customers and German tastes, and so we are still here."

She seemed to have a very good grasp of the business. Since I assumed she was hardly born when the first Daitokai opened in Düsseldorf, I asked how long she had been working here.

"Twenty years here," she said, "And a year before that at the Frankfurt outlet."

I didn't want to keep Takeda from her duties for long, so I asked her if there were things about operating a restaurant in Germany that she enjoyed, maybe things that were different from what it would be like in Japan. It did not take her long to think of her answer.

"In Japan, there is a very clear distinction between the staff of a restaurant and the customers. We call the customers *o-kyakusama*, honored guests, and we treat them like special guests in our homes. We say *o-kyakusama wa kamisama desu* (the customer is God) But here in Germany things are more relaxed. In general, I would say that there is much less distance between the owner, chef, and customers. You feel closer to the customers, and it is a friendly relationship. I enjoy that aspect of this business."

"Many customers are not used to the Japanese way of doing things. So, for example, when we hand them plates it is always with two hands, because that is polite. They see that and later hand the plate back to us using two hands. It's a very small thing, but it makes me feel good because they are trying to be polite. It seems natural for German customers to show respect for another culture and try to emulate it.

Hearing footsteps approaching, Takeda stood up and introduced me to her head chef, Mr. Kobayashi. He stepped forward to shake my hand, dressed in a white chef's outfit, complete with white kerchief and a tall, pleated toque. Like Takeda, he had a name tag with his last name in block letters that customers could read, and the word KIKKOMAN printed above. He looked surprisingly young, with smooth features and a pleasant smile. It was hard to imagine him performing high-speed surgery on a piece of sirloin with razor-sharp knives that looked more like short swords. As soon as he sat down I inquired about his background. He began to speak in a lively, friendly tone:

"When I was a kid, my family used to take me to a *teppanyaki* restaurant in Japan. I loved it. I thought those chefs slicing up steak were really cool. Then, when I was around sixteen or so, my dad was sent to Germany by his company. I decided to go to Germany with him, and I lived with him for a while and studied German. When he went back to Japan, I stayed on, getting more comfortable with German culture. Then I went back to Japan and studied at a cooking school. I heard about an opening for someone to work at a Japanese restaurant in a hotel in Düsseldorf, so I signed up. That's where I got my first experience working the grill at a commercial *teppanyaki* restaurant. I stayed there for a few years, and eventually I heard about Daitokai. When the time came to move, I was ready. Now I have been here seven years, and I'm happy."

While we were talking, a number of regular customers had come in and other staff were showing them to tables. Gradually we could hear the buzz of conversation start to rise and I could see that Takeda-san was looking over her shoulder anxiously. I felt bad, because I had come here with a representative of Kikkoman, which to her meant The Boss Is In The House. Now she was treating me as Kikkoman's honored guest, which I wasn't, and both she and Kobayashi were neglecting their real guests. I looked at Sato and said that I was getting hungry. He smiled and asked if we could have a table somewhere in the back.

"I already have a table ready for you," said Takeda, rising to her feet, a look of relief on her face. She guided us deep into the restaurant, to a large table in the rear.

Teppanyaki is an interesting cuisine. It is all prepared on a flat griddle (*teppan*) that occupies most of each table top, usually surrounded by a wooden area for normal things like plates and glasses and utensils. Everything is cooked (that's the *yaki* part), not eaten raw, and it is prepared by a skilled chef, not cooked by the patrons themselves, like many of the *o-konomiyaki* restaurants I had been to in Japan. Even today many Americans expect teppanyaki to be more about entertainment than dining, because of the Benihana chain that turned an ordinary meal into a dazzling dinner show. Benihana opened in New York City in the 1960s and spread internationally in the decades that followed. They introduced customers to an unusual form of teppanyaki theater, with chefs who chatted or cracked jokes with the customers, all the while twirling their knives, slicing meat and vegetables as dramatically as possible, and flipping pieces of meat in the air while they cooked. It was entertaining, but not very Japanese. Daitokai, as I knew already from the Kikkoman logo on their name tags, was something more traditional. We sat down at our table, just two of the eight open seats, and Kobayashi himself came over to be our chef. I dimly noticed Takeda-san back towards the front of the restaurant, greeting customers with a little bow and personally showing them to tables.

Looking around, I saw that the place was filling up quickly. I noticed some people were wearing white T-shirts and blue jeans, while others were in business suits. There were couples obviously out on a date, families going out for an evening together, and several groups of friends with lots of beer on their tables. A pretty Japanese waitress in a gold-colored kimono was helping to tie a bib napkin around a gentleman's collar while his wife looked on in mock disapproval. Everyone seemed to be enjoying themselves.

As there was no one else at our table, and Kobayashi was still spreading cooking oil on the griddle, I decided to continue our previous chat. He said he liked being here, in Köln and in Germany. Did he really enjoy working here?

"Absolutely!" he replied immediately. "I love to cook. What I mean is, I have always liked cooking, but more than that, I like cooking *for* people. I like to hear people say 'That's good!' or 'Wow, that's delicious!' It makes me feel good. Most chefs are stuck in a kitchen and they only hear about customer reactions if something goes wrong. With teppanyaki you are right up front, close to the people you are cooking for; you can see their faces and hear their reactions immediately. I cook, they eat, I know instantly if they liked it or not. That's what cooking should be all about."

I got his point, and we talked a bit about the interaction with customers.

"Once some German customers told me that they loved the food I had made, and they asked me to pull up a chair and sit at their table as their guest. They even gave me some of their wine to drink. It was great to share that experience with my customers, but it doesn't happen often." Kobayashi thought a moment. "In Japan it doesn't happen at all."

While we were waiting for the meat dishes to come out, we were served a surprising assortment of sashimi and other small dishes. As a rule, I always tell people to avoid Japanese restaurants that try to do too many things. A good sushi shop is not the best place to go for tempura, nor will a soba shop have great *unagi* (eel), nor a tempura restaurant have good sushi or noodles. Thus, I was genuinely surprised when the sashimi and other delights that came to our table were excellent. The sashimi would easily have done credit to a fine sushi restaurant, and I noticed Sato had picked out a good brand of *Nihonshu* (sake), which is the only thing to drink with sliced fish. We toasted each other and consumed several small glasses of the sake, which was, just as I'd expected, delicious.

"Do Germans drink sake?" I asked our chef.

"Yes, in fact it is beginning to become popular," he replied, putting the first cuts of meat on the grill now. "Some of them drink it when they are entertaining clients. And more people are asking the chefs which sake to order, what goes well with this or that food, or whether wine might be better? What is interesting is that most Germans like *atsukan* (heated sake). They drink *atsukan* even in the summer. They sometimes drink German beer and *atsukan* together. It looks strange to us, but if they are happy, I am happy."

He was cooking now, his practiced hands slicing meat and vegetables, sequestering each bit to its own part of the grill, his left hand reaching out for the half-dome copper cover to put over the steak and let it cook evenly. In between, he was shaking on salt and oil, his hands always in motion but his face calm and relaxed, a man enjoying himself.

We settled down to eating rather than talking, and I was suddenly grateful that Kikkoman was taking me out tonight. I would not have discovered this restaurant on my own, and if I'd seen it listed in some guide book, I would have dismissed it as a weak attempt to offer something that looked Japanese but probably tasted terrible. Instead, I was having a fabulous meal and probably the best teppanyaki I'd ever tasted. The quality of the meat was excellent and Kobayashi's preparation was superb. I told him so and thanked him for his efforts. He bowed and thanked us for coming. All very standard Japanese manners. But I could tell that he really enjoyed talking about his work and why cooking mattered to him.

All too soon we were finishing our dinner. I thanked our chef once again and remarked that it had ended too quickly. He took my comment more seriously than I had intended it and replied, "Yes, here in Germany we prepare the food much faster than we would in Japan. Our customers are not expecting dinner to take hours, and they don't want formality; they want good food and big portions and they like to see it cooked in front of them. So we do cook faster than we would in Japan. I'm sure it is the same at teppanyaki places in America or elsewhere."

Click! Just as Kikkoman molds itself to local cultures, Japanese culture, too, is molded into different shapes by contact with other peoples. The world becomes more interesting the more of it you see. I thanked Takeda-san on my way out and asked Sato (who had consumed far less sake than I had) to drive me back to my hotel.

On the way back to Düsseldorf, we talked about my brief but interesting visit: the KTE offices, the warehouse next door, the cooking school, the cathedral in Köln, the beer hall, and the wonderful meal we'd just had at Daitokai. He said there were other Kikkoman Group offices in Europe, but I had already visited the big factory in the Netherlands and the sales office in Germany. I was beginning to feel I could keep going to more and more offices and meet more people, but I would just hear the same stories repeated again and again. I needed to make a bigger break, get out of the Old World paradigm of Europe and the U.S. and go see something different. I think I surprised Sato by telling him my next stop was Asia.

"We have various operations in Taiwan and China, Thailand and Australia, and all over Asia," he said. "But the original location is probably the best: Singapore. That's the one you should go to."

I told him I was way ahead of him on that. I had done my research. I knew that Singapore, not Folsom or Sappemeer, was Kikkoman's second overseas factory, and I had a feeling that if I understood what the company was doing in Singapore, I would have a pretty good handle on what it was doing throughout Asia. That night I went online and booked myself a ticket out of Düsseldorf, headed for the mysterious Orient. The excellent sake in my system helped me to fall asleep almost as fast as my head touched the pillow.

Singapore

My flight was long and tiring, but enjoyable all the same. It had been years since I had visited Asia, and I was frankly happy to be back. The final leg of my flight touched down smoothly at Changi Airport around 10 am, and I felt an old thrill as I walked through the terminal. Changi has won more awards than any airport on the planet — in 2015 alone it won twenty-eight different "Best Airport" awards and has collected all sorts of accolades from travel magazines and business flyers. I enjoyed my short stroll to collect my luggage, passed quickly through Immigration, and stepped outside to get a taxi. Of course, the difference in temperature between the inside and outside is at least 10 degrees Centigrade, and the humidity differential much higher still. Ten seconds outside and I was ready to turn around, go back inside, and camp in the airport. Fortunately, a taxi pulled up just in time, and the driver jumped out and stuffed my bags in the trunk. I gave him the name of one of the big hotels downtown, and we were off to the races. Literally. He had a very heavy foot. I tried to calm myself by looking at the blur of scenery go by.

In each trip I've made, Singapore looks different to me. That's remarkable considering what a small city it is, only about 720 sq. km (less than 280 sq. mi), making it a little smaller than the land area of New York City. In fact, you could easily fit three Singapores inside Tokyo — not Greater Tokyo, which is roughly the size of Jupiter, but the inner city.

Within this small space live 5.5 million people, earning on average over $80,000 each.[5] That's a lot of income. And they need it to pay their rent. Singapore is regularly ranked as either the most expensive city in the world to live in or a close runner-up. What is not so well known is that the city ranks at the top of the global livability index (for example, complete public safety is taken for granted, something unimaginable in Western cities). The World Bank ranked Singapore as the best place to do business for seven years in a row. In short, it's a great place to live and to run a business, but it's also cramped and expensive.

Singapore is famous for its shopping, its food, its cleanliness, and its location. But to me, the biggest attraction is the people. London and New York often claim to be cultural melting pots, but the reality is that they are more like cultural salads — lots of different peoples living close together with very distinct cultural identities, and not always "melting" into a unified whole. Singapore is different, as was confirmed for me by one of the city-state's most eloquent philosophers, my garrulous Indian cab driver.

"The rest of the world, they want what we have in Singapore," he said in response to a question about the weather. Clearly, this lecture had been well prepared in advance and was simply waiting for a captive audience. My New York reflexes suddenly switched to Alarm mode: *Warning: Possible crazy person! Potential for violence unknown. Proceed with caution!* I glanced at the door locks to see if they had sealed automatically when I got in, then looked at the highway speeding by. No chance to jump; my best bet was to listen to whatever crazy rant was about to come, then bolt as soon as the cab stopped for a red light. But there weren't any red lights, it didn't stop, and neither did he.

"What we have here in Singapore is very special, something you see nowhere else on Earth. Here you got Chinese and Indians and Malaysians and all sorts of people living side by side. No one fights, no one makes a riot. Do we know that the person sitting beside us on the train is Indian or the lady selling tea is Chinese? Of course we know! But we don't care. Race is unimportant; religion is unimportant, skin color is unimportant. Unless you are looking for a certain kind of restaurant, you never think about race. We all live here together, we work together, we respect together. Because we are all Singaporean. We are one country, one people. No hate crimes here, no persecution, no war. You take those Arabs and Jews, those people in Ireland and Eastern Europe and wherever, you bring them to Singapore. Let them see what life *should* be like. We have accomplished something nobody else has done! You bring the Pope here and show him. This is how people should live. He should tell people: Do it like they do in Singapore."

He went on at length for most of the drive to my hotel. By the time we arrived I had stopped thinking about my chances of surviving a leap from a car going 100 kph and begun to realize that this man might be a true taxi savant – a genius social critic stuck behind the wheel of an aging sedan, his lecture hall a soft bench seat in back where a maximum of three students could squeeze in. But his speech really struck me because it matched perfectly with what I had seen on my previous trips here. I hadn't grasped the point so clearly or articulated it intellectually, but here it was, summarized and delivered in the *lingua franca* of the modern world, broken English.

Indeed, Singapore was a mishmash of cultures, Chinese, Indian and Malay being the most prominent, and there were certainly cultural enclaves within the confines of this small island which, as my peripatetic professor said, are best known for their cuisine (Little India is justifiably famous). The populace consists of Buddhists, Muslims, Hindus, Taoists, Christians, and others, all living in close proximity without any obvious tensions. The first national language is English, not the native tongue of any of the ethnic components of the country, but essential if Singapore is to punch above its weight in the international arena. Malay, Mandarin Chinese, and Tamil are also official languages.

I was happy and a bit relieved to reach the Pan Pacific Hotel in one piece. I checked in smoothly and went straight to my room, which was just as I expected — clean, spacious, and comfortably cool. I kicked off my shoes (I'd remembered that it's foolish to wear tied shoes in Asia), and just sat on the bed. Very comfortable. A whole lot more comfortable than the airplane had been, and I wasn't even flying Steerage on this project. I swung my legs up onto the bed just to check out the feel. Pretty nice. After a long flight, much of the time spent working on my laptop instead of watching movies, eating MREs disguised as real food, and drinking lots of red wine to keep both the food and stress level down, it really felt good to stretch out for a few minutes...

You know the rest. The next thing I knew, a phone was buzzing much too loudly inside my head. I sat up. No, the phone was next to the bed, and the clock beside it insisted that I had been out for almost an hour. I picked up the phone and discovered it was one Priscilla Wang, an assistant to Mr. Otani, the general manager of Kikkoman Trading Asia, the sales and marketing side of the operation. Priscilla was asking if I was planning to take a taxi or walk to their building. I was still pretty fuzzy. Walk? Did people walk in the tropics? "Yes, if you'd like to. We're only about ten minutes from your hotel. Or you could easily catch a cab right there...?"

I told her I would walk — mostly because I needed to clear my head. I got up, jumped in the shower, changed my clothes, and headed out.

—§—

Priscilla had given me an address downtown and assured me it would be ten minutes or less on foot from my hotel. I enjoy walking, and I looked forward to seeing a little of Singapore on foot. Because it is usually quite warm in the daytime, and for much of the year, hot and humid in the afternoon, people prefer cabs or buses or the colorless but efficient metro system.

My walk took me on a roundabout route to a building called Parkview Square. Priscilla had said I would know it when I saw it. What did that mean? All the big office buildings downtown looked pretty much the same. But five minutes later, when I approached the building, I understood her little joke. Yes, it was a tall, beige-colored office structure with some nice landscaping, but there the similarity to any normal office building stopped. It was a massive, over-the-top, Art Deco-on-acid architectural burlesque. There was no section of the building that was not layered with extra folds of stone, no surface left plain when it might be ornamented with a projection of some kind or a rectilinear mosaic of metal. It was "Modern Times" on steroids.

I entered through the elaborate main entrance... and stopped in my tracks. If the outside was ornate, the interior was mind-blowing. The lobby was dominated by a two-story cafe/restaurant done in the same over-the-top Art Deco style, even including the carpets. The bar was one of the most ornate I had ever seen, and behind it towered a massive, three-level pipe organ-like wine cabinet of what looked like burnished gold. The wine was stacked so far above ground that only an Art Deco giant could reach the bottles. And they had a few of those in the room as well, both human-sized mortals in togas and giants in classic Deco-style faux-Greek-god nude poses. On the walls above the bar, large Deco-Greek figures in bas-relief seemed to be climbing among the tops of featureless skyscrapers. I had never seen anything like it and was sure I never would again.

Trying to shake off the overwhelming sense that I had just stepped into some strange movie set, I made my way through the lobby to the elevators. Of course, the halls and even the directory listing the building's tenants were done in a 1930s style. The tenants, however, were very modern, and on the sixteenth floor, I spied Kikkoman Trading Asia Pte Ltd.

Fortunately, the elevators were not of the same vintage as the artwork, and just a moment later I was being greeted by a short, bubbly Chinese woman who introduced herself as Priscilla Wang, the person I had chatted with on the phone earlier. She gave me her card, which informed me that she was the head of sales for Kikkoman Trading Asia Pte Ltd. I mentioned what a remarkable building this was, and we started chatting about the design while we waited for her boss, Mr. Otani. She said he was on an international phone call but would be with us in just a moment.

I took the opportunity to ask Priscilla about her own situation. She told me she only joined Kikkoman a few years ago.

"I came from a completely different industry," she said. "It was an okay job, but I didn't feel any passion for it. I love to cook and I love food, so this job was perfect for me. I wish I had come here sooner."

I asked her to elaborate. What was so good? What made her happy here?

"I have a real passion for food, and I love to share my interest with other people. I love soy sauce and I enjoy talking about it to my friends. I tell everyone in Singapore that Kikkoman is healthy, with no preservatives, no additives. I'm so proud to tell my friends about it."

So she uses *shoyu* at home?

"Of course!" she said with a big smile. And then, looking around to make sure we were not being overheard, "But you know, Chinese cooking is very salty. I usually add a pinch of salt to the Kikkoman sauce. The local brands here are very salty, and that's what we're used to. Younger people are more health conscious, so they may use less salt than older people, but still, many people want a more salty taste."

We talked about the three big ethnic groups in Singapore and the corresponding food cultures. She told me that both Chinese and Malay cooking used soy sauce, and the Indians less so. But ethnic Chinese make up more than half the population. She started talking about Malay cooking and the similarities with Chinese-style cooking, but halfway through my lesson on multicultural cuisine, a solidly built man in his fifties appeared. He had a round face and a big smile and was dressed in what I was already starting to think of as "Singapore formal," a comfortable-looking, cool green suit with an open-collar white-on-white striped shirt. For some reason, he made me think of Paul Sorvino, the urbane Mafia boss in *Goodfellas,* and I tried to imagine him with a cigar in one hand.

Of course, as soon as he began to talk, the Hollywood images evaporated, and he invited me into his office. The first thing I noticed was the view of downtown Singapore, which even from the sixteenth floor, was gorgeous. From this vantage point there was more green visible among the gleaming hotels and high-rise office buildings. Then we settled down to business.

Takeru Otani's card said that he was the General Manager of Kikkoman Trading Asia, so he surprised me when he started off by talking about the U.S.

"I lived in America for eight years before coming here," he said. "One thing I noticed in the U.S. is that Americans now accept soy sauce as part of everyday cooking. They use it on anything — meat, fish, stews, pasta sauces, whatever. In that sense, the North American market has been Kikkoman's greatest success, because we have finally convinced people that soy sauce is a universal seasoning.

"But here in Southeast Asia, people see *shoyu* as something you use on Japanese food. The problem is that they don't go out to Japanese restaurants often, and they never make Japanese food at home, which severely limits our sales. Therefore, our main challenge is to teach people to be a little more Western — that is, to add Kikkoman to all sorts of recipes they are already familiar with.

"Also, when we say *shoyu*, we mean the basic style of Kikkoman *shoyu*, or at least the standard taste of naturally brewed *shoyu* in Japan. But every country in Asia has a different culture, and some have multiple cultures within a single nation. And every one of them has its own food culture. In general, Southeast Asian and Chinese people like their soy sauce sweet. For example, Chinese people always prefer a sweeter style than Japanese. Indonesians like it sweeter still, and Malaysians like it even sweeter than that. Did you know that Indonesians put chili sauce on sushi? I'm not saying that's bad, just that it's unusual, it's different. Every country is different and every country has its own food culture. From Kikkoman's perspective, that's wonderful, and we deeply respect that, but from a food business perspective, it presents a huge challenge for product development and marketing.

"In Singapore, fish-based dishes are standard for most meals. A while ago we went to the biggest supermarket in Singapore to do a sales promotion, and we let people taste different Kikkoman products on various dishes. So we had chicken teriyaki, and *chahan* fried rice, *yakisoba* fried noodles, and salmon teriyaki, and a couple of other dishes. It wasn't just a sales promotion for us, but also market research. I watched their faces while they were trying different food combinations and tried to judge their responses to each dish. What do you think they liked most?"

I looked up from my notes and shook my head. I really had no idea.

"Only one thing really got them excited, and that was the salmon. They loved it! The idea of teriyaki-style salmon hasn't caught on in Singapore yet, but trust me, it will. Fish-based dishes will always outsell all others, and everyone here loves salmon."

"Wait," I asked incredulously, my mind filled with images of fish swimming vigorously up ice-cold Canadian streams. "Is any salmon caught here in Singapore?"

"No, not at all. It's all imported, but people like it anyway. In every big supermarket here there is a sushi corner now, and a lot of the sushi is salmon. The bottom line is that you have to go out and meet customers face to face to get educated."

I looked up again, quizzically.

"I mean, how do we learn? We learn when our customers teach us what they like. Retail customers, distributors, restaurants in a dozen different markets — they all tell us what kind of tastes they like, and we have to respond.

"Our biggest issue here, as you will hear again and again, is price. Kikkoman is more expensive than Chinese-type *shoyu*. In Singapore it's only a little more expensive, but if you use a lot of *shoyu* (and restaurants and big families certainly do), the price difference can become significant. In Singapore, people already have a higher standard of living, and it is continuing to rise. Young people are willing to spend a little more for a high-quality product, like a gourmet-style *shoyu*. But in places like

Thailand and the Philippines, our soy sauce can be as much as three times the price of the chemical types, and consumers don't have the income flexibility to buy Kikkoman. What can we do?

"To succeed in those markets, we must offer something that is affordable to our customers. You have been to our factories, you know that we can't take shortcuts with the process, which means we can't cut prices any more than we already have. Our solution is to package the product in smaller containers. In a nutshell, our strategy in Southeast Asia is "smaller and sweeter," because that is the combination that is most attractive to consumers in those markets. They teach us, we respond."

I asked Mr. Otani about marketing. Where was his focus, geographically speaking?

"Well, India is a huge potential market, but Indians are not big meat-eaters, which holds down our sales growth. India will take some time. Indonesia, however, is very interesting. Indonesian people are open to new ideas and influences, and there are many foreign restaurants. In fact, there are lots of Japanese restaurants in Djakarta, and it's a very big city. As you know, the population of Indonesia is very large, so that could be a big growth market for us in time. And Indonesians eat beef, which will open up a range of products for our marketing efforts.

"As I noted before, every country is different, every culture is different, and every market is different. We have to constantly learn from our customers and look for new ways to appeal to them. That is the best route to long-term success."

I enjoyed talking to Mr. Otani, and he had the kind of practical, down-to-earth approach that I was coming to expect from this company. But I also wanted to talk to people who did not work directly for Kikkoman. I needed to get more of an outside perspective on the company. I mentioned this to Otani, and he immediately brightened.

"Yes, I almost forgot! I am about to take you to meet Manjo Trading, one of our top distributors. The head of the company not only knows all about Kikkoman, he's also a very typical local distributor. You'll like him."

I said the schedule sounded fine. We got up and made our way through the Art Deco museum to the street, and Otani hailed a cab.

—§—

We rode for about half an hour, eventually reaching a kind of industrial park with multi-story concrete buildings that looked like airport parking garages. We turned into the entranceway of one of them and climbed up four or five floors, going round and round in circles as if it were a parking garage. I noted lots of trucks on each floor, no two with the same company's markings. At some point we stopped climbing and Otani directed the driver through the dim, grey concrete interior until he finally found what he was looking for and abruptly asked for us to be let off. The inside of the building looked like it was full of giant storage units, and I saw that many of their clients used this as warehouse space.

We got out, and I looked around to see where we had stopped. Looking towards the outer side of the building, I saw a small warehouse area and a small office within. The outer wall was decorated with a full-color photo poster that had to be four meters high. A full lineup of Kikkoman bottles was parading around against a bright orange background. There were flavors I had never seen before alongside old familiar labels. Things like Roasted Garlic and Honey & Soy marinade were marching alongside Tempura Noodle Sauce, Spicy Teriyaki Sauce, Less Salt Soy Sauce, Teriyaki Marinade, and dominating the photo, two large bottles with elongated necks that looked nothing like the traditional Kikkoman bottles I knew. The Chinese label said these contained "Manji Shoyu," which I remembered was a trade name Kikkoman used for Chinese customers. At the bottom of the poster were two big red cartons of Kikkoman *shoyu*, each marked "Pro Pack" containing eighteen liters.

Otani led me into the small, open-front warehouse. Walking inside, past rows of neatly stacked sacks of rice, we reached the tiny office, just a couple of very small metal desks and an aging metal fan wheezing as it tried in vain to keep the place even slightly cool. It was here that we met Mr. Clement Tang (at least that was the English name on his business card). He was short and very thin, with a weathered face and a bush of white hair that said he might be sixty or seventy, but wasn't anywhere near retiring. He wore a blue check shirt, open at the collar, black pants and comfortable shoes. At first glance, he struck me as a man devoted to his work. We shook hands. Otani explained my purpose in being here. Tang stared at my card all the while, listening and nodding intently. I asked him the usual first question.

"I have been with Kikkoman for thirty-three years as a distributor," he said in heavily accented English. "My old boss retired and I went independent. Kikkoman and I both started same time in Singapore. First years were tough. I had one or two staff, which is not enough. I had to load trucks and make deliveries myself. It's hard to manage a company when you are driving truck. Kids today can't imagine what life was like for us thirty, forty years ago."

I looked around. There were cases of shoyu in all different sizes, piled on pallets going up well over my head. There were cases of other Kikkoman brand products, such as Teriyaki Marinade, also stacked up, and all sorts of other foodstuffs and cases of green tea piled high. On the floor in the center of the room were pallets of 50 lb. (22 kg) sacks of rice, with brand names such as Tamanishiki Super Premium (JFC's most famous brand, in gold-yellow sacks) and Kokuho in white sacks, and Botan in white and blue with a red peony (*botan*) in the center. Each of these pallets had seven layers of five bags each, or just under a ton of rice per pallet, and I saw five stacks that were three-pallets high along the far wall. Mr. Tang had enough food here to feed an army. Or a small city-state with hundreds of Chinese and Japanese and other Asian-style restaurants.

He then began to explain his operation to me in slow, clear, spicy English. "Only five people here, move millions of dollars of product every year. Everyone has key to our warehouse. In my business, no bosses, no workers; we are all same."

That was as clear as it could be, no problem with communication. I complimented Mr. Tang on running such a thriving business so efficiently.

"I want my son to take over healthy business and grow it for next fifty years!" he said proudly. Looking at the huge amount of food crammed into this small space, and guessing that his average stock turnover was measured in days not weeks, I figured his son's biggest worry would be getting a good tax accountant.

I asked Tang about the product breakdown. Rice seemed to take up most of the physical volume of the space. He said no, *shoyu* was his main product, accounting for about 70 percent of business, followed by rice, which was about 20 percent, and all the other products together made up about 10 percent of sales.

"Is *shoyu* — Kikkoman *shoyu*, the Japanese kind, the expensive kind — really selling that well in Singapore, where there are so many cheaper Chinese options?"

Tang said the demand for Japanese *shoyu* just keeps going up. He always keeps plenty of stock on hand, because there is no way to know how restaurant demand will fluctuate from one week to the next. "We support our customers," he said proudly. "If they need something on short notice, we bring it! We always have driver on standby every day."

Since he was not an employee of Kikkoman but had been working in one way or another with the Group for decades, I waited until Otani stepped outside to make a phone call, then asked Mr. Tang about his relationship with the giant Japanese company.

"Kikkoman not like other companies," he said clearly. "Kikkoman taught me about value of trust, trust-based partnership with customers. Now I have same relationship with my customers." What a surprise, I thought, not at all surprised.

Tang also told me that Kikkoman's advertising and the cooking classes it sponsors are having an impact on younger people. He said the biggest changes he sees are in customer attitudes. In the 1970s and '80s, people thought of Japanese food as only raw fish, and everyone thought it was very expensive. No one had money to spend on Japanese food. Tang says even he never went to Japanese restaurants back then because it seemed like a waste of money. Now, kids think Japanese food is just another kind of food. They like it, and no one worries about the price.

"Younger customers want healthy foods," Tang said. "Old people always say Kikkoman products too expensive. I think if you wait one more generation, you will see Kikkoman take off. Big time."

I would have been happy to chat with him longer, but Otani returned and pointed at his watch. I thanked Mr. Tang sincerely, shook hands with him again, and assured him that we would find a place for him in the book I was writing. Much to my surprise, a cab was already waiting for us a dozen meters away. I guessed that Otani had used his phone to arrange for our transportation. We jumped in, and I saw Mr. Tang still standing in front of the giant Kikkoman poster at the front of his mini-warehouse, waving goodbye as we pulled away.

"Your hotel is closer than my office," he said. "I will drop you there and Mr. Hibino will come to meet you." From my notes, I already knew he was referring to the general manager of Kikkoman's local production facility, and the idea of getting out of the warm, muggy air and back to my hotel room for a short break was quite attractive. During the ride, we chatted more about Kikkoman's sales strategy in Southeast Asia, about the differences between his sales side of the business and Mr. Hibino's manufacturing responsibilities, and about the pleasures of living in Singapore.

14

From Factory to Beer Garden

An hour after leaving Mr. Tang, I was completely refreshed, sitting in a coffee shop in the Pan Pacific lobby, enjoying a second cup of good coffee and reading the *Straits Times* when my cell phone rang. It was Hibino-san, the head of the local Kikkoman factory, saying he would come to pick me up. I cheerfully said I could leave any time, how soon would he arrive? He paused, a bit embarrassed, then said he was already in the lobby and would wait for me to come down.

I finished my coffee, folded my paper, and walked across the lobby. I had no trouble locating the only Japanese, who was sitting in a comfortable chair, looking around the room. He jumped to his feet when he saw me approaching. Only a little shorter than me, I guessed he looked about forty, which of course meant he was at least fifty, dressed in a blue-and-white striped short-sleeve shirt, no jacket, and dark khaki slacks. A man well adapted to life in the tropics, I thought, but the button-down shirt gave something away.

"You must be the General Manager," I said, all my deductive powers in high gear.

Smiling, he shook my hand and reached in his shirt pocket for the card he had already prepared. Of course, I hadn't brought my *meishi* case with me (a failing I would have to rectify if I were hoping to go to Japan), but I took his card with two hands and stared at it for the appropriate amount of time. It read:

Hisanobu Hibino, General Manager, Kikkoman (S) Pte Ltd

"I have my car," he said, pointing out the front door to a Toyota Camry parked nearby. We got in and he gently pulled out onto a main road in front of the hotel, then sped quickly out of the downtown area.

"Shall we go straight to the plant?" he asked, and I assured him I was looking forward to seeing his plant. Of course, I had already seen a few Kikkoman factories, but now I was in Asia for the first time and I wanted to see what, if anything, might be different.

In a few moments we were speeding along a highway. He told me that automobile taxes in Singapore are ferociously high. This seemed strange to me, as the roads were full of cars and the roads I had seen so far were all new, clean, and well maintained. Clearly, Singapore was a good place to drive, just not a good place to own a car. The government must be worried about the rapid increase in vehicles, especially in the central business district. Singapore obviously did not want an air pollution problem like Beijing or Shanghai, so there was a strong disincentive tax to keep people from buying cars.

"It isn't working," Hibino noted, pointing out the number of Mercedes, BMWs and even Lambourghinis along the road. "You cannot imagine how expensive those are here," he said. "Yet still, people keep on buying them."

We drove for half an hour or so on a high-speed road going north towards the edge of the main island of Singapore, just across a narrow waterway from Malaysia. On the way, Hibino and I talked. I asked about his personal background.

"I came here about four years ago," he said. "I started out in the company's Hokkaido factory, then worked in Brazil, Walworth, Noda, and other places in Japan. Then I came here as the General Manager."

Did he like living here?

"Yes. Singapore is an easy place to live. Sure, it's expensive if you want to live like a Japanese manager would back home, but it's fine once you adapt to the local lifestyle."

What about his products? Is Kikkoman well known in Singapore?

"Of course!" He sounded surprised, then reflected a moment. "Well, not everyone knows Kikkoman, but a large part of the population here is ethnically Chinese, and they all know the Kikkoman brand. But–" he paused and smiled. "What brand do they *buy*? That's the problem. All those Chinese mothers grew up using the soy sauce that their mothers used."

I knew that the predecessors of *shoyu* originated in China, but I knew nothing about the modern Chinese-style product.

"There are basically two types," Hibino explained, still looking straight ahead as he drove. "There is a dark type, which by Japanese standards tastes very salty, much more so than any Kikkoman product; and then there is the light type, which by Japanese standards is too thin and lacks flavor. In other words, once you get to appreciate Japanese *shoyu*, you won't be happy with either of the basic Chinese versions."

So, other than tradition, what accounts for the continuing popularity of the Chinese sauces?

"The main thing is the price. It's cheaper. Kikkoman is always more expensive, and I'm sure you know why. You have seen our production process. It's the same in Noda or Singapore or Wisconsin. We don't cut corners, and now that our plants are all automated, there isn't much room to squeeze more efficiency out of the system. The costs are largely fixed, which means our sales people have very little room to cut prices. The result in Singapore is that our products look expensive.

"On the other hand, the locals know that Kikkoman products are extremely high-quality, and in Singapore everything that's really good costs a lot. The older people don't want to change their habits, but I think more young Chinese wives are trying our products and deciding that the small increase in cost is well worth it in terms of superior flavor. Also, there is a sushi boom here, and that is helping our marketing tremendously. People go out to restaurants, they eat sushi and dip it in Japanese soy sauce — almost without exception Kikkoman — and they like the taste. Chinese recognize immediately that it doesn't taste like the soy sauce they're used to. It's deeper and richer but not so salty."

We had turned off the main road now and were in a large industrial park, though nothing like the green, rural area in Sappemeer. There were dozens of warehouses and office/warehouse combinations lined up on both sides of the road, mostly low, white concrete buildings. Hibino swung into a driveway next to a low, red brick wall with the letters "Kikkoman (S) Pte. Ltd.," and behind it a small complex of white, two-story buildings. I noticed that the Kikkoman plant stood out noticeably on this block for looking so clean and presentable. I was not surprised.

I had to remind myself that this was Singapore — an energetic nation crammed into a large city, as if all of Japan wanted to do business inside downtown Tokyo. That meant that land was at a premium, and it also meant that the Kikkoman plant here would look different from any that I had seen before. And yet, much to my surprise, the similarities were more apparent than the differences. While some of the other facilities on this street were clearly showing their age, the Kikkoman facility was well maintained, spotlessly clean, and shining bright white in the Singapore sun. You could have dropped it in Folsom or Walworth or Sappemeer and it would not have looked out of place. At a quick glance, the whole complex was a bit smaller than those others, but not really small, just more compact. Everything seemed designed to economize on space, outdoors as well as indoors.

As soon as we stepped inside the office building I could smell that familiar smell, and I knew I was in a *shoyu* factory. I asked Hibino if he would postpone the welcoming speeches and coffee and get right down to the grand tour. He seemed happy to oblige. In my brief experience, I had noticed that most Kikkoman general managers and all production managers are more comfortable walking the plant floor than sitting behind a desk. Hibino was no exception. He seemed to become at the same time more relaxed, more animated, and more comfortable as we walked through the plant.

Of course, everything was exactly as I'd expected it to be. The same long, empty corridors, same big *koji* bin, same tall *moromi* tanks, same pressing and filtering area, the same basic bottling operation. While this plant seemed a little more compact, it was unquestionably the same basic process, and I knew it was all managed and quality-controlled in exactly the same way as other plants around the world. Product variation and quality fluctuations were not a prominent feature of Kikkoman's brewing style. I also remembered Nicolaas back in Holland telling me that after his training in Japan he was sent here to Singapore for several weeks of follow-up study, so Kikkoman must see this plant as a good place to learn about its production process.

As we walked through the storage and loading areas, dodging fork-lifts carrying pallets of heavy-looking cartons, I asked my guide about the company's history in Singapore. Hibino explained that this was Kikkoman's second overseas plant, set up in 1983, only a decade after Walworth. I had learned that fact before but forgotten it. Now it seemed surprising. I said it was interesting that the company wanted to establish a plant in Asia before building a second plant in the U.S. or opening one in Europe.

"Yes, it is indicative of Kikkoman's global strategy, I think," Hibino said. "This facility opened its doors fifteen years before Folsom and Sappemeer. And it was export-oriented right from the beginning. That is probably the main reason for building in Singapore — from here you have a solid base in a politically stable, business-friendly nation that thrives on international commerce. Singapore is strategically important for us. This factory supplies much of the Asian and Oceanic markets, which means we don't need to build a factory in every country.

The taxes on our business are low and international shipping is very easy. We currently export to more than forty countries, including places like Brazil, South Africa, the Mideast, and North America."

That also surprised me. With two plants now functioning in North America, was there still room to import more product?

He pointed to a pile of cartons with green labels marked "Gluten-free Soy Sauce" in English. "Guess where that is going?" he asked rhetorically. "North America."

After a short pause he continued. "It takes us a long time to develop a new product, and then prepare the factory to produce that new product, and then we must wait at least six months for the first batch to be ready, bottle it, and ship it," he explained, moving through the stacks of boxes as he did so. "For obvious reasons, we cannot respond to every nutritional trend. At first we did not think the gluten-free movement would last, but it gradually became clear that this was important and we needed to respond to it appropriately. So we created a gluten-free *shoyu* by substituting rice for wheat in our process. This is not as simple as it sounds and it definitely creates new challenges in our procurement-storage-production flow, but it is important to make products that our markets demand, so we do it. We make lots of gluten-free soy sauce and ship it to the U.S, to supplement the production there."

He added that this one factory ships 260 different products. I knew that Kikkoman doesn't make as many as that, and I called him out on it.

"I mean that we make products under hundreds of different labels to export all over the world. We also supply all sorts of products to many famous food companies and other businesses. I can't tell you the names, of course, but..." He glanced upwards as we walked, and I saw row after row of boxes marked with some of the most famous names in the global food business. Some were the same as I'd heard about in the U.S. and Europe, but some were new to me.

We had wandered through the plant, up and down stairs, through the shipping area and out to the loading docks, and now found ourselves back outside again. He pointed to the office, and we headed back there. We sat down in a meeting room and *bento* lunch boxes soon appeared on the table. We talked while we ate. I explained the nature of my book project in detail and, apologizing for my rudeness, said I wanted to talk to some of his employees as well as suppliers and other people not on the payroll. He said he perfectly understood my point and not to worry about it. How soon did I want to get started?

I said, "Right now!" Without replying, he picked up the phone and asked to speak to a Mr. Chu, who I guessed was still on his lunch break.

A few moments later a serious-looking middle-aged Chinese in a white coat came into the room and I asked him to sit down. Hibino looked at me, I nodded toward the door, and he half bowed and stepped out to get a cup of coffee.

The gentleman across the table from me introduced himself as Chu Chien-Ming and said he was a technician. Despite a heavy accent, his English was very understandable.

"I maintain the machinery here." he said. "I studied at ITE [the Institute of Technical Education, one of Singapore's many schools of higher learning]. I know technology."

I asked how he came to Kikkoman

"After university I was looking for a good-paying job at a solid, stable company. I think the food business is very stable, not like semiconductors or other industries we see. I decided I wanted to work for Kikkoman here in Singapore, and they accepted me in 1991. My parents supported my decision. They knew this was a good option for me."

What about the company? Why does he think it is a good company?

"I wanted a life that's stable and also gives me some flexibility. Kikkoman is good for me. Here I could work in the day and study at night... And Kikkoman has lots of growth potential. You see, we always have roughly the same number of workers, but productivity always goes up... Also, there is room for advancement here. In time, I think I will get promoted. I want to work here until I retire."

I asked if his family uses *shoyu* at home.

"Yes. We make fried rice with shoyu and put teriyaki sauce on chicken dishes. My wife used to use Chinese-style *shoyu*, but now only Kikkoman. And she tells all her friends how good it is. People learn about *shoyu* from word of mouth, not from advertising. My family is proud that I work here and proud of Kikkoman soy sauce."

Mr. Chu had been looking at his watch the entire time, so I decided to cut our interview short, thanked him, and let him get back to what I guessed was a half-eaten box lunch that Hibino's call had pulled him away from. I had a feeling that if I could meet all the employees, I would probably hear the same kind of story several times over. Just an Asian version of tales

I had heard in Wisconsin and California and the Netherlands. I wanted something different.

I went back to Hibino's office. He was just hanging up the phone.

"I have another interesting gentleman for you to meet," he announced, and led me to the meeting room. A thin man with Chinese features, wearing a jacket and printed shirt but no tie, Singapore style, stood up as we entered. He introduced himself simply as Mr. Chua. We exchanged cards, and we all sat down. His card said his name was Alvin Chua and he was the Managing Director of SuperPet Plastic Pte Ltd.

I began by asking him how long he had known Kikkoman.

"I have been supplying Kikkoman for twenty-seven years," he said proudly in strongly Chinese-inflected English.

"With what?" I asked.

"With bottles!" He looked surprised. "I make the bottles for Kikkoman products. So many different bottles. I make over twenty different plastic bottles for Kikkoman: 1 liter, 1.6 liter, 2 liter, 1 gallon, many more.

"My company has worked with Kikkoman for years to develop new containers. For example, Japanese used to use a lot of 1.6 liter glass bottles. The old general manager asked me if we could make a PT bottle the same size. It took time, but we developed a 1.6 liter bottle that met all Kikkoman's requirements, and we replaced the old glass bottles. Now they use only this plastic bottle. We also developed a 3 liter plastic bottle. Very good."

Hibino leaned in to explain to me, "The 1.6 liter plastic bottle was a big advance for us in packaging, and it's still very popular. We ship a lot of them to Australia and China, and the 3 liter bottle also goes to Australia, mostly for big warehouse stores like Costco."

Mr. Chua was definitely not finished. "Quality is very important for Kikkoman," he said, then began educating me. "In the early 1980s, around the time Kikkoman set up this factory, there were over fifteen soy sauce makers here in Singapore. Many failed. Of the ones that are left, many have problems with quality and maybe all of them have problems with consistency. We have no such problems." He made the last statement with great pride and looked at Hibino, who smiled and nodded agreement.

I asked him to give me a little background. How did he meet Kikkoman? How did he start working for them?

"Long ago, before Kikkoman even came to Singapore, the government here sponsored me to go study in Japan. I went to Nagano Prefecture to study at a famous machinery company. I studied injection molding machinery. I learned a lot. I saw how Japanese go crazy if anything is not right, if there is one tiny screw missing on one unimportant part of one big machine. They do not accept 'almost perfect.' At first I thought this was insane, but now I understand. Now I trust Japanese machinery over all others. I would guess maybe 90 percent of the equipment in our factory is Japanese.

"When Kikkoman first came to Singapore, they spent a few months checking us out. They reviewed every step in our production process and looked at every corner of our factory. In 1987, the General Manager himself came to inspect our plant. He stayed until 10:00 that night, no dinner, just examined our work. He was very, very tough. He said he wanted a 'perfect' bottle, nothing less. We stayed up late that night to make exactly the kind of bottle he wanted.

"We finally became an official supplier to Kikkoman, and then we started to grow. We invested a lot of money in mold-making equipment to satisfy Kikkoman's needs. Now we are very proud of our equipment, and we use it for many other clients. What Kikkoman cares about is quality and hygiene. Everything must be perfect and germ-free. It was not easy, but we did everything they asked. Now I have over thirty customers, but they are No. 1."

"Is Kikkoman a good customer to work with?" I asked, ignoring the fact that Hibino-san was sitting right next to me.

"Very good customer," Mr. Chua replied without thinking. "They want a long-term relationship. They have a win-win approach. That is very rare."

Somehow we got to talking about Chinese people in Singapore. He said his wife still uses Chinese-style soy sauce, although he said he likes to eat Japanese food with Kikkoman sauce. He added, "Many mainland [China] people come here, buy Kikkoman in Singapore and take it home because they like the taste and because it makes a good gift." We started talking about China, and suddenly he said, "I spend one-third of my time in China."

"Why?" I wondered. "To see relatives?"

"No, my factories. I supply the Kikkoman plant in China."

"From here in Singapore?"

"No, no. I have a plant in China that supplies Kikkoman over there. I am doing good business in China. I have three joint ventures over there now, and one of them is growing very fast. My China plants have eighty times the capacity of my Singapore plant."

He continued: "Doing business in China is very difficult. But Kikkoman is the secret to my success."

That caught me off guard. Why did he think so?

He became increasingly animated: "Kikkoman taught me importance of crazy quality control. Now I teach Chinese. They are like me: they don't understand at first, then they begin to understand, then they see this is best way. Once you demand total quality, you have no rivals. Kikkoman very demanding, but their demands helped me succeed in China!"

We chatted some more, then Mr. Chua stood up, shook my hand, and apologized to Hibino for having to leave so soon, but I assured him his stories were very interesting and Hibino and I both thanked him for coming in.

Sitting down again, I noticed that this was turning into a long day.

"I have another interview for you, just a short one with a member of the government," Hibino said jovially. "After that we will go for dinner, and then there is someone special I want you to meet. By the way, there is an Indian restaurant on Orchard Road that has what they call a Kikkoman special dish. I hope you don't mind having Indian food this evening...?"

I told him that sounded good to me. Singapore is a pretty good place to eat Indian food. However, Hibino hadn't mentioned the Little India neighborhood, but instead, Orchard Road, the single most famous shopping street in Singapore, a glittering avenue lined with famous-name fashion stores. I wondered what he had in mind.

This time we did not get back into Hibino's Camry, but instead took a taxi. We headed downtown, towards the very heart of old Singapore, and ended up on North Bridge Road, a major business street downtown. The cab pulled up in front of the Raffles City Tower, a skyscraper full of offices overlooking the iconic hotel of the same name.

We entered the lobby and Hibino gave both our names to the Security desk. The receptionist called upstairs, confirmed our appointment with something called the Economic Development Board, and directed us to an elevator. Upstairs, the EDB waiting room was impressive without being intimidating. Comfortable chairs, lots of magazines, coffee and soft drinks, and a panoramic view of downtown Singapore. I stood almost mesmerized at the windows, looking out over the city. There were dozens of tall office buildings, but they were not clustered together, Manhattan style. Instead, they seemed to be spread over many blocks, with lots of older, lower buildings in between, and even vest pocket parks and lots of trees on the streets. I couldn't help but think, "Very livable town. I can see why people like it here."

Almost as soon as we arrived, we were greeted by a charming young woman who introduced herself in perfect English as Joyce. Her card said she was the "Senior Officer, Marketing and Communications." I assumed she was our contact and started right in talking about Kikkoman. After a short time, she looked embarrassed and said to me, "I'm sorry, I don't know the answers to all those questions. I think you'd better take that up with Mr. Chan. His English is quite good."

What? The Senior Officer of Communications was not our contact? And if her faultless English was nothing to brag about but his was "quite good," what kind of person were we going to meet? I looked at Hibino, who seemed nonplussed by the whole thing. I continued to look out the window until a few minutes later Joyce came to call us. "Mr. Chan is ready to see you now."

We walked through a connecting door, down a hall, and into a small, nicely decorated meeting room. Like everything else I had seen on this floor, all the furniture looked as if it had been purchased yesterday, the pictures on the wall were all very tasteful, the carpet was clean, and the staff were a little scary — smart, personable, well bred. Where were the government functionaries, the mindless bureaucrats constantly quoting rules and regulations?

The gentleman who greeted us was medium height, slightly built, with a dark suit and tie (the first one of those I'd seen in Singapore), hair neatly combed, and thin, wire-framed glasses. He was probably in his early forties and could easily pass for a decade younger at a quick glance.

"My name is Chan," he said, handing us his card, which informed us that he was both the Deputy Director of Marketing & Communications and Deputy Director of Consumer Businesses.

"How do you do?" he said in impeccable, unaccented, and perfectly inflected English, the kind of speech that no native speaker learns naturally but television newscasters back in the day were taught how to master. "How may I be of help to you today?"

He asked us please to sit down and we obliged. A female staff member silently brought in coffee and departed, reminding me of my years in a Japanese company. If only she'd bowed slightly to us as she backed out the door, this would be Tokyo. Was I getting nostalgic for Japan now that I was in the Pacific once again? Or was it Kikkoman's influence?

Hibino explained the nature of my visit and stole my opening by asking about the history of EDB and Kikkoman. I simply kept quiet and got out my notebook.

Mr. Chan began by saying that he wasn't at the EDB thirty years ago and could not speak from personal experience about things in that era, although there certainly were people here who could do that if we needed it. All the same, he was very well informed about the history I was looking for, and I assured him we would not need to bother anyone else in his office.

He began, "We've had a long relationship with Kikkoman. In the 1980s, some Japanese companies started looking at Singapore as a place to establish a base. Kikkoman was one of the early firms, and in some ways it was a pioneering firm.

"Kikkoman executives first contacted our office in Tokyo and then here. Singapore was looking to promote high-end man-ufacturing, so Kikkoman was a good fit from our perspective. When we find a company like Kikkoman, we are happy to say, 'How can we help you to grow?'"

I asked him what the EDB saw in Kikkoman.

"The EDB is not merely looking to help foreign companies set up business here. We aim for two-way growth; we learn from foreign investors, and that helps us to better manage Singapore's growth. We want to help companies like Kikkoman because we understand that successful businesses support a whole ecosystem of related firms. For example, Kikkoman is localized. They could easily import everything from Japan, but they don't. That means they have a significant, positive effect on our economy. In addition to providing good jobs for local workers, the company uses local bottling, shipping, packaging, wholesaling, advertising, PR, and other services. The company is closely connected with the Singaporean economy, and we have been pleased to see that relationship grow and develop over time."

We talked more about the EDB and what it does, and then I brought the conversation back to the subject at hand. How is Kikkoman perceived by the government?

"We see Kikkoman as an unusually responsible company. Lots of companies talk about CSR, but very few actually walk the walk, so to speak. Kikkoman management takes its commitments very seriously. Singapore has grown up a lot and Kikkoman has evolved together with Singapore, including in terms of its contributions to the community. For example, in the 1990s they contributed to the arts — simple, well-placed monetary contributions to support good causes. By 2014 their approach had grown much more sophisticated. In that year they made a significant, long-term contribution to our natural environment by contributing to Kingfisher Lake, part of the Gardens by the Bay nature preserve. That was an ongoing contribution that benefited the environment and provided something of real value for all our residents. I believe Kikkoman wants to be part of everyday life in Singapore

"In conclusion, you want to know how we view the company? My colleagues see Kikkoman as a very honorable firm. I think we have a relationship of mutual respect, and we value that relationship. We try to help them in any way we can. If Kikkoman ever has a situation involving some other government agency, we will do whatever we can to help."

Hibino signaled to me that we should keep this short. I was sure that Chan was a busy man, and we were lucky that he had taken time to speak to us. We got up, shook hands all around, and made out way to the door.

"Interesting fellow?" Hibino asked when we reached the lobby.

"Very interesting," I replied, and I wasn't exaggerating. "Where to next?"

He smiled. "*Indo*," he said, the Japanese word for India, and raised one hand to hail a cab. We took the taxi to Orchard Road, not very far away, and I wondered why a man with his own wheels who obviously enjoyed driving would switch to a cab. Who knows? People do all sorts of things for reasons I can't fathom.

Hibino directed the cab to a 2 km-long strip that looked like 5th Ave. and Ginza-dori rolled into one. In just a short distance I saw shopping centers full of familiar names, plus huge signs for Louis Vuitton, Prada, Cartier, and a dozen other world-famous brands. Want discounts? You're in the wrong part of town. People come to Orchard Road to spend money, and Orchard Road does not disappoint.

Hibino directed the driver to turn down a small side street and let us off. We walked along that little street, which later opened onto a long, open courtyard with a raised wooden floor packed full of tables and chairs. Both sides of the street were lined with good-looking, inexpensive restaurants. He steered us toward a place in the rear. We sat down at an empty table and he waved for a waiter from a place called Maharaja nearby. The waiter, a large, friendly Indian, came over to our table and beamed when he recognized Hibino.

"It is good to see you again," the man greeted him. "You want some beer to start with?"

I looked at Hibino, who seemed to be weighing the pros and cons of having a cool beer on a hot afternoon. I suddenly realized why we had come by cab and left the Camry at the office. I decided to make it easy for him.

"I'm thirsty. What do you say we have a beer to start?" I suggested.

A subsequent chat with the waiter somehow turned our pair of glasses into a pitcher. Well, work was done for the day, so why not? When the pitcher came, I toasted Hibino-san with the traditional Japanese *o-tsukaresama deshita* (you've been working hard; you must be tired), and we started drinking before we even looked at the menu. In a moment he called the waiter back again and asked if they still had the special Kikkoman curry. The answer was of course they did, and we decided to split a large order and mix it with several other curries.

Now I could really relax. Beer in hand, food on the way, no more real work to do today. There was a subway stop only two blocks away. That meant I could say goodnight to Hibino when we were done and maybe even get back to my hotel early and get some much-needed rest. After some serious drinking, of course.

I said as much to Hibino, who suddenly looked serious and confessed, "Please don't be angry. We have one more person to meet." He looked at his watch. "She should be here in a few minutes. I think you will like her."

What? Oh, yes, I'd half-forgotten already, he had said there was someone he wanted to introduce. But who was this person? A friend, an associate, an interview subject for me?

"She is our main PR person. She is very smart and very good at her job. She has helped Kikkoman tremendously in Singapore. She speaks good English, she has a good sense of humor, and she likes to talk about PR. I think you two will get along just fine."

I was pretty sure I would get along with anyone after I had consumed a few more beers. The only question was whether I would be able to read my notes tomorrow morning. One problem at a time. Hibino and I lifted our glasses again.

Twenty minutes into our drinking and talking session a Chinese woman of indeterminate age approached our table and smiled broadly at Hibino-san. He stood up and greeted her, then introduced me. We did the Japanese thing and exchanged cards immediately. I could tell by the way she handled that small task effortlessly and correctly that she had been working with Japanese companies for a long time.

Her card said that she was Chew Lee Ching, Managing Director of Mandate Communications (S) Pte. Ltd. This was interesting. I had talked to both the marketing manager and outside PR consultant in Düsseldorf, and here I was meeting the head of a local PR agency in Singapore. She sat down and said she would rather have a glass of wine than share in the second pitcher of beer that had somehow mysteriously appeared. Once her wine arrived, I asked how did she get hooked up with Kikkoman?

"I got to know Kikkoman more than twenty-five years ago when they were looking to launch their product here. At that time it was perceived in Singapore very much as a Japanese company. As you know, soy sauce is an important ingredient in Asian cooking. But we had a lot of other brands here already. So Kikkoman was not the top product by any means. I met the general manager, who said his goal was to build brand recognition. He wanted the name to be in people's minds even if they were buying another brand. The other thing was that a lot of people think that Kikkoman soy sauce is only good for Japanese cooking. That means it is not suitable for Chinese cooking or for other types of food. We needed to change that perception. So these were our two big hurdles.

"We created a multi-pronged strategy. Part of it was a campaign using both English and Chinese newspapers, as well as radio and TV, and we tried to inject a little humor into the campaign. We created a series of ads in which vegetables and other ingredients in a wok or a saucepan would talk to the Kikkoman sauce. We wrote funny dialogues where the food and the soy sauce talk to each other. We also put these simple, catchy images on double-decker buses. We coupled that with a cooking program. One of our themes was, 'A kiss of Kikkoman,' because the idea was you don't need to drown food in soy sauce, just a little touch of *shoyu* makes it better. It was very successful. Suddenly people started to take notice of Kikkoman.

"After a year or so, we hired a company to measure the results of our various campaigns, and they reported that the brand's recognition had shot up from 3 percent to nearly 70 percent. At the end of two years we started to see successful trial conversion, meaning that people went from knowing the brand name to buying and trying our product. We knew that we could not get older people to give up their favorite sauces, but perhaps we could get their children to try something new and use both of them from time to time."

I was already impressed with this woman. She was smart, she knew her business, and she knew her market. I couldn't help but think Kikkoman should put her and Hans Fuchs from Düsseldorf and Gigi Scholler from Vienna together in a room sometime to discuss global marketing and PR strategy. I asked her how she felt about her relationship with this big Japanese company after so many years.

"My relationship with Kikkoman has been and continues to be very satisfying. I have seen the brand grow roots here. Over the years I have seen how the brand has developed from something that people barely knew to one that is respected and has earned a lot of goodwill. And I don't mean just by consumers. Even the government departments think quite highly of Kikkoman. I went to one state function some time ago, and a government official was complimenting the company to someone right in front of me.

"I am also happy to say I have had excellent relationships with many key people in the company, both the executives in

Tokyo and the GMs in Singapore, and they have all been very supportive of what we do here. They know that I am always concerned with what is good for their company. The client always comes first. Frankly, I don't charge Kikkoman a lot, because this is a journey for me and for them, and I think of it as something I *should* do. I take my profit in other ways."

I was happy to let her do most of the talking because our curries had come, and I was enjoying my 'Kikkoman special' — a beef curry with a dash of *shoyu* to bring out the various flavors. It was very good, and it kept my cold beer company.

I remembered what the manager at the EDB had said just a few hours ago about Kikkoman's CSR stance. I asked our guest if Mandate Communications was involved in that in any way?

She smiled and sipped her wine.

"From talking to the executives here, we learned that Kikkoman has a very highly developed, well-articulated CSR policy. That is very unusual. They are one of the very few companies that have been doing CSR for a long time and they take it quite seriously. I thought, there must be a way to work that into their long-term image building.

"For their twenty-fifth anniversary in Singapore, I wanted to do something with lasting impact, not just sponsor a concert or whatever. We wanted to promote the message that Kikkoman doesn't just make good products, but is also a really good corporate citizen. I know that Kikkoman does well all over the world, and it wants to give back to society in every country where it operates. So why not tie it in to this big anniversary?

"At that time, something called Gardens by the Bay was just being developed. It's a 250-acre nature park, with two lakes and raised walkways around the lakes. By the way, it's absolutely beautiful, and if you haven't been there yet, I recommend a visit.

"Anyway, Kikkoman is always talking about the importance of clean water, so I started thinking about the lakes. They're right next to the Marina reservoir, and they play an important role in capturing run-off from within the Gardens and act as an 'eco-filter.' One of them, Kingfisher Lake, was still available for sponsorship. I thought this would be an ideal opportunity for Kikkoman and they agreed. Kikkoman made a very substantial initial contribution to help develop the lake and support the whole ecosystem. It was a big deal. We had to organize every-thing from planning the groundbreaking event to getting gov-ernment ministers to come right in the middle of an election, and — let me say, it wasn't easy. But it worked out beautifully."

I had finished my curry by now and was well ahead of Hibino-san in the beer department. I finally realized that he was being a good sport drinking with me, but he really wasn't in the mood to drink much tonight. I, on the other hand, was in the home stretch of my round-the-world tour and was enjoying the refreshing coolness that appears so unexpectedly in the evening in Singapore. The tropical breezes were a good enough excuse to finish most of the second pitcher myself.

I asked if Kikkoman's donation was well received.

"Oh, absolutely" she said. "Everyone is still impressed, because this is very unusual, a private company supporting the natural environment of Singapore. The Kingfisher Lake area has become a popular visitor attraction."

I asked her how Kikkoman is viewed in the community now, after more than three decades of activity.

She paused to think for a moment. "I would say that today people see Kikkoman more as a local company than an outsider, and people see them as a really good company. That is not my doing; that is simply Kikkoman being Kikkoman."

I said that she, like her client, was being too modest. If the company's image had changed so significantly over the years, some of that success must be due to its very creative, hard-working PR agency. She thanked me and said once again that the relationship had been very good for both sides. Her company had learned a lot from Kikkoman and she felt grateful for the experience.

We talked for another twenty minutes or so about everything other than Kikkoman, and all of her stories were interesting. I felt privileged to have met someone who was intelligent, motivated, hard-working, loyal to her clients, and proud to be helping her country. I once again concluded that she really was an impressive woman. I was just about to order her another glass of wine when she apologized, stood up, and said she had to be going.

After she departed I thanked Hibino for introducing us. He looked at me seriously, "You said you wanted to meet people who knew about our business but were not Kikkoman employees. She is one of the best people I could think of for you to meet."

Yes, the best people. I had met a lot of "best people" in my travels. Sitting there, at an outdoor table in the heart of commercial Singapore, slowly turning my nearly empty beer stein, I thought back on all those interesting people I had met in the Kikkoman universe.

At first, back in Walworth, I thought perhaps Kikkoman is like a magnet that attracts these good people, but in short order I realized that it is much more than that. Kikkoman not only brings in the best people it can find to join its family, it also brings out the best in the people it touches. How often do you find a company like that? I felt lucky to be researching a company that had so many good people in its extended "family" for me to meet on my travels.

Once again, I looked back on the strange route that had taken me across America and then to Europe and now to Singapore. Then I realized that something had been tugging at me for a while now, and being here in Asia at last was making it seem more imperative than ever. I was now certain that the Kikkoman story was not just a story of all the interesting people I had met, but also, I sensed, a story about one man, though as yet I had not met him. One man made all this happen, and one man turned his vision into a global empire, bringing all these people into his extended family and turning his company into an international giant in the process.

If I was going to complete this mission and really get to the heart of Kikkoman, I would have to visit Japan and try to meet this man. I had been all around the world and seen his foot-prints and his handiwork everywhere, but I had not talked to him directly. The only thing to do was to stop wasting time and get on a plane to Tokyo.

I told Hibino my plan, and he poured me another beer, smiling.

"Yes, I think you are right," he said. "Good luck."

It was only later, back at my hotel, that I began to wonder what he had meant by that.

Tokyo Connection

15

J had come to understand that the best way to really understand Kikkoman and get the inside story on how things like the "miracle of Walworth" had come to pass was to meet the DNA face-to-face. That is, I had to meet the man who embodies both Kikkoman's centuries-old DNA and its future strategy, and that meant getting a meeting with the former president and now honorary chairman, Yuzaburo Mogi.

With that goal in mind, but no idea how to achieve it, I booked a flight to Tokyo. When I landed at Narita Airport, I felt all the old feelings coming back. I lived here for a few years, and they were very happy ones. So I was thinking more about my own past and not much about Kikkoman as I stared out the window of the Narita Express train that whisked visitors into Tokyo. I mindlessly watched as the rice fields gave way to houses, then to towns and then to warehouses and finally, office buildings. I got off at Tokyo Station, one of the largest and busiest in the world. It had changed a lot from when I was last here, but it was still an amazing sight. I got a cab in front of the station, and on the way to my hotel I began to focus again on the mission in front of me.

From talking to Japanese managers overseas and from my own research on the Web, I knew that Mogi was elderly but still very active in the company. In fact, I'd heard that his daily schedule would tire out CEOs half his age, which meant that his days were booked solid. What were the chances he would make time to see an independent foreign writer who was merely interested in learning about Kikkoman? That's what companies have PR departments for. I knew that if I called or wrote for an appointment, I would never get near the CEO's office, much less get face-time with the Honorary Chairman.

However, in my days as a business journalist I'd worked with many big Japanese companies, so I knew that anything is possible but the direct approach is usually a waste of time. Going in the back door would be much more effective. I needed to talk privately to someone close to Mogi-san, someone whose opinions he trusted, but also someone who would sympathize with my situation.

As soon as I settled into my room at the Mandarin Oriental in Nihonbashi, I opened my laptop and scanned the list of executives on the company's website, but came up with nothing. Not a clue where to start. Next, I mailed Ron Yates in the U.S. and explained my predicament. Could he suggest anyone? A short while later a reply arrived:

"Find a guy named Narusawa. He used to be a hot salesman, then I heard they rotated him into Accounting or something, and I don't know where he went after that, but I'll bet he's somebody important in the company by now. Very smart, speaks

English better than you do, and knows everything there is to know about Kikkoman. Come to think of it, I heard a rumor he was Mogi's right-hand man for a while. He's a super-nice fellow, and he's your best bet — maybe your only bet — to get in to see the Big Guy."

Ron's text included an old email address and phone number for Hiroki Narusawa, which he warned me might not work. Japanese companies rotate staff around to many different departments for the first couple of decades of their service. I knew that phoning the old number would be a waste of time, but there was still a good chance that the email might reach him. What did I have to lose? I wrote to Narusawa, explained that I was writing a book about soy sauce and specifically about Kikkoman, that I was a friend of Ron's, and that he had strongly recommended that I contact him. I told him that I desperately needed to talk to someone who knew a lot about the company and might be able to help me talk to senior management. I did not mention Mogi's name.

Sure enough, my mail was answered the same day in perfect English. "I cannot say that I know a lot about the company," was the reply. "But if you are a friend of Mr. Yates I would be pleased to meet you."

He asked if I wanted to meet him at the Tokyo headquarters or perhaps after work somewhere else. That in itself was unusual. People in major Japanese companies don't usually set up a first meeting outside the head office. I said, if it was all the same to him, I'd rather meet outside the building. I knew that getting an employee away from the group-think mindset inside his office is the first step to getting more straightforward answers to questions, and if possible, getting him to talk in English would be a huge advantage. Japanese literally change their personalities when speaking other languages, and the transformation that takes place in someone who has a reasonable fluency in English is remarkable. If you understand the Japanese language well enough to hear the person talk to friends or colleagues in his own language, and then talk to him in English, you could be forgiven for thinking you're witnessing split personality disorder — there seem to be two different people inhabiting the same body.

So, my rules for getting information from Japanese mid-managers, especially those who have worked overseas, are:

1) get them away from the office
2) speak only in English
3) administer large quantities of alcohol

That trio had seldom failed me in the past, so I asked Narusawa if there was a place we might have a beer after work. He quickly suggested that we meet two days hence in a traditional Japanese *izakaya* pub in Shimbashi, a crowded business district in the center of the city. Shimbashi is famous for the number of inexpensive watering holes there. I knew that Kikkoman's Tokyo HQ was located on the upscale western edge of Shimbashi, while Narusawa had chosen a place on the heart of the old, funky, after-hours side. So far, so good.

Two days later I was waiting at the bar at 6:30. Narusawa had said "between 6:30 and 7," and my guess was he would be late. Japanese workers seldom leave the office before 8, and I vividly remember my old mentor instructing me on Day 1 at my new job in Tokyo that, "unless you have some reason to stay late, normal working hours are 9 to 9." He was joking, but not much.

The place Narusawa had chosen was a typical *izakaya*, one of only a few million in Tokyo — old wooden tables artlessly crammed in between older wooden posts, not smoothly carved and artistic as I had seen at Daitokai in Köln, but rough-hewn, grey, and slightly dirty, creating an atmosphere that assured you the place had been serving *yakitori* and beer since before the war — the Russo-Japanese war of 1905. The green plasterboard walls were covered with a couple of faded calendars and a dozen or so posters from beer companies, featuring female pop stars from another decade. Here and there were handwritten signs informing patrons of today's specials. I ordered a big stein of the house draft and waited.

Narusawa arrived at 7:00 sharp. He was tall and slim, with close-cropped hair, and most unusual for a middle-aged Japanese, did not wear glasses. He looked like he was in his mid-forties, though I knew appearances were very misleading. He greeted me in impeccable English and we exchanged cards. Then we both sat down, he called to a waitress and pointed to my glass. "Two more of these and a large assortment of *yakitori* please," he said. I noticed he was polite even to the wait staff, not a universal trait among Japanese men.

Of course, I studied his card for a few moments as a sign of respect and discovered that he was now in the company's CSR department. "I thought you were in Sales?" I said, just to get his story started.

"I was in Sales for a while, yes," he replied. "But as you may know, in Japanese companies people get rotated around several different positions to learn how the company operates. Over the years I have worked in Sales, Accounting, PR, Human Resources, IR and even our International Department."

I asked him how he learned to speak English so well. I always think the way to work with people is to show genuine interest in what they have to say. Narusawa and I had just met, but I wanted to build a connection quickly.

"It's a long story," he said, looking down at his beer.

"I've got time," I told him. "Did you go to a language school here or did you live overseas?" I asked.

"Both," he said. "I began to study English at home when I was very young, and later I spent time overseas with Kikkoman."

He paused to reflect a moment, then continued. "After university I wanted to join a big, international firm, but there weren't so many to choose from. The normal course would have been to join a general trading company [*shosha*] or maybe a big bank, and hope to get posted overseas. But I happened to get my hands on a book by Mr. Mogi that talked about international business, and it changed my life. He talked about the importance of bringing something quintessentially Japanese to the outside world. His words moved me, and I gradually determined to become some kind of a bridge between Japan and the outside world. So, I went to a company interview at Kikkoman. I think they were impressed with my English skills, but also with my passion for wanting to visit and understand other cultures. When I got hired, I was sure they would immediately assign me to some overseas post far away from the company headquarters." He laughed to himself now at the memory.

Narusawa told me that the very first step for all new recruits back then was to undergo a two-month training program wherein they learned how soy sauce was made, and not by studying textbooks. Each employee, regardless of whether they would soon be assigned to work in retail sales in some faraway prefecture or corporate planning at the HQ, was sent to Noda City in nearby Chiba Prefecture to work at the company's oldest and most famous factory. Noda was the company's birthplace and is still the site of one of its two headquarters. More importantly, the Noda factory, which embodies 400 years of company history, remains its spiritual center.

The young Narusawa worked hard learning the process that makes the company's main product. As he recalls it, by the end of each day even his hair smelled like soy sauce. But he and all the other recruits also derived a feeling of pride in the high quality of the naturally fermented soy sauce that they had helped to make. Now they, too, felt like generations of Kikkoman craftsmen, charged with preserving and maintaining a tradition that now had a special meaning for all of them. Even today, he told me, all new recruits undergo a one-month training period, not only learning how to make soy sauce, but also visiting a domestic winery or a tomato farm, as those are two more Group businesses now closely connected with the Kikkoman brand. I made a note to ask him later about how wine and tomato products fit into the company's operations.

After postings in other cities, he was moved to the HQ in Tokyo. His first assignment was to manage the Japanese staff already assigned to international posts, in other words, managing people overseas rather than going overseas himself. He was also told that he would be the unofficial assistant to the head of international operations, the very same Yuzaburo Mogi whose book had inspired Narusawa to join Kikkoman in the first place. Mogi was a director in the company, but not yet senior enough to rate a personal secretary, so Narusawa became his unofficial assistant, booking travel arrangements and preparing documents for every foreign trip. It was in that position that Narusawa had a chance to travel the world and get to know Mogi's thinking first-hand.

"Mr. Mogi was in his late fifties when I first met him," Narusawa remembers. "Reading his book, I had developed great respect for him and wanted to impress him. But he was quite strict — strict with himself and with those around him. If I made even a single mistake in a business document, he would tell me to do it over again. Looking back on it now, I realize that I had grown up in a fairly lax environment; I expected that my small mistakes would be overlooked and that the overall quality of my work would outshine the small errors. Mr. Mogi understood that in business any error was a major error, that mistakes might be tolerable in children, but not in international commerce.

"Now I look back on it and realize that he was an excellent teacher and I was a slow student who had no idea how much more he still had to learn. Strict teachers are the best teachers."

We ordered more drinks and I encouraged him to tell me more. I was learning things about the Chairman and about Kikkoman as I went on, and I doubted that I would find anyone in the head office with as much knowledge as Narusawa, much less anyone who could explain it to me in such good English. He was exactly the kind of source every journalist dreams of.

He told me his stint as Mogi's secretary was short-lived and that he moved on to several other positions, including being stationed overseas himself. He lived in Europe for a while and then in the U.S., sometimes alone and sometimes with his family. The latter periods were very happy years, he said.

We talked for about an hour, and I made sure the beers kept coming, although I noticed that his drinking pace slowed rapidly after the second round. Several other customers had come in, usually in groups of three or four, men in white shirts carrying their jackets slung over their shoulders, all laughing and talking loudly as they entered the bar. The background noise was increasing minute by minute, so I decided it was time to get on with my research. My top priority was to learn more about the man I had heard so much about in my travels. Did Narusawa have any other direct contact with Mogi?

"Yes," he said. "For a short time I served in the President's office after Mr. Mogi was promoted to President and CEO."

Once again Narusawa said he had an opportunity to work closely with the man who was now a legend within Kikkoman. During that time he met the President often and got to know him a little better than before. Narusawa told me several interesting stories about those days, but none of them shed any new light on Mogi as a man or as a chief executive. I decided to stop wasting time and put all my cards on the table. I told him that I wanted to ask for a very big favor.

"Of course," he said pleasantly. "I will do whatever I can to help you come to know our company better."

I explained that I had traveled all over the world and talked to many people in the Kikkoman world, including dozens of employees, managers and outside suppliers. I was impressed by two things — the very strong personal character of just about everyone I met, and the nearly universal feeling of a family-like bond among them. I said that I wanted to tell that story as much as the ancient history of the company and the tale of its growth in various markets. To do that, I still needed one more key interview, and it might be a difficult one to arrange.

"With who? I can contact our PR Dept. or, if it is someone I know personally, I can arrange for them to talk to you myself." He wasn't pulling my leg; Japanese can be extremely naive sometimes. I thanked him but said that it wasn't like that. I needed to talk to Mogi-san directly. Was there any way that I could get an appointment to see him?

For the first time Narusawa's face clouded, he looked down and fiddled with his glass.

"That would be difficult. The Honorary Chairman is extremely busy these days. So many people want to meet with him and there are so many things around the world that require his attention. In addition, there are all the events and social affairs that he needs to attend here in Japan." He paused, and now the smile and the positive glow returned to his face. "As you probably know, Kikkoman is now a first-rate biotechnology firm. Sometimes I think we should have poured all our resources into cloning Mr. Mogi. One of him is not enough."

He laughed and I smiled at this attempt at either humor or distraction, but I wasn't letting him off the hook. I pressed him again. There must be some way for me to get in to see Mogi, even for fifteen minutes. I told Narusawa that after all my travels and all my interviews around the world, I knew for certain that this man embodied the living DNA of Kikkoman. He *was* the company, and regardless of how very talented its executives were in the future, and regardless of how many Mogi family heirs followed in his footsteps, the company would never be exactly the same without him. The Japanese sometimes talk about *fushi*, the bumps that look like joints on stalks of bamboo. They signify major growth spurts, and in that respect the term can be more useful than our trite "turning point." Viewed up close, Mogi's reign at Kikkoman was arguably a major turning point for the company. Yet viewed from a 400-year perspective, it was just another, admittedly big *fushi*, a vital step in the company's ongoing, healthy growth. But how long would it be until the next big one came along? Mogi was one of a kind.

So, how could I get to meet this man? Did I have to be a king or a queen of some European nation? Did I need to be the governor of an American state or an ambassador or what? I asked again.

"Narusawa-san, I have traveled all around the world. I have visited several of your plants and sales offices and talked to your suppliers, PR agents, distributors and restauranteurs. I probably know as much about Kikkoman as any foreigner who has not worked for your firm. But I have not met Mr. Mogi. Now I have come to Japan and I am ready to visit your headquarters, because my journey is not complete. I cannot finish this book without meeting Mr. Mogi face to face. It doesn't matter if his title says CEO or Honorary Chairman or Special Advisor. I know now that he is something beyond titles. Western companies like to talk about their 'corporate DNA,' but that is usually some nonsense cooked up by their PR or marketing departments. In

Kikkoman's case you have the company's real, living DNA right here. He *is* the past, the present, and in some sense, the future of the company all in one. I must meet him."

His head turned up slowly.

"Yes, he is the DNA of our company, in a very real sense..." His voice drifted off, then snapped back to hard reality. "But no one gets to see Mr. Mogi without an appointment, and it is almost impossible to get an appointment."

"I have not done all this research and traveled once around the planet just to talk to people in your damn PR Department!" I blurted out in semi-drunken frustration.

He looked pensive. "I said *almost* impossible. That does not mean impossible." He was staring into his beer, lost in thought. "Perhaps... if I ask the right people... I can arrange for you to meet him — briefly. It might not work, and if it does, it will take time to set up. I assure you it will not happen this week or next. If it does, it may happen very suddenly, perhaps when someone else cancels an appointment. If you are ready to move quickly, we just might succeed."

"What? Of course! I will do whatever is necessary to get in to see him. Just tell me what to do and when."

"I will call your hotel next week with an update. I should know more by then," he said, standing up. We shook hands and headed for the door. He reached for his wallet, but I stopped him. I was glad for his help and did not want to spoil the relationship. I had let the company take me out to dinner in Köln and Singapore and give me rides here and there, but that was enough. I did not want to owe Kikkoman anything.

I paid the bill, thanked the woman at the register, and stepped outside. Narusawa was waiting for me politely. He bowed and said goodbye, then hailed a taxi and a moment later was gone.

With a real possibility now that I might actually get to meet Mogi, I thought the Tokyo air seemed somehow fresher and more exciting than it had a couple of hours ago. I went back to my hotel, opened my laptop, and started to write a thank-you mail to Ron Yates.

16

Meeting the DNA - Part I

One evening early the next week, I was working in my hotel room when the phone rang. It was Narusawa.

"I might be able to arrange a short meeting with the Honorary Chairman." I knew he must be in his office because he referred to Mogi by his title instead of his name. Even in English, this is important in a Japanese company. "Would you be able to come to our building on Thursday? That's the seventh."

"Sure," I said. "What time is good?"

"He will receive you at 8:30 sharp, before his business day officially begins. You will only have a few minutes to talk... That is the best I can do."

I thanked him twice, silently pumping my fist in the air. YES! This was a major coup. As he had said, you don't get to see Mogi without an appointment, and no one gets an appointment. Well, I just got one, and I felt as if I'd just won a gold medal at the Journalism Olympics.

When I first started to investigate this story (it seemed like ages ago), it was all about taste. I wanted to explore umami, a taste sensation I knew nothing about. At least my brain knew nothing about it — Barb Stuckey insisted that my tongue knew all about it before I was even born. From that innocent beginning I had pursued the mysteries of high-quality soy sauce, and that had led me to Ron Yates in California and the opening of a door into one of the world's oldest continuing businesses and one of Japan's first and most successful international companies. Now I had traveled around the world, and discovered a global enterprise growing by leaps and bounds and a group of employees spanning a dozen different countries who had never met each other but felt as if they all belonged to the same family.

All of this growth and energy and familial feeling ultimately stemmed from the seeds planted by one man, and that man was now so well regarded in both his home country and his many adopted nations that he seemed to be constantly speaking, traveling, and joining in events around the globe. Getting in to see him seemed something that only CEOs of big companies, government ministers, or heads of state achieved without enormous effort. I had heard from some employees overseas that when he visited their plants he would occasionally chat with line workers and ordinary staff. But here, in the company headquarters, he was loaded with important responsibilities.

It was totally understandable that he would not have time in his schedule to meet with a virtually unknown visitor such as myself.

And yet, here I was, with an appointment to see the Old Man in less than a week. I mentally thanked Ron for introducing me to Narusawa-san. The latter had proven to be a good friend and much more influential inside the company than he ever let on.

—§—

On the appointed day, I put on my best suit and took a taxi to the Kikkoman headquarters building a little after 8 AM. I wanted to be sure that I arrived on time. I walked through the small lobby, but I didn't see anyone at the Reception desk. I paced around in front of the giant, inflated Kikkoman soy sauce bottle, big enough to be a child's float in a swimming pool. Around 8:15, two women in prim uniforms appeared, and I presented my business card and said I had an appointment with Mr. Mogi. They both tried to appear nonchalant, but I could tell that this was a big deal — an American showing up at the office early in the morning to meet with the Honorary Chairman. One of them made a phone call, and then asked me please to sit and wait for just a moment. In less than that time, Narusawa appeared and ushered me to the elevators. He looked nervous for the first time since I had met him, and he talked as if he were still acting as one of Mogi's personal assistants.

"Remember that you only have a few minutes," he said. "Mr. Mogi may be feeling *genki* this morning, or he may not, so pace your questions accordingly. Do not rush him, and if he appears not to want to answer something, just let it go. We don't want to disturb him or upset him. He has many important meetings today..." He went on in that vein all the way upstairs, down the carpeted hall, and into the big room where the meeting was to take place. As is the custom with Japanese companies, I was shown where to sit, and I obediently took my place in a large, man-eating leather armchair. Mr. Mogi would sit directly opposite me, a low coffee table in between us. I asked Narusawa if he would be there for the interview. In fact, I wanted to be left alone with Mogi, but I doubted that would be possible.

"The decision is not up to me," was all he said.

We waited until just a couple of minutes past the scheduled time, then the door opened suddenly, and another uniformed woman held it open for the Honorary Chairman, who strode into the room energetically. Mogi wore a dark suit with a white shirt and soft blue tie, as conservative as any of his peers among Japan's corporate elite, but his stride, his smile, and his demeanor were something altogether different. He held out his hand to me.

"How do you do?" he said in clear English.

I greeted him and thanked him immediately for taking the time to see me.

"Not at all," he said, sitting down and facing me with a big smile. "I am always happy to meet people who are interested in Kikkoman." His face was lined but not wrinkled, and once again I thought he looked younger than the age my notes indicated. His eyes were lively behind gold-rimmed glasses, and though his hairline was receding, he was far from bald. My overall impression on first meeting him was one of vitality, exactly the opposite of what I had expected.

He looked over at Narusawa and greeted him like an old friend. They chatted for a few moments, and I saw the younger man relax visibly. I inferred that he would be staying for this meeting. No surprise there.

"So what do you want to talk to me about?" Mogi said, sitting up straight in his chair and reaching for a glass of the cool barley tea that another uniformed employee had left on the table. "Or perhaps you would like to tell me how you came to be interested in Kikkoman?"

"Well, sir, it's a long story," I began, not sure where to start and keenly aware that we didn't have much time. "One night several months ago, I heard a talk at Columbia Business School by a woman who runs a food research company."

"What? Did you say Columbia Business School?" His eyebrows shot up. "I went to Columbia Business School! I was the first Japanese to receive an MBA from that school, way back in 1961!" He looked positively animated now.

"Yes, sir, I am aware of that. In fact, I also went to Columbia, though not to the business school."

"You did? Well why didn't anyone tell me? So we both went to the same school!"

"About three decades apart, sir."

"Doesn't matter. It's an important connection between people. So, what about this woman?"

"She convinced me that I should begin to study soy sauce... and that there was no point in wasting my time looking at inferior quality soy sauce, so I should start right away with Kikkoman."

"This woman sounds very intelligent," he interrupted with a big smile.

"Yes, sir. Anyway, I followed her advice and began to look into your company. I met with Mr. Ronald Yates in California. He gave me lots of good advice and asked some people here to help arrange for me to visit some of your factories and offices around the world."

"Excellent! First, please tell me, how is Mr. Yates? Do give him my very best regards when you speak to him next. Second, where did you go? Which plants have you visited?"

"I've been to Walworth, Folsom, Sappemeer, and Singapore, and I've visited sales offices in Düsseldorf and San Francisco. I also went to the Daitokai restaurant in Köln, and in addition to your staff, I've talked with all sorts of suppliers, distributors, and PR people who help support Kikkoman around the world. I also met with Mick Neshek and Governor Thompson in Wisconsin and Martin Brink in Amsterdam."

"Very good, very good! I see you have traveled a lot and talked to the right people."

"Yes, I have met many very interesting people. And the more I traveled and the more people I talked to, the more I saw that it was you who made this company what it is today. That's why I wanted to come here and meet you."

He shook his head and waved his hand from side to side.

"No, I am just the Honorary Chairman. The really important people are the managers and staff you met, the people who run those companies and make the products and sell them and promote them. They are the essence of Kikkoman."

Okay, now I needed to add Modesty to his list of attributes.

"Mr. Mogi, there is one thing that still impresses me more than anything else, and that is the decision to set up a factory in America back in the early 1970s. Considering this company's long history in Japan, it seems almost strange that you decided to go overseas, and especially at that time, when no other Japanese firms were doing so and when there was still anti-Japanese sentiment left over from the war. What made you decide to become an international company?"

He thought a minute, looking to one side and rubbing his jaw with one hand, then looked back and me and began to speak.

"First of all, I didn't make Kikkoman into an international company; it was operating internationally before I was born. The Kikkoman brand was legally registered in California in the 1870s, even before it was legally trademarked here in Japan, and a few years later it was registered in Germany. Back in 1883, Kikkoman won a gold medal at the Amsterdam World's Fair, and it had received recognition in other world's fairs before that. That gives you some idea that our business was not confined to Japan, even back then.

"Early in the twentieth century, the predecessor of what is now Kikkoman Corporation exported roughly ten percent of its total production overseas — mostly for Japanese people living in Asia and Hawaii. We began exporting again in 1949, but there wasn't enough capital to invest in overseas factories. Our new focus was selling to customers on the American mainland. By 1957, we were shipping enough *shoyu* to California that we felt confident setting up a sales company in San Francisco, then offices in LA and New York. The U.S. company even ran television ads as far back as 1956. Can you believe there was a Kikkoman ad on the TV news coverage of President Eisenhower's reelection? That's another tradition we have upheld for more than a century — good advertising.

"In any case, we were very serious about developing the U.S. market, but we were doing so by exporting *shoyu* in bulk and bottling it in California. That was a satisfactory way to move a product into a growing market, but not a good way to develop a company the way that I knew Kikkoman needed to develop. To me, the next step was obvious — do what we had done before and open a production facility close to our main overseas market. So you may say that my proposal to build a factory in Wisconsin was radical. I assure you, the company's board of directors in 1971 would have agreed with you. Or you may say that my ideas were very much in line with the international business traditions of Kikkoman stretching back at least a century. In that case, I would agree with you. I think the only thing radical about my suggestion was the timing. And yet, in retrospect, even the timing looks fortuitous."

I was taking notes on all of this, not much of which is readily available, even on the company's website.

"Mr. Mogi," I said, "even with the background that you've just explained, it still seems like a huge step for a company that is only exporting and has no overseas production capability to build a factory from scratch in a challenging market like America. How did you personally come to believe in Kikkoman's international destiny? How did that become your personal mission?"

He thought for a moment.

"Let me see, let me see. I don't often tell this to people, but when I was young, I really wasn't much interested in the family business. Yes, I knew all about the history and the Mogi family tradition, and my father was an important person in Kikkoman, but frankly, it didn't really move me. I went to Keio University in the 1950s, and like most young people at that time, the old ways and ancient traditions of Japan seemed less exciting than the new world of technology and social change that we saw coming from America. Like a lot of my peers, I wanted to be more international. I joined the company — it was still called Noda Shoyu Company back then — in 1958, right out of university, and almost immediately I applied to Columbia so I could go abroad and study American ways of business. You might wonder how modern American business strategy could possibly be of use to a nearly 400-year-old Japanese enterprise, but to be honest, I wasn't too concerned with those questions. I just wanted to travel and study and see the outside world for myself.

"I had to work very, very hard at Columbia. We had a lot of reading to do, which was quite a challenge for me, but I studied hard. And while I was there, I happened to attend a trade show in Chicago, where I saw a food tasting demonstration by our sales company — you know, one of those things where they let people try new types of foods. They were dipping meatballs in just a bit of *shoyu* and serving it to American consumers, and the reaction was quite surprising — people *liked* the taste of foods they were familiar with, but seasoned with *shoyu*. Until that time, I had always thought of *shoyu* as a purely Japanese seasoning, something tied to our past, not a wave of the future. But in that instant I realized that *shoyu* was in fact an *international* seasoning, not in any way limited to Japanese culture. When I went to other demonstrations in supermarkets, I saw the same thing. American housewives right in front of me tasted soy sauce on their favorite foods and liked it. What if *more* people had a chance to taste it?

"Suddenly the whole context of my family business changed. I began to understand that I was in a position to help bring this traditional taste from Japan to the rest of the world, starting with America. It could be my mission to internationalize *shoyu*, and *that* really was interesting! That was exciting. It was a big challenge, of course, but a challenge worth doing. Now I was becoming very interested in the family business!"

I looked over at Narusawa, who was scribbling notes faster than I was. I gathered that some parts of this story were news to him, too.

"After I went back to Japan, I was just another new recruit at Kikkoman. Like other new hires, I was sent to Noda to work in the factory for six months. We all had to go through a complete training in *shoyu* preparation. Now, our new employees spend only a month learning how *shoyu* is made, but it is important for every employee to have that experience.

"Anyway, after my six months' training was finished, the Personnel Department called me in and asked me where I wanted to work in the company. My father was a specialist in labor relations problems, so they asked if I wanted to do something like that. I said, 'No way!' I wanted to work in Corporate Planning, which was a lot closer to the kinds of strategy and financial planning that I had studied in business school.

"The fellow in Personnel said I couldn't just go straight into corporate planning — that was a relatively high-level job. First, I should work in some area like Accounting for a while. So I was sent to the Accounting Department for about two years. But I never stopped thinking about corporate planning and the kinds of strategic thinking I had learned in grad school."

At this point a young woman came in and handed Mogi a small slip of paper. He nodded, handed it back, then said something quietly to her. She disappeared. I looked at Narusawa, who was pointing surreptitiously at his watch. He had to be joking — we had just started talking, and I'd barely asked a single question. All the same, it would not do to break the rules that had been carefully explained to me. Not if I wanted another chance at this.

"Mr. Mogi, I am very grateful for your time, but I know you are busy. Perhaps we should talk some other time..."

"Nonsense!" He waved his hand as if shooing away a fly. "I have lots of time. I just made some more time, so don't worry. Now, where were we? Oh, yes, corporate strategy.

"At that time many Japanese companies were making long-term plans, but as far as I could tell, Kikkoman didn't seem to have one. I decided that the fastest way to get myself promoted to the Corporate Planning Dept. was to come up with a viable long-term plan for the company. Another young guy and I would develop it and show it to the brass and see what happened.

"Now, at that time Kikkoman was already selling *shoyu* in America, as I told you. We knew that shipping thousands of glass bottles from here to California was incredibly expensive, so we tied up with an American firm to do the bottling over there. We shipped *shoyu* across the Pacific in giant 200 kiloliter tanks to a little company in Oakland, and they bottled it for us. We had the sales office in San Francisco to promote and arrange distribution for us. It sounded good on paper, but even with the bulk shipments we weren't making money. The American operation was a cost center rather than a profit center, and I knew that wasn't sustainable. And on top of that, roughly 90 percent of the wheat and soybeans used in Japan were imported from America. That meant we were importing raw materials from the U.S. and exporting finished products back to the U.S., and in the process paying shipping costs, insurance, import duties, the whole thing — just to send processed soy and wheat back to the States. On a very small scale, it might make sense, but not at the levels I was thinking about. I felt sure that the North American market had huge potential, possibly bigger than the Japanese market if we approached it correctly.

"So I helped to put together a plan to turn our international business into a profit center. I pointed out that shipping *shoyu* from Japan to the U.S. in any form, bottled or bulk, was not a viable long-term strategy, and the company could not and should not support a money-losing business. My solution? Even way back then I said that we should build a factory in America and be up and running there when the demand for *shoyu* began to grow.

"Of course, I did many simulations, just the way I'd learned in business school. I looked at all sorts of variables and possibilities, examined sales growth in the U.S. up until then, and potential sales figures for coming years. How much would it cost to buy suitable land and build a new factory? How much to hire workers? How much to transport raw materials in and finished product out to the market? I looked at many factors and put them all into my business models. The result I came up with was indisputable: if we built a factory and sales rose at anything close to the rate I anticipated, we would break even in just a few years and turn a profit shortly after. More than that, we could stop shipping *shoyu* to the U.S. and cancel our bottling contract with the U.S. company. Any way I looked at the numbers, it all made sense. But I think what was really at work was my... what do you say?... my gut. I knew deep down that we *had* to internationalize. Even in Japan the demand for *shoyu* had weakened as people turned to more Western diets, so I knew we needed to become an international business. We *needed* the international market. To me, that was the only viable future for our business."

I already understood why people called Mogi a visionary, but I had never understood just how much of a visionary he was at a very young age. In big, conservative Japanese companies even today, and back then much more so, junior execs are rewarded for keeping their mouths shut. If they have any brilliant ideas, they are smart enough to keep them to themselves. For Mogi to propose such a radical and risky plan would be career suicide in many firms.

"Did you actually go ahead and suggest that the firm build a plant in America?" I asked, already knowing the answer.

"Absolutely! Somewhere around 1965 I gave them my original plan. Of course, no one took it seriously, and in retrospect, I don't blame them. The sales figures in America at that time were still not enough to support the costs of building a factory there. I was counting on demand to grow, but... not everyone shared my enthusiasm."

"So what happened? What changed?"

"Over the next five years, demand for *shoyu* in the U.S. **did** grow steadily, just as I knew it would, and my resolve to build in the States grew with it. Both the current sales figures and the potential sales growth made my plan seem less and less risky. Then," he chuckled to himself, "I guess you could say the Osaka Expo 1970 was a turning point for us."

I looked puzzled.

"You see, back at Columbia I knew an interesting fellow named Malcolm Pennington."

My ears perked up. There was a name I had heard often in my travels, someone who I knew had been essential to the company's growth, but who I would never get to meet, as he had died more than a decade earlier.

"He and I were classmates, although we didn't really know each other at first. We met at the campus Toastmasters Club. You know what that is — people get together a couple of times a month and are given topics about which they have to make impromptu speeches, then everyone critiques them. We enjoyed those sessions and we all drank gallons of cheap, awful California wine. Remember that this was the early 1960s, a long time before anyone thought California wine was drinkable.

"In any case, Pennington and I got to know each other at Toastmasters and we became good friends. He was a natural talker and his speeches were very good. I had a harder time because I was trying to do this all in my second language, so it was a real challenge for me. I can tell you this, though: All those evenings of being forced to stand up and give an ad hoc speech on some topic came in very handy later on. Over the next several years, I had to do a lot of speeches in English, and I was much better prepared thanks to my days in Toastmasters.

"Anyway, Pennington and I stayed in touch after graduation. I visited America once around '69 and we chatted, but that was about it. Then I heard that he and his wife were coming to Japan for the Osaka Expo '70. I invited them to stay at our house, and they accepted. Pennington and I had plenty of time to talk about all sorts of things. At one point, I mentioned my idea of building a factory in the U.S. We discussed it for a while, and then I said, 'I'd like you to help me.' He agreed almost immediately, and a plan was born.

"By the way, you may not know this, but Pennington was a first-rate corporate planner himself."

I had already researched Mr. Pennington and had his file in my notes. The classmate whom Mogi met at Columbia Business School had been a systems analyst for IBM before joining the MBA program, and before that was Maj. Malcolm W. Pennington, USAF, having served with distinction as a bomber pilot in the Korean War. In the same year that he and Mogi began talking about the possibility of building a *shoyu* plant on U.S. soil, Pennington established Marketing and Planning Group, Inc., a pioneer in corporate strategic planning. He later helped to found *Planning Review*, the official journal of the North American Society of Corporate Planning, and co-wrote a two-volume textbook called *Corporate Planning: Techniques and Procedures.* It would be perfectly normal for Mogi, a foreign visitor in America, to turn to one of his school buddies for help in starting a business in the U.S., and it would be just as normal for that classmate to prove completely inadequate for the task at hand. In Pennington's case, it is a safe bet that there was no better person in all of the United States for Mogi to turn to for advice. Had the Fates determined long ago that Mogi was "doomed to succeed"? The more I heard, the more I wondered.

Of course, I enjoyed hearing about how he and Pennington had banded together to create the Master Plan for building Kikkoman in America, but I didn't want to get lost in that story when we had so little time to talk. My biggest question, the one that had nagged me since first visiting the huge plant in Walworth, was the one I really wanted to ask him today.

"Considering how long ago this was, and how traditional and conservative Kikkoman was as a company, and that you were quite young and also one of the very few people in the firm with any kind of overseas experience, how did you ever persuade the company to take this huge, risky step?"

Mogi sat for a moment and sipped his tea. He seemed to be enjoying these reminiscences, and Narusawa's frantic note-taking reassured me that these were not stories that were told every day. Finally, he looked up, his customary smile in place and his eyes dancing.

"A few months after the Osaka Expo, Pennington and I traveled around the States, looking at potential sites. That information was essential to include in my proposal, which I prepared at the beginning of the following year, in 1971. Of course, that big a project needed to be decided by a formal meeting of the Board of Directors. I was only a mid-level manager at the time. I did not have the right to attend a Board meeting to present the proposal, so I gave it to my boss, who had a seat on the Board, and he presented it.

"By my calculations, the new factory would cost at least 40 *oku* in Japanese yen [an *oku* is 100 million yen, a very large sum back then], and possibly more. At the time Kikkoman had about 32 *oku* in paid-in capital."

I had to stop him here.

"So you were asking the company to gamble more than its total capital base on a gigantic overseas project that only you knew anything about?"

"No!" He suddenly sat bolt upright and his voice took on a sharper tone. "It was not a gamble! A risk, yes; there is always risk in business. But risk is not bad, only poorly understood risks. I had examined all the numbers, I had done hundreds of calculations, and I was sure that the new factory would break even within five years." He quickly returned to his normal composure.

"But all the calculations were really a way to prove something that I knew in my bones. Again and again, I had seen American housewives' reactions when they tasted *shoyu*-seasoned foods. I *knew* for certain that people would like the product and that demand would grow. It was just a matter of time."

Mogi was clearly remembering the past vividly. I wondered how long it had been since he had explained this history in English. Or had he ever? He took a long breath and started again.

"In any case, it did seem, as you suggest, a very risky proposition to the Board members. They did not vote Yes or No, but simply tabled the matter to discuss at another meeting. I was disappointed but also just a bit relieved. They could have said No outright, but instead they had left the door open. That was in February. The next Board meeting was in early March, and it produced the same result: Decision pending. But at that March meeting one board member suggested that they ask our main bank for an outside opinion."

I tried to hide my smile even as I was writing notes. So much like big Western firms today, I thought. When the company needs to make an important decision but no one wants to go out on a limb, what do you do? Hire a consultant, of course. Because a consulting company knows more than you do? No, of course not. Many of them know less than the clients they work for. From what I have seen, consultants are often paid to provide an outside "expert" opinion, which a CEO can then follow or ignore with impunity: If things go well, everyone is happy; if things go badly, you can always blame the consultant. Considering how appealing that kind of face-saving approach is in twenty-first century America, imagine how appealing it must have been in a Japanese boardroom in the 1970s, where face-saving was practically a religion.

"So our director in charge of finance contacted our main bank to give us an opinion. But the bank didn't know anything about this kind of overseas investment — remember, no Japanese company had built a factory in the U.S. at this time, so they had no reference data to start with — and the bank knew absolutely nothing about soy sauce production or how to project future sales growth in a foreign market. The simple fact was that the bank was not capable of rendering an opinion.

"Of course, the bank was not going to tell an important client that they had no information upon which to base an opinion—"

Certainly not. Face-saving at work again, I thought.

"—so they searched for someone who understood the *shoyu* business and also had experience in the U.S. market." Pause. "That person was a junior staff member in our company, someone knowledgeable about these matters but conveniently not part of the Board of Directors. And that person was, of course, me." Now he was smiling from ear to ear, his whole face lit up with the irony the Fates had sent his way, or perhaps with the inevitability of his plan working out.

"And so, the bank used my data and my analysis to prepare their answer to my proposal. They told the Board that it was reasonable to build a production plant in the U.S., but with certain conditions, which had to do with limiting capital investments during the start-up phase. But at least they gave my proposal a green light. And I went back to my boss and lobbied hard not to change the initial capital investment plans. I explained why this funding was so important in the start-up phase and why reduced expenditures would cripple the business before it got started. He understood, and he took the idea to the next board meeting."

"And the rest is history," I interjected with one eye on my watch. "You got the Board's approval and it went ahead."

"Not exactly. The bank's recommendation convinced them not to oppose the idea. But that didn't mean they favored it or wanted to go on record as favoring it. They left the final decision up to the president."

"Did you know the president," I asked.

"Yes. He was my father."

There was a moment of silence in the room. I noticed the soft hum of the air-conditioning equipment for the first time.

"Well, that was a good thing." I said. "He must have understood your proposal better than any of the other directors."

"No, he did not. Of course, we were father and son, and we lived in the same house, but as a rule we never talked about business at home. He didn't like to talk about work with the family. He left his job at the office when he came home. And I respected that and never once discussed my international strategy over the dinner table. So the only information he had about my plan came from the presentations my boss had made to the Board of Directors."

"And the entire future of your company rested on your father's decision," I said.

"Yes."

"If his son was wrong, if this overseas expansion plan didn't work, it might very well bankrupt Kikkoman, and end a centuries-old tradition that he and the other founding families had spent their lives trying to preserve?"

"Yes."

The air-conditioning seemed even louder than before. I knew I should keep my mouth shut, but there were so many questions bubbling up in my brain, and besides, I've never been good at keeping my mouth shut. Questions just started pouring out:

"So why did he vote Yes? Why did he take that risk with his company's future? Did he trust the bank's opinion? Or did he trust your opinion? ... Did he understand that the only future for Kikkoman was to go overseas? ... Could he see that this was maybe a once-in-a-century opportunity? ... Or did he understand that neither he nor anyone on his Board had a clue about international business and his only rational choice was to bet that his son, who had lived in the United States and learned English and gone to Columbia University, was a pretty smart guy, and then decide to trust him?"

Mogi looked at me a moment, still smiling. He spread both hands, palms up, with a look that seemed to say, "Who knows?"

Or maybe he meant, "Does it matter?" I will never be sure. In the next instant the door opened and a worried-looking assistant came in and handed him another piece of paper. He nodded and she stepped back, her hands folded primly in front of her.

"I'm sorry," he said, standing up and smoothing his suit, "I have things I must attend to."

I was instantly on my feet, as was Narusawa.

Mogi shook my hand firmly. "But I have enjoyed your questions, Mr. Russell. Perhaps we can meet again sometime?"

I was nodding rapidly, not quite finding the words I wanted. He headed to the door, which his assistant was holding open. Suddenly he stopped, one foot out the door, and turned back to me. "Have you been to Noda?" he asked.

"No, not yet," I said, feeling stupid.

"Why don't you go visit Noda? Then let's talk again." He nodded towards Narusawa, who did a quick half-bow, then he was gone.

Narusawa and I were both still standing. He gestured for me to sit and he did the same. He took a very deep breath.

"That went very well," he said.

"What? I didn't even ask him anything. I mean, I asked him maybe one question…"

"It wasn't the question. It was you, an American, reminding him of his days at Columbia, and then triggering his memories about Pennington and starting up the business in the U.S. I think he enjoyed that."

"Why does he want me to go to Noda? I've seen four Kikkoman factories already. Is there something in Noda that you don't do anywhere else? Is there some special process or technology or something I have to see to understand Kikkoman?"

"No, not really," he said, looking out the window behind my head, apparently lost in thought. "I think he just wants you to visit Noda, to breathe the air where the company was born, and see the place where the business began. Perhaps he wants you to get an idea of what he put at risk when he asked his father and the Board to bet the whole company on a crazy scheme to build an overseas factory."

"Can you arrange for me to see the Noda plant?" I asked.

"Anyone can see it. It's open to the public and there are half a dozen tours every day. But we will do better than that. I will guide you around the Noda facility personally. Then, as the Honorary Chairman has instructed, I will arrange another meeting for you."

This meeting was over.

17

Noda

I left Tokyo right after breakfast. Narusawa-san said he lived in the suburbs, so he would not come into Tokyo to meet me for the ride to Noda. Instead, he would meet me at the factory and be my personal guide.

I arrived at Noda station a little before noon. To my surprise, it was even smaller than I thought, almost like the tiny railway outposts I had seen in the far north of Japan ages ago, places where the train station is a single wooden building in the middle of nowhere with a road in front of it but not a shop or hotel or gas station anywhere in sight. Here, the station was two buildings, with a small convenience store next door. There was a small local intersection, with what looked like two shops on one street and a couple of restaurants on another, all closed at the moment.

If this was a company town, so to speak, the original head-quarters of one of the world's largest food companies, we might expect it to look like a bustling metropolis with every store, street, and office a dazzling tribute to the company that owned it all. Instead, Noda looked like any other sleepy little town, where people went about their business in a quiet way. I knew from my research that the Mogi family had lived here for generations, that their company had long ago contributed heavily to build the rail line that brought me here, as well as a hospital and many other public facilities that made Noda a more livable community. The histories of the Mogi family and Noda city were so inextricably intertwined that it was hard to know where one stopped and the other began.

Narusawa said all I had to do was to get off the train and walk towards the silos with the Kikkoman logo. When I looked up, I could see a row of half a dozen grey steel silos off in the distance, with a giant red Kikkoman logo floating near the top. As I walked closer, I noticed that there were really a dozen silos, not six. And when I looked behind me, on the other side of the station, I saw a matching double six-pack of grey silos and another giant Kikkoman building off to one side, looking like a big warehouse. This part was just like I'd imagined: everything over two stories tall that I could see from the station had a Kikkoman logo on it.

I followed my instructions and kept walking in the direction of the first set of silos I had seen. Soon I reached the entrance to the Noda plant. There was a little guard station just inside. I gave my name to the guards, and they directed me to the main building about a hundred meters straight ahead. As I approached, I detected a faint smell that I knew well. Perhaps most tourists would not recognize it, but I knew the smell of *shoyu* brewing.

As I walked across the parking lot, I noticed on my right a small, very traditional Japanese building, with a hewn-stone foundation and above it bright white walls, and a tiled roof. A small, shallow moat surrounded the building and a curved vermillion bridge led up to its heavy wooden door. I had a pretty good idea what this small building on the factory grounds must be, but I thought I would ask Narusawa, because I saw him standing in front of the main entrance to the plant, waiting for me. He was wearing a blue blazer and casual slacks and, I was relieved to see, an open polo shirt. If he had worn a shirt and tie for this occasion, I would have felt like a customer being "managed" by an official company rep. But Ron Yates had assured me that he was no PR flack. His attire and his manner suggested that he really wanted this to be a casual and enjoyable experience. I was grateful for that.

We shook hands and almost immediately I asked about the little building I had just passed.

"It looks like something out of an old samurai movie," I said.

"Yes, perhaps it does." He was laughing now as he guided me inside. "That is the *Goyogura*, which literally translates as something like 'Imperial storehouse.' It may look centuries old, but it was actually built in 1939 to preserve the old-fashioned process of making soy sauce. We can go there later if you like."

We stepped inside the main building, and the cool air massaged my face. Suddenly I was in no hurry to go outside again to visit the Goyogura or anything else. I paused to mop my forehead with a handkerchief. I noticed that we were standing at the end of a long hall whose walls were decorated with photos and drawings. We walked down the hall, past pictures of salt and wheat and soybeans on one wall and dozens of smiling children from all over the world eating different dishes on the opposite wall. The photos of happy kids surrounded a bit of text called the Kikkoman Promise: *To fill the world with the joys of food by delivering wholehearted flavor.* The slogan was a bit stiff, no doubt an attempt to stay close to the Japanese original, but the spirit of the message came through loud and clear. Kikkoman was all about using food to help people enjoy life more. That seemed close to the message I had heard wherever I went.

At the end of the hall the walkway turned right, leading to a spacious lobby. A group of noisy parents and children was just forming up as a tour guide ushered them into a small theater off to the right. The guide was a woman in her thirties with a headset microphone and a small amplified speaker slung over her shoulder, like an old-fashioned portable radio or CD stereo. When she spoke, her voice was clear and easy to hear, nothing like the sound of a blaring PA system. All very professional, I thought.

"All the tours generally start with a video," Narusawa explained.

I said I wanted to see what it was like, and he took me up to the entrance to the little theater and gently opened the door so we wouldn't bother the visitors inside. I stood in the doorway for a minute or two and watched the show. It featured a lot of animated characters representing wheat and soybeans and enzymes and bacteria, all doing their job. Even the chemical processes of proteins being broken down were graphically explained so that both children and their parents would easily understand them. It wasn't condescending, just clear and memorable. Unfortunately, I have a short attention span where cartoons in a foreign language are concerned.

"Enough," I said, "Let's see the good stuff." And we moved on..

I'd been to several Kikkoman factories already, so I knew the layout and the process fairly well, but this was a whole different experience, not like any of the other plants I'd visited. It wasn't just that this was a large-scale facility; it was also more visitor-friendly — there were enclosed hallways just so tour groups could walk in and around the production areas and enjoy learning about how *shoyu* is made without bothering anyone on the plant floor. There were large, mural-sized posters on the brightly colored walls and stand-up displays where visitors could "sniff test" the aromas of different stages of *moromi* aging, and wall-mounted videos here and there to better show off key points in the manufacturing process.

There was a series of numbered murals to explain the production process in detail. The first one showed the raw ingredients — soybeans from the U.S., wheat from the U.S., and salt from Mexico. So, most of the *shoyu* made in Noda came from imported ingredients? I didn't know that. And obviously, in addition to all the huge purchases made domestically for the Wisconsin and California plants, Kikkoman was also a major importer of U.S. agricultural products.

One wall poster showed greatly enlarged photos of the three microscopic elements that must be added to these ingredients to produce fermentation: yeast, lactic acid bacteria, and the famous Kikkoman aspergillus mold. For the first time, I saw a picture of the latter, which looked like a tiny head of broccoli. So that was the family's secret ingredient from centuries past?

We walked down the hall to poster No. 2, which showed how the raw ingredients were processed. Narusawa pointed at the pictures.

"In Walworth and Folsom and the other plants, I think people showed you big tanks, or at least rooms where this processing is being done. Here, we explain everything with these drawings, because looking at the outside of this equipment is not very informative.

"You remember that the soybeans we buy are screened and then steamed. Do you remember why they have to be heated?"

"To make them softer," I said.

"That's more of a result than a goal, but yes, it does make them softer. The real purpose is to change their chemical structure. Soybeans are full of proteins, but in their natural state those proteins aren't likely to ferment. In the same way, wheat is loaded with starch, but it, too, is not ready for the fermentation process. We steam the soybeans and roast and crush the wheat to make it easier to start the enzymatic reactions that are part of the fermentation process. Then, once we add the Kikkoman seed mold, things begin to happen."

We had been walking slowly, and now Narusawa stopped in front of two long glass windows, similar to ones I had seen at every plant overseas. I already knew what was inside: the big, circular *koji* tank. I also remembered from visits to other Kikkoman plants that this was always viewed through a window, just as I was doing now. No one wanted uninvited germs floating around in the *koji* room.

"The *koji* room is usually kept dark," he said, pointing to a small video screen up on the wall. "To help visitors understand what's going on, we have this video, which is much brighter and easy to see." The video was running in a loop, showing a well-lit, *koji* tank, a shallow vat about 16 meters in diameter, turning slowly while an arm with a conveyor belt moved in and out, depositing layers of mixed ingredients evenly over the surface of the *koji* bed. I looked at the real thing through the window. It was dark inside, and I agreed that the video was a big improvement for visitors.

"We keep the *koji* in a warm, humid environment, we monitor the temperature and humidity very carefully, and we stir it slowly," my guide explained, although I remembered this part well from my very first experience at Walworth. "In that environment, the mold multiplies and produces various enzymes. Those enzymes help to break down the proteins and starches in the mix. This is the beginning of the fermentation process."

There was something I'd never asked before. "What exactly is the *koji* mold, the special Kikkoman mold everyone talks about?"

"It's part of a very common family of molds called Aspergillus. As you know, molds are a type of fungus. Aspergillus is very common, and people breathe in its spores every day."

"Is it dangerous?" I asked without thinking.

"Not for you and me," he replied casually. "In very rare cases, certain highly sensitive people might have reactions to it, just as some people have bad reactions to sunlight or to the thousands of varieties of germs that you and I breathe in every day. There is nothing in Aspergillus that is any threat to your health."

We continued on, climbing up to the second floor.

"I'm sure you remember what happens to the *koji*," he asked, like a teacher helping a student review for some test.

"Sure. It sits there for three days, then it gets doused with salt water and sent to fermentation tanks for the best part of a year."

"Exactly. We add brine — salt water — and mix it up. Until now, the *koji* has been dry, but adding the brine makes it more of a light-colored mud. That is what we call *moromi*, and it is pumped into giant tanks to ferment."

As we walked along, Narusawa stopped in front of a large picture window with a view outside. Some distance across from the building where we stood, I could see several gleaming stainless steel tanks, not as tall or as dirty as the raw ingredients tanks I had seen when approaching the plant. These were shiny, and ribbed, and tapered at the top. Narusawa explained that these were the *shikomi*, or fermentation tanks, the vats where the wet *moromi* mash would sit for months on end.

"That is where the real fermentation takes place," he explained. "After a couple of months, the light-colored mash starts to darken and begins to develop fragrances and flavors that resemble soy sauce. After half a year, the mash gets darker still. We continually mix the mash by puffing up air from the bottom, and we carefully control the temperature by circulating hot or cold water around the outer edge of the tank. Basically, it's a very slow, natural process that we can control but never synthesize.

"When all the raw materials and microbes have completely mixed and acted on each other, the result is a symphony of hundreds of subtle fragrances and flavors like nothing else in the world. Sometime, just for comparison, you should taste soy sauce that is made the other way — with a quick, inexpensive chemical process, avoiding all this time-consuming fermentation."

"Tastes like chemicals?" I ventured.

"Worse. It tastes thin and artificial and lacking in any depth of flavor or aroma."

If Narusawa were a paid PR guy, I wouldn't say anything, but he had been upfront with me and I felt I could talk to him as a friend rather than as a representative of Kikkoman. So I stated what seemed like an obvious fact, especially here in Asia: "Of course, I agree with you, but don't tens of millions of people use that chemically produced soy sauce every day? And they don't seem to mind it."

"Quite right." He seemed almost grateful that I had splashed some other perspective on the discussion while he was busy eulogizing the virtues of natural soy sauce. "However, you won't find any gourmet chefs using it, not in North America or Europe or even in Asia. And remember, those tens of millions of consumers who have not yet enjoyed our style of soy sauce are *not* in any way our competition. They are all future customers." His face lit up again. Was he making a joke or a prediction? Or both?

Resuming his tour guide demeanor, he pointed down to the floor where we were standing. There was a large, orange semi-circle painted there, and we were right in the middle of it.

"Just for your reference, this is the size of the biggest of those tanks over there."

I looked down. Thirty or forty people could easily stand in this half-circle where we were now. And this was the diameter of one of those big *moromi* tanks? There were no visual aids like this at plants overseas. "Just how big is it?" I asked.

"The big one is 330 kiloliters."

I tried to do the calculation in my head. I knew that a kilo-liter is over 250 U.S. gallons, about the amount of water in a child's swimming pool, which is a lot of water. Multiply that times 330... "That's about 80,000 gallons!" I blurted out.

"About 87,000," he replied with calm, Spock-like precision. "And that's only one of the tanks. We have a lot of *moromi* fer-menting at any one time."

We walked on, up a staircase to the second floor and down another hallway. Now we were at a different window, smaller and on an interior wall. From this vantage point I could see one of my favorite parts of the process, the filtering and pressing room. I always enjoyed watching the light brown filtration cloth flow out of a giant spool on the floor and pass upwards towards the ceiling, being evenly drenched with *moromi,* and then being neatly folded by mechanical arms into a tightly confined tower two stories high. The difference is that here we were standing behind glass, outside spectators to a process that I had seen up close on my tours at some of the foreign plants. But there were benefits to this child-and-housewife-friendly enclosed tour. For example, there were samples of the filtration cloth out on tables for visitors to pick up, touch, and pass around. I didn't hesitate. It was thinner than I'd expected, but very tough, like synthetic canvas.

"Nylon," Narusawa explained. "We used to use linen, but this is stronger. The filter cloth inside is almost 3 meters wide and the spool is 2.8 kilometers — about a mile and a half long." He pointed to the cloth moving smoothly through the system, being folded in neat sections by machine, and stacked hundreds of layers high. "First, the weight of two stories of piled *moro-mi*-soaked cloth presses out a lot of the sediment," he said. "Then the entire stack is gently moved over to the pressing machine over there for mechanical pressing." He pointed to one of the large metal towers to one side of the room.

"The hydraulic press squeezes that big stack of folded cloth very slowly, exerting a pressure of 2,000 tons. That removes whatever fluids were not already excreted by the gravity method. You may have seen before that the *moromi* that is applied to the filtration cloth is a dark brown sludge like mud. The pressing process here takes almost a whole day for one stack, but even then the result is not clear *shoyu*."

Yes, I'd seen it all before, but it was still impressive. Then I remembered what I had learned overseas. The dry sediment that is squeezed out by the press is called "soy cake" in English, and that can be used as livestock feed. But there was another by-product, called soy oil, which was still a part of the fluid collected after filtration. I wondered about that.

Narusawa walked me down the hall to an outside window and pointed to another series of large tanks. "The filtered, raw *shoyu* goes into those tanks to settle for about three days. Because the soy oil is a different density, it floats to the top. Most of the solid wastes have been pressed out as soy cake, but there is still a small amount of sediment, which naturally sinks to the bottom. What is left in between is pure, unpasteurized soy sauce, what we call *raw shoyu*."

"How do you dispose of unwanted byproducts like soy oil?" I asked.

He laughed. "We don't dispose of very much in this plant — everything is reused, recycled, or sold off, like the soy cake, for someone else to use. We use the soy oil as fuel in the boilers that heat the raw ingredients. As I'm sure you noticed in Wisconsin and elsewhere, all our plants are very environmentally friendly. *Shoyu* is born from natural ingredients, and we really do think of Nature as our vital partner in this process. That's not some slogan dreamed up by our PR people, it's true. We work very hard to minimize our environmental impact, and if you look closely, I think you'll be surprised at how thoroughly we keep that promise. Even the bottles and caps we use are made of plastics that can be easily recycled, and the cartons we pack them in are designed to use the minimum amount of materials.

"Kikkoman starts with natural ingredients like wheat and soybeans and salt, then processes them using other natural ingredients, then waits a long time for Nature to do its work, which allows us to produce a very pure, wholesome product. The by-products of that process are put to good use, and we even clean the air that circulates inside the plant before we let it outside again."

This was not the first time I had heard about Kikkoman's commitment to leaving a very small environmental footprint, but in my previous research I had been focusing more on the process itself. Now that I knew how *shoyu* was made, I could focus on other things, and how a giant factory like this works to protect the environment was a very important "other thing."

I also realized that the overseas plants always needed to be concerned about visitor safety, which is something no one can guarantee absolutely, and also with the small but very real risk of some well-meaning visitor showing up with a head cold or something worse and introducing germs or a virus into the plant. One nasty sneeze could in theory contaminate the soy sauce and/or the equipment, which would be catastrophic. That explained why the plants I had visited went to such great lengths to see that all visitors wore special clothing, hair nets, beard nets, shoe coverings, and so on, kept them at a safe distance from the machinery, and never ever let them come close to the ingredients or the product until it was sealed in bottles.

Thinking back, I had seen *koji* rooms through windows and seen *moromi* tanks, but never the *koji* or *moromi*, up close. Noda had gone one step further, insulating the entire production process end-to-end from outside contaminants brought in by visitors. And I had to admit that, much as I missed walking the plant floors with the local Production Manager, chatting with the workers we happened to meet, it was much easier to take this simple, educational tour with a knowledgeable guide and lots of pictures, text, and video to augment what you could see through the windows. It didn't take long before I realized that I had seen the best of both worlds in my travels, and I was (and still am) very grateful for that.

All too soon, we had wandered back to the lobby where we started. I had enjoyed the tour and Narusawa's detailed explanations along the way, but now I wanted to see the one place I hadn't visited yet. I told him I wanted a tour of the *Goyogura* next door.

He thought a moment.

"All right, I think we can do that." He pulled out his cellphone and made a quick call. Then we both set off along a path of bamboo trees for the little red bridge leading to the small building that looked like it just came through a time tunnel straight from 17th century Edo (old Tokyo).

Narusawa walked up to the big wooden double door that formed the entrance to the old building. The big doors were bolted from the inside and so heavy that I doubt we could have opened them if they were not locked. But he stooped down and pushed a square section of the door that came up roughly to my chest. It was a door-within-a-door, also something from an earlier era. He pushed it open and stepped through, holding it for me to follow. I managed to whack my head trying to step through gracefully. I noticed an elderly caretaker standing inside, who closed and locked the mini-portal as soon as I was through.

Inside was a short walkway to the entrance, all nicely landscaped with bamboo trees, just like the exterior leading up to the building. Stepping inside the glass doors to the Goyogura, I noticed the mixture of old and new: inside was a simple museum-like display of equipment used a century ago to prepare the raw ingredients. Behind it I could see the stone foundations and spotless white walls of the exterior. So we were inside the compound and inside the entrance, but not yet truly inside the old building.

Narusawa took me along the display of the ancient equipment, narrating as we walked.

"The ingredients and the basic process for making *shoyu* have not changed much over the centuries. Only the technology has changed, which more than anything else, has increased efficiency and production capacity" he said. "Even in the Edo period [starting around 1600], soy sauce was made from wheat and soybeans, salt and pure water. The biggest difference between now and then is the quantities of ingredients that could be processed at one time.

"For example, soybeans were put into a metal cauldron like this—" he tapped a heavy-looking grey tank about four feet high and three feet wide with a thick metal lid held in place by a dozen strong latches. "—and then soaked overnight. Then the water was drained out—" he pointed to a small pipe protruding near the bottom of the tank, "—and the beans were steamed, just like we do today. The wheat was roasted in a device like this—" he pointed to the next item in the line, a short brick oven-like structure with a metal box and feed chute propped on top and a couple of temperature gauges and pressure valves sticking up, "—then the ingredients were sprayed with the Kikkoman seed starter, that is, the special Aspergillus mold, and carefully mixed by hand."

There was a small open space with shovels and a dozen empty wooden trays about an inch deep that Narusawa informed me would be used to hold this mix when it went into the *koji* room.

I stepped back and looked at all the equipment in this display. None of it was large or impressive in terms of scale. Quite the contrary, it made me realize that until the early twentieth century *shoyu* was made in small quantities entirely by hand. It was heavy, physical labor and probably unbearably hot, not only in the summer, but for months afterward, as much of the process involved cooking raw ingredients that could only be harvested in the fall, then heating the *koji*, keeping the *moromi* warm, and finally, heating the finished product. To the average farmer in Noda, it might have looked slightly better than rice farming, but not by much.

Narusawa was motioning for us to step inside the building proper. There was an opening in the stone wall, and we passed through it. It was much smaller and a bit darker than I had imagined, much like a real *shoyu*-making facility must have looked like centuries ago, although back then it would have been lit by candles and must have been even darker than this. Narusawa showed me twin giant vats made of Japanese cedar (*sugi*) their vertical staves wrapped tightly with five bamboo ropes so thick I could barely get my two hands around one. But the real treats were up the small staircase. To the left of the stairs, he showed me the *koji* room, a tiny red brick sauna with piles of the wooden trays I had seen downstairs stacked on both sides of the brick walls and a two-foot-tall metal stove, actually more like a fire box, in the middle.

"The *koji* mix is put into these trays," he said, "And then it is heated with a fire in that stove. We monitor the temperature and humidity and adjust them by opening that window in the back." What I had taken for the doors to some kind of wooden cabinet mounted in the rear wall were in fact the shutters to open a window to the outside. The whole room was so small I doubted that two large men could even work in there comfortably.

To the right of the stairs was a glass wall, and beyond it the open tops of ten vats of *moromi* that must extend down to the floor below. Now I was very aware of the glass partition allowing visitors to stand only a meter from an open vat of fermenting mash. No hair net or surgical mask needed; a kid could sneeze in here and not affect the product on the other side at all. The walls and floor of the room on the other side, and the outer few inches of the vats protruding from the floor were all painted a bright crimson, while the interior of each vat was black.

The milk chocolate color of the *moromi* in the tanks told me it was still in the first couple of months of aging. I could see a window in the back of the room, clearly a means to aerate the mash naturally and modify temperature and humidity depending on the weather. Remembering that the giant steel *moromi* tanks at the main plant use air jets to mix the mash, I asked how the *moromi* in these vats was stirred. Narusawa pointed to a pair of long wooden implements hanging on the wall nearby. They looked like oars for a large rowboat. "Workers had to stir the mix by hand, and I assure you, in the early stages at least, it was a slow, hard, back-breaking job. For hygiene reasons, we don't have men go in there and stir each vat any more. It would take a week or two each time, and it would not do the job as well as using air—" he pointed to one of the vats in the interior. I could see small bubbles breaking on the surface. I nodded and we walked back down the small staircase.

Down below, I saw an early mechanical press for squeezing out the filtration cloth and more giant cedar barrels where the soy sauce was manually separated from the soy oil, then heated and pasteurized in a caldron. There was also a small glass tank with pipes running in and out. A sign explained that this was a measuring tank used to check the finished product before it was bottled or, as was the custom from ancient times until just after WWII, put into small wooden casks (*taru*) with bamboo wrapping on the bottom and a big Kikkoman logo on the side, their lids tied down and the whole thing ornamentally wrapped with thick rope. I pointed to one on display and commented about how artistically they were made and wrapped.

"They look beautiful," Narusawa said, "And they worked fairly well for centuries, which tells us how effective they were. But once bottling became standard, and especially once airtight plastic bottles appeared, the wooden casks had to be retired."

We had come to the end of the very short tour. Once again, I was surprised what a small facility this was and yet how much of the old process was still on display. I paused as we were once again stooping to pass through the little half-door to exit the museum area, because I remembered that the *moromi* tanks I had seen upstairs were all full.

"Do you actually make *shoyu* here?" I asked. "I think it's a wonderful thing to show people, but isn't it ferociously expensive to make soy sauce by hand using this old process? Just for an educational display? Does that really make sense?"

"Using the old process is only part of the cost." He pointed back at the main factory as we stepped back outside. "Most of the ingredients that go into that process are imported. We bring in high-quality soybeans and wheat and salt from overseas. But all the ingredients here—" he pointed to the little building we had just exited, "—come from Japan. Japanese soybeans, Japanese wheat, and Japanese salt. Of course it is more expensive, but it also makes a very special product."

"And who buys that very special product?" I asked half in jest.

"The Imperial Household," he said with unexpected gravity.

"What? So you are making *shoyu* here for the Emperor and Empress of Japan?" Suddenly I remembered the sign out front: *Imperial Storehouse.*

He bowed his head slightly and in a softer voice said, "We are very proud to be able to make products that are selected by the Imperial Household Agency." His English was following his posture now, taking on a decidedly Japanese tone.

I got the message. This was not just a working museum or merely a PR device, but a real, functioning part of the Noda complex, and one of which the company was rightfully proud. What a perfect way to end a tour.

I suggested that it might be time for me to head back to Tokyo. He agreed, and said he would accompany me back into the city.

18

An Educational Train Ride

***N**arusawa and I walked back to the little Noda train station and waited for a train heading in the general direction of Tokyo.

While we were standing there, I mentioned that I was glad I had seen the company's operations in Noda. He began to chuckle. "You have seen only a fraction of the company's operations in Noda," he said. "But at least it's a good start."

Puzzled, I asked what else there was.

"To start with, there's the bottling plant and also other production facilities, plus our R&D center, biotech research labs, a few other buildings of historical significance, and an excellent museum that would tell you everything you could want to know about the history of soy sauce."

Now I began to see the bigger picture — Noda was the ancestral home of the companies that eventually became Kikkoman Corporation, but Tokyo is the capital of Japan and the right place to be if you want to do business.

He continued: "Also, not all of the company's businesses have been centered in Noda. One in particular is based on the other side of Tokyo, in the hills of Yamanashi Prefecture."

That stumped me. Yamanashi was known for three things — Mt. Fuji, mineral water, and fruit orchards. Its grapes and peaches were famous nationwide and sold for ridiculous prices in the food sections of Tokyo department stores. What did any of that have to do with Kikkoman?

"Yamanashi has the best vineyards in Japan," he explained. "That is where we created our wine business."

"Wine business?" Now I was surprised. I remembered that there was a big wine boom in the 1990s when I was living in Tokyo, and people said it had been growing steadily for a couple of decades. In addition to lots of independent wine importers, all the big Japanese beer companies started importing wines from around the world, and by the time I was getting ready to leave Japan the market was flooded with imports from France, Italy, Spain, California, Chile, Argentina and more. It sounded as if Kikkoman was one more company jumping on the band-wagon, and I ran that past Narusawa to see if my impression was fairly accurate.

"Not... exactly..." he said, and paused for effect. "To put it simply, we started the bandwagon. What we think of as the wine 'boom' started in the 1990s, but its roots go back to at least the 1970s. And even before that, back in 1962, Kikkoman set up its wine business, called Mann's Wine Company, and unlike other firms, it was focused on producing rather than simply importing. It grew its own grapes in Yamanashi Prefecture, which was already famous for growing grapes when Mann's set up its first vineyard.

"Back then, most Japanese not only had no interest in European-style wines, they actually disliked the flavor of those wines. Around the time that Mann's was established, the total amount of Western wine imported each year equaled roughly one tablespoon per person — not the beginnings of a wine boom by any stretch of the imagination."

I could see that we were straying from my main interest, the soy sauce business, but any discussion of wine catches my attention, and the idea of Kikkoman getting involved in making wine seemed somewhat odd, so I asked him, "Then why start a wine business?"

"Because even back then, Kikkoman understood the need to diversify. Other companies were diversifying into all sorts of businesses unrelated to their core business. Kikkoman chose a different path. Our idea was to diversify, both domestically and internationally, but to stay close to things we knew well.

"In staying close to our core business, we also looked at our strengths, which obviously involve fermentation. We could have easily started a beer company, but Japan's beer market was already well served at that time. The opportunities for a new beer company would have been very limited. However, the wine market was, as I said, very, very small.

"I can't imagine how you could get a whole country to start drinking wine if they didn't even like wine to begin with," I said, now becoming caught up in his story.

"I said it was an opportunity." He looked out the window, too. "The company understood it as first of all, a marketing problem, and that, too, is part of our core competence. Just as we successfully showed Americans the pleasures of using *shoyu*, we showed Japanese that they could enjoy drinking wine, not only in restaurants, but at home, instead of beer or sake."

"And then the wine boom grew?" I asked.

"Not exactly. It took time... decades, in fact. Sales didn't begin to take off until after the World Expo in Osaka in 1970."

"What did the Expo have to do with it?" I wondered.

"The Osaka Expo was a follow-up to the Tokyo Olympics in '64. It was a chance for Japan to stand proudly on the world stage and show off its achievements. It also meant that thousands of foreigner tourists poured into the big cities, so there was a growing sense of internationalism. For more than a decade, many Japanese had wanted to look more Western, go to Western movies, listen to Western music, and eat more Western foods. The Osaka Expo became a promotion of Japanese culture to Western visitors and a display of Western culture to Japanese people. Kikkoman set up a restaurant at the Expo, and we served both red and white wine with the meals, Western style. The food and wine pairing created an ambience of sophistication and modernism that was exactly what Japanese people were looking for.

"After the Expo was over, the trend towards a more sophisticated, more urban, more 'international' lifestyle was ready to take off. And drinking wine, both at home and in restaurants, became an integral part of that image. Kikkoman launched a huge ad campaign to show that wine was not only something that businessmen could enjoy in fancy restaurants when they were entertaining important clients, but something good to be enjoyed at home with their wives. One of our ads showed pictures of a popular Kabuki actor drinking wine over dinner with his wife. That in itself was a radical step."

I could imagine. Even today, equality between men and women in Japan exists only on law books. However, thirty or forty years ago, when men were expected to work long hours six days a week, forego vacations, and play golf on Sundays while their wives managed their households and waited patiently for their exhausted husbands to return, it was almost scandalous to say that a man should enjoy life at home with his spouse.

Narusawa continued: "In the end, we encouraged Japanese consumers to try wine in much the same way as we encouraged Western consumers to try *shoyu*. The results in both cases were gratifying. Not overnight successes by any means, but as you know, Kikkoman is a company with a long history, which means we have learned the value of combining strategy and patience. We are always prepared to take a long view to growing a market so long as our strategy is sound and our sales growth is steady. That is exactly what happened with Mann's Wine. We basically created a mass market where there was very little demand before, we advertised our products heavily, and we made sure that they were readily available to consumers.

"In short, our expansion into the wine business was nothing like an opportunistic investment. It was a smart, strategic step in a long-term plan for diversification."

I had to ask the blunt, journalistic question.

"So, is Kikkoman responsible for the wine boom in Japan?"

Narusawa shifted position uneasily.

"I am not an expert on social trends or marketing, nor was I actively involved in our wine business in any way, so I am not the right person to comment. What I can tell you are simple facts. When Mann's Wine was created, there was virtually no market for Western-style wine in Japan. In just one decade, we created consumer interest in the product, greatly expanded distribution channels, and developed major advertising campaigns. Over the next two decades, from 1973 to 1993, wine consumption in Japan increased about seven times. And Mann's Wine's annual production in those first three decades increased roughly 100 times to meet the huge growth in demand.

"No one would say that Kikkoman single-handedly created the wine boom. I think we have talked too much about wine already — it is really only a small part of our domestic business. What I wanted you to see is how winemaking is a perfect example of a company leveraging its core competence — not only its production strengths, but also its advertising and marketing strengths — to diversify strategically."

Okay, I got that. Still, I enjoyed the short digression. It was interesting to get a new perspective on the wine boom of the late twentieth century and to see that it wasn't foreign winemakers so much as a domestic foods company that brought about the change. From my meager understanding of the way things get done in Japan, that was a much more believable story.

But if getting into the wine business was a purely domestic move, and even then not a huge one, what other types of diversification were important to the company?

"One of the important ones is biotechnology," he continued. "As you know, Kikkoman had the first real laboratory in the domestic food sector almost a hundred years ago. The company's R&D in certain areas is world-class. As a result, Kikkoman's biotech researchers have created and commercialized a number of useful products that are currently at work in industries here and overseas."

"Okay," I said. "What else? Biotech is interesting, but I know there's something bigger and also international. I saw a big Del Monte logo on one of the Kikkoman warehouses back in Noda, and I meant to ask about it but forgot. What's it doing there?"

"Yes, I was saving that. When we talk about diversification, we should certainly talk about Del Monte. You already know the Del Monte name, I assume?"

I nodded. It was a household name in the U.S. from way back when.

"In its more than 100 years in business, Del Monte has become a leader in the packaged food industry and one of the world's premium brands. It is best known for tomato products, but also for a wide range of canned fruits and vegetables—"

"Wait, so Kikkoman is tied up with Del Monte?"

"Yes we are, in a very significant way. But let me put this in the perspective of diversification, because that's what we're really talking about. Go back to 1963, the year after we created Mann's Wine, and try to grasp how long ago that was — John F. Kennedy was still president, the Tokyo Olympics were still a year away, and the Beatles were unknown in the United States.

"Kikkoman saw that Western foods were more than a passing fad. The trend was still just beginning, but Kikkoman saw the future very clearly. And so, in 1963 it created a subsidiary to select, pack, and distribute Western foods in Japan.

One of the key product lines was tomato-based items, so they obtained a license from Del Monte Corporation in the U.S. to produce both ketchup and tomato juice locally under the Del Monte brand. The strategy was very successful, and Kikkoman soon captured a large share of the domestic market for tomato-based products.

"But that was only the beginning. In 1990, the firm acquired the rights to the Del Monte brand name for all products throughout the Pacific, from Japan to Australia and all of Asia except the Philippines. It was a huge coup for Kikkoman and a major step in the company's diversification. Today, we operate Del Monte production plants in China and Thailand and have a Del Monte sales base in Singapore to manage this division's operations. Our Overseas Foods segment includes a separate Del Monte division. It is not as big as soy sauce, of course, but it makes a significant contribution to our consolidated sales and profits."

I agreed that the tie-up with Del Monte was an excellent business strategy even if Kikkoman did not need to diversify. The company had done well to develop both its domestic wine business and its Asia-based Del Monte brand business. Looking out the window, I realized that we were almost back to Akihabara, the final stop on this line.

"There's one more big one we haven't mentioned, and we don't really have time to discuss it, but you already know the company," Narusawa said.

I looked blank.

"JFC. You met with them in Düsseldorf and must have talked about them a little when you were at Kikkoman Sales USA in San Francisco."

I told him I had visited JFC in Europe but had not gone to LA to see their U.S. headquarters. Was JFC really a big contributor to Kikkoman's bottom line? And how did that diversification come about? I knew we didn't have much time to talk, but...

"Back in 1969 Kikkoman invested in something called Japan Foods Corporation, which about a decade later became JFC International. In '69, Japan Foods Corporation was already a major supplier of Oriental foods on the West Coast of the U.S. By acquiring JFC, Kikkoman not only gained access to a rapidly expanding retail chain just before the years of increasing interest in Asian food were beginning, but it also diversified its revenue base far beyond *shoyu*. Today, JFC has eleven branches in the U.S. and three in Canada, plus separate sales offices in both countries and a sales office in Mexico. And, as you already know, there are JFC operations all over Europe, Moscow, Hong Kong, Singapore, China, Australia, and beyond. In addition to branded imports, the company has its own brands, and it now represents around 10,000 different products, all of them Asian in flavor, but not necessarily imported from Asia. For example, JFC has contracts to produce its own house-brand rice in California."

I remembered seeing pallets stacked with JFC rice at the distributor's mini-warehouse that I visited in Singapore.

"As to how much of a contribution that makes to the bottom line, we book that segment under our Overseas Foods Wholesale business, and it has been growing at an average annual rate of nine percent for the past decade."

I did a quick mental calculation and noted, "That means their sales are doubling roughly every eight years. Not bad!"

We were just gliding into the station now. It was a big, modern, underground complex typical of Japan's newer train lines. Narusawa looked at me as we stepped off the train and started towards the escalator.

"That business segment now contributes more than one-third of Kikkoman's total global sales. How important is our diversification strategy? If you can build an expansion business into a unit that accounts for a third of your total worldwide sales, that's a successful strategy."

I thanked him and said I needed to meet someone at the Foreign Press Club.

"Wait! We haven't even talked about our soy milk or health food or several other ventures that are part of our more recent business diversification."

I shook his hand and thanked him. Between wine, bio-tech, Del Monte, and JFC, I felt I had a pretty good handle on Kikkoman's diversification strategy. My main focus now was on the man who had told me to go to Noda in the first place. I wanted a second chance to talk to the company's living DNA.

"I hope you haven't forgotten that Mr. Mogi said he wanted to talk to me again, after I'd been to Noda," I added, hopefully.

"I hadn't forgotten," Narusawa said softly, his understatement making me a bit embarrassed for even mentioning it. "I will contact you when something is arranged."

We shook hands as friends and parted. I was starting to feel that I had a better grasp on the company's history and growth. But two big questions were still percolating in my brain: How did the miracle in Walworth really come about, and what was left for Mogi to accomplish now that he had made Kikkoman a popular worldwide brand?

I planned to get the answer to at least one of those questions at our next session before our face time ran out.

Meeting The DNA - Part II

19

I received an email from Narusawa a few days later. He said that he had talked to the Honorary Chairman's current secretary and tried to work out a schedule so that I could see him again soon. This was way beyond what I had hoped for when I first came to Japan, so I was already excited by the news. I called Narusawa to tell him that I would be happy to meet Mogi anywhere and anytime, morning, noon or night.

Narusawa said he could not predict what time the appointment should be. But later that same day I got another brief mail: "Friday morning, same place, 08:00."

I replied that I would be there and also, being an impertinent foreigner, asked if early morning was really the best time. Sure, I would get up and have three cups of coffee and be at the Kikkoman building by eight, but wasn't everyone just a little slow in the morning?

Narusawa's reply was to the point: "Not Mr. Mogi. He goes for a thirty-minute walk every morning. He says it makes him feel good. Then he comes to the office early and full of energy. You are actually lucky that he has agreed to meet you early."

—§—

I took a taxi to the Tokyo head office just as before, only this time Narusawa was waiting for me in the lobby. He was dressed in a dark suit, subdued tie, and polished shoes — exactly what you'd wear if you're going to be wandering around on the executive floor of any big Japanese company.

"Good morning," he greeted me, a bit formally. I guessed it was the suit and the thought of where we were going. He ushered me to the same elevator and upstairs to the same floor. A female employee was waiting in front of the elevator when the doors opened. She bowed in greeting, then escorted us to the same meeting room as before.

"The Honorary Chairman will be with you in just a moment," she said softly, bowing as she backed out of the room.

I was more relaxed than at the previous meeting. I immediately wandered over to the windows on the far side and gazed out at downtown Tokyo. I had just turned to Narusawa and was about to say something incisive about the hodgepodge of architecture that makes up the cityscape when the door sprang open and Mogi strode in with what I now took to be his usual sprightly gait. He looked even more energetic than at our previous encounter. He shook my hand vigorously, adjusted his grey, checked suit, and made himself comfortable in his favorite chair. He was barely seated when a cup of cool tea appeared on a tray beside him, but only after a cup was placed next to my chair. Of course! I was too nervous to pay attention to such details the last time I was here. Japanese protocol demands that I, a lowly writer from abroad, be served ahead of the Honorary

Chairman who practically built this company with his own two hands, because I was *o-kyaku-sama*, an honored guest. There are some things I will love about Japan all my life, and the genuine politeness people show to each other, regardless of rank or station in life, is one of my favorites.

In any case, this honored guest ignored his tea and instead picked up his notebook and pen. Mogi was looking up at me expectantly. As long as he wasn't looking at his watch, that was a plus, I thought. Still, I had learned long ago not to assume anything in an interview. Get the ground rules out in the open right away.

"Mr. Mogi," I began, my voice not as calm and relaxed as I'd thought, "What is our time frame here?"

He looked puzzled.

"How long can we talk this morning?"

He looked absentmindedly at his watch, perhaps remembering subsequent duties and appointments.

"Oh, I think we can chat for half an hour or so. Is that all right?"

I was overjoyed.

"That would be wonderful, sir. Let's get started..." Bad idea to jump right into a serious topic, I thought. Warm him up first. "Mr. Narusawa tells me that you go for a walk every morning."

"Yes, that's right. Every morning. I walk briskly for at least thirty minutes, longer when I can. It helps to wake me up, clear my mind, and get me ready for the day. I come to the office feeling full of energy. I feel *genki*!"

"I can see that," I said, not patronizing him at all. He really did look *genki* (energetic, full of life). "But your bio says you were born in 1935. Even with my poor math skills, that makes you over eighty now."

"And what's wrong with that?" he retorted, his humor lighting up his face. "I hardly even noticed when I turned sixty; a man still has a lot of work to do when he is sixty. And at seventy I was still strong and *genki*. Now that I am past eighty I am perhaps not so strong, but I am still *genki*!" He laughed out loud. I had to admit that I had interviewed executives at least a decade younger than Mogi who were already so far past their primes that they should not have been managing anything more serious than a shuffleboard game. Here was Yuzaburo Mogi, no longer the official president of the firm, but undoubtedly the most important voice in the company and the ultimate in-house advisor on any long-term global strategy. I hoped that I would be this *genki* when I was his age. I returned to my notes.

"Mr. Mogi, when we spoke last time you told me how the company came around to the momentous decision to build a soy sauce plant in America. That was in 1971. Only two years later you were standing at the grand opening of the new plant in Wisconsin. That seems a very short time from green light to ribbon cutting. And I am still curious why the first Japanese factory in the U.S. wasn't built in California, close to Japan and close to your sales office in San Francisco? Why the Midwest?"

"A good question," he said, obviously sorting through a jumble of memories and answers to similar questions that must have been asked many times. "Yes, we did move very fast in building that first plant, and the main reason is that I did not want to wait. In my mind, the decision had already been made back in the sixties. When Pennington came to visit me in 1970 was the first time I discussed it with him, but I had already decided much earlier. He understood that this was no passing fancy of mine, that I had thought about it seriously and examined all sorts of simulations. He knew me and knew that I was not being impulsive about such a large-scale project; he knew that once I resolved to make it happen, it would happen sooner or later, so he was quick to agree to help.

"In fact, he and I went to look at possible sites for the plant later that year, in 1970, which was before the Board even voted, before my proposal was even made. I had no doubt that the future of this company lay overseas, and particularly with expansion to North America.

"Obviously, we had strong ties to the West Coast, and particularly to California. At that time, there were not yet any Japanese factories there, but there were lots of Japanese and American-born Japanese living there, lots of people who spoke our language, shared our culture, and so on. Also, as you said, we had been operating a sales office in San Francisco for some time. As a result, many on our Board wanted to build the factory in California. I understood their feelings and did not disagree with any of their arguments. But I was opposed to the West Coast plan. I think my biggest objection had nothing to do with transportation or raw materials or tax incentives or anything of the kind. It was a gut feeling of mine..." He paused, his gaze now somewhere in the middle of the table between us as he searched his feelings and his memories.

"I felt it was important to create a feeling of *independence* for the new U.S. production facility. You can't run a business by remote control. In order to succeed, the company needed to be independent. I didn't want it tied to the head office's apron strings, and I think that was my biggest objection to the West Coast option."

He paused, took a sip of tea, then continued.

"I truly believed that our new business in America would grow and that Americans would gradually take to *shoyu*, and sales would rise. But we only had one shot at it. We couldn't run around building factories here and there all over the country, and if the first one was not a success, as you have already observed, it would have been disastrous for the parent company. So we had to pick the right location and build the right factory and hire the right workers and have everything go right from the very start. We needed to hit a home run our first time at bat. And I believed we could.

"Location was a very important factor for me: I felt that our first overseas plant needed to be centrally located and able to supply the whole country. We looked at the East Coast, but it was just too far away from markets out West. The West Coast had the same problems in reverse, and as I have said, I did not want to build the factory there because I was afraid it would be remotely managed from Tokyo. That only left the South, which was far from sources of raw materials, and the Midwest, which we didn't know much about.

"Pennington was very helpful there. He even contacted a law firm in southern Wisconsin that could help us with the process of scouting for places. That was Godfrey and Neshek's firm, and they soon became much more than just our legal counsel. In fact, those two partners became key players in helping to develop and implement our U.S. strategy. I would say that, together with Malcolm Pennington, Mick Neshek and Tom Godfrey were among the most important people helping Kikkoman to internationalize in the twentieth century. The four of us formed a team that did everything. We started with about sixty possible sites in several different states, including Michigan, Illinois, and Wisconsin, then boiled that down to six, mostly in Wisconsin. We visited the sites, we looked at them from every angle, we even flew over them in a helicopter, and finally, in the summer of '71, we thought we'd found the perfect site, a 200-acre dairy farm in the small town of Walworth, Wisconsin."

As he talked, the full story emerged. It was easy to understand why the Kikkoman board of directors preferred California, or at least the West Coast. There were many good reasons for a Japanese firm to set up shop there, and while Mogi and friends were looking at possible sites in the Midwest, Sony got a jump on them, setting up an assembly plant in San Diego. Within the next two decades, dozens of Japanese companies would rush into California for exactly the reasons that Mogi had named: proximity to Japan, easy air and sea transport, and a large local Japanese-speaking population. The decision to go to the Midwest seemed strange, even to me. Why would anyone want to build a new factory, especially one producing a Japanese food product, in one of the most rural parts of the country where people do not welcome outsiders even from other U.S. cities, much less "invaders" from overseas?

Mogi explained that Kikkoman had five key criteria for its first U.S. plant:

2138229752)Access to raw ingredients
2138229753)Access to clean water

2138229754)Access to local markets and a national transport hub

2138229755)Availability of a hardworking labor force with a strong work ethic

2138229756)A strong sense of community in the locale

The site in Walworth met all five: Soybeans were available right there in Wisconsin, wheat was grown nearby in North Dakota, and salt could be easily brought in from Canada. The quality of the water was famous, one of the reasons that Wisconsin was home to over 300 breweries a century ago. As for markets, Chicago was a little over an hour away, and it was also a central rail hub. From Chicago, goods could easily be shipped east, west or south. As for labor, the people in southern Wisconsin were mostly either full-time or part-time farmers, which meant they had a very strong work ethic, and the area around Walworth had a strong community spirit. In sum, it was an ideal location.

None of this was really news to me. The people in the Walworth plant had told me bits and pieces of the story and helped me to understand the area's attractions. I had to admit that it still seemed strange not to build the first overseas plant in California and then a second one in the Midwest instead of the other way around, but Mogi's comments about wanting to hit a home run the first time at bat made sense, as did wanting independence from the parent company. I decided to focus on the main story I wanted to pursue, the "miracle" in Walworth.

"Mr. Mogi, I understand the reasons why you wanted to set up the company in Wisconsin, and they certainly make good sense," I said. "What I'm really interested in is how you managed to build a successful company in the middle of the American heartland. In the early 1970s, most Americans were not wildly pro-Japanese, and farmers in a small southern Wisconsin community were likely to be even more insular, parochial, and even prejudiced."

What I was getting at was obviously a sensitive topic, and educated Japanese beat around the bush even when topics are not so sensitive. Yet the elephant in the room was the fact that WWII was still fresh in many people's minds. A hit TV series called *Combat!* had just finished a successful five-year run, and the Hollywood war epic *Tora! Tora! Tora!* was released just before Mogi went real estate shopping in the Midwest. There must have been quite a few WWII veterans living in Wisconsin and many more families who had lost loved ones during the war. It is hard for us today, in the twenty-first century, to imagine what life was like in 1970s America, much less what it was like in a rural farming town in Wisconsin. At the risk of being offensive, I asked Mogi directly about the lingering anti-Japanese sentiment.

"I don't think people were fundamentally anti-Japanese," he said. "I don't think they were angry at or worried about having Japanese neighbors, and I know they weren't against soy sauce because they didn't even know what it was." He was smiling, always genial even when confronting a rude foreign writer in his own office. "The real problem, you see, was the land itself. The farmland we bought was zoned as prime agricultural land, which meant we needed to rezone it, and that was the source of the opposition. Wisconsin has some of the best farmland in America, maybe in the world, and you don't just plow that under to make room for a big factory and parking lots and a railway line. That is almost blasphemy up there, and I could totally understand why the local people were against a factory, any factory, being built on such good land. A lot of the towns-people were committed to preserving the agricultural identity of the area, which they had every right to do."

"So what did you do?" I asked. "When I was in Walworth, Mick Neshek told me a little about the history, but he was a bit vague. He said that you 'persuaded the local people to be more receptive to your plan.' That didn't tell me much. How did you persuade them?"

He sat back, both hands together, fingertips joined, almost as if he were praying. "I went to a *lot* of meetings," he said slowly. "Big meetings and small meetings and everything in between. I think there were seven town meetings altogether, and I can't count all the meetings with farm groups, church groups, the local Grange, the Rotary Club, 4H Club, ladies' social clubs, you name it. I don't like to make speeches, and I certainly didn't back then, especially in English. But I did want to talk to people face-to-face and let them see who I was and know that I was being honest with them. I wanted them to see that Kikkoman was a group of good people who wanted to become caring members of their community.

"First, I tried to get them to understand that we were also an agricultural business, not their nightmare of a big manufac-turing firm. I explained that soy sauce was a natural product, essentially made of four things: wheat, soybeans, salt, and fresh water. I explained that our business involved brewing, which was a major industry in Wisconsin back then. Most of all, I promised them that we would be a pollution-free plant, that we were not going to build a factory, pollute the environment, and run away. Mick Neshek's partner, Tom Godfrey, even flew to Japan and went out to our Noda plant just so he could say that he had seen a Kikkoman factory in action, that it didn't smell bad and it didn't pollute the air or water. He and Mick helped me convince the locals that Kikkoman sincerely wanted to be a good neighbor and wanted to get along with the community. I explained that Kikkoman has been doing business in a little town called Noda for over 300 years, and we learned a long time ago that to survive and prosper you need to coexist with the local community. I said that, based on past experience, if Kikkoman and Walworth could get along well, we would both prosper. Of course, none of this was PR; everything I said was absolutely true."

"Yes, but did they believe it?"

"A lot of them did. But it took a lot of work, and not everyone was won over at first. I think the final vote on the zoning board was roughly 50 to 10 in our favor. In another sense, though, talking to so many people was actually a good thing. It convinced me that we needed to be even more American if we were to succeed. For example, I knew that the thinking in Tokyo would be to ship everything from Japan — people, parts, raw materials, and more — until the plant was up and running smoothly. And I saw immediately that such a plan would not work; it was exactly the *opposite* of what we should be doing. We needed to 'buy American' as much as possible, use American labor, and make every possible effort to blend into the community.

"That last one was an especially important point, but also a little difficult for our own staff to accept at first. I knew that our

Japanese staff would want to live together in a little Japanese enclave somewhere not too far from the factory. They would socialize with each other, not improve their English much, and naturally be seen as aloof and alien by the local community. I decided right then that I would not allow that. I decided to spread our staff out geographically, to physically separate them, let them live in local neighborhoods, talk to their neighbors, send their kids to local schools, go to local social events, and be accepted as members of the community rather than as outsiders. Anything less would be a failure in my eyes."

I looked up from the notes I was writing.

"Well, isn't that exactly what happened?" I said. "The locals finally came around to accepting Kikkoman, not only as a local industry but also as a good neighbor, and your staff, both then and now, have been accepted as valued members of the community. I would say your policies were a big success. And I assume the business took off just as you predicted."

He laughed and shook his head.

"No, no it certainly did not." Now he looked down, almost wringing his hands as he remembered discouraging times.

"We got the rezoning, we established Kikkoman Foods, Inc., in Wisconsin, we built the plant starting in 1971, we hired excellent workers, and everything seemed to be going exactly according to my projections. Then, a few months later, the oil shock hit. It was a devastating blow to the American economy and to our business as well. Not just oil, but all consumer prices skyrocketed, and so did the prices of everything we needed — raw materials, shipping, utilities... everything just rose again and again. Here we were, trying to introduce a whole nation to the taste of *shoyu*. What could we do? When you are trying to introduce a new product, it's not a good time to suddenly double the retail price."

"Couldn't you borrow funds to cover your budget short-fall?" I asked.

"We wanted to, but interest rates were up around 20 percent. It was not a good time for business."

"So what happened? How did you survive?"

He took a deep breath.

"To put it plainly, we lost money. This was one of those big unknown variables that weren't included in my simulations. We lost money in Year 1. And we lost more money in Year 2. Everyone was asking me if we would be all right, would the plant survive? They all thought I must be seriously depressed or getting ulcers or I don't know what. But you know the truth?"

He looked up at me, his eyes dancing and his smile back in place.

"Even in that situation I was not frightened. I knew that the effects of the oil shock would fade in time, that prices would return to normal, and the economy would go back to the way it was. We had already seen the worst of it. I knew that we would be okay, and I told my staff to believe it. And sure enough, by 1977 we were actually turning a profit, and after that we never looked back. Production increased on average by 7 percent every year and has continued that way for over forty years. Sales took off, just as I knew they would, and North America became the main engine for our ongoing business growth.

"From that rocky start in Walworth, we now earn about 70 percent of our total profit from our international business.

We opened Kikkoman Trading in Germany in 1979, and our second overseas plant in Singapore in 1983, just ten years after Walworth. In 1990 we did a tie-up with a prominent Taiwanese company to set up a factory, and that business became our doorway into China. Two years later we had a marketing operation in Australia. Then, 1997 was a very big year — we opened our first factory in Europe, in the Netherlands, and broke ground for our second U.S. plant in Folsom, California. If someone had told me in 1970 that someday we would open two major factories overseas within a year, I wouldn't have believed it."

I noticed that his thumbnail sketch of company history did not include 1995 — the year he took over as president and CEO of the company. As many people around the world had told me, Mogi was not much interested in self-promotion. This was part of what Martin Brink meant when he said that Mogi had the ability to look down from the balcony and see what was happening on the stage. He had a long-term, global perspective that put his company and its achievements above all else.

I told him that I had heard stories about the Walworth and Folsom plants during my travels, but I had never heard how the company chose the Netherlands to be its European production base. I asked Mr. Mogi if there might be an interesting story there, and he did not disappoint me.

"Oh, yes. Well, by the mid-1990s we had already built a factory in the U.S. and two in Asia, so it was no secret that we were looking at Europe as our next major market. Until that time our only business in Europe was in Germany. We had a trading company in Düsseldorf and a handful of restaurants in the major cities. It would not have been at all strange for us to build a factory there in Düsseldorf and ship in all directions, from England to Moscow."

"Why didn't you?" I asked.

"I was contacted by the prime minister of the Netherlands, and he said he wanted to talk. So I flew over to the Hague and met with the PM and the Minister of Finance. They showed me a map of Europe and started to explain why the Netherlands was the best place to site a company. They were very persuasive. I should mention that Denmark also approached us directly, and we seriously considered both countries as candidates. Both had access to clean water and well-educated working populations. English is a business language in both countries, which is important for us. We Japanese already have to study English, and we don't want to study yet another language to communicate for business. Of course, our staff who are stationed overseas are expected to try to learn the local language, but the only necessity is that they can do their jobs in English, as that is the common language — what do you say? the *lingua franca* — of international business.

"However, one of the other key things we were looking for was ease of distribution to the rest of Europe, and there the Netherlands slightly trumped Denmark. Ultimately, we found a very good location, with excellent water and a good local labor force, and we were able to purchase it for a very attractive price, so the decision was made.

"One of the wonderful things about doing business in the Netherlands was the tremendous support we received from the government, both national and local. Do you know where we held our opening party to celebrate the opening of Kikkoman Foods Europe B.V.?"

I looked blank. When I was talking to people in the Netherlands, it never occurred to me to ask about their opening party. It wouldn't have been in the Royal Palace, of course, but maybe some prominent conference hall, or even, was it possible? The Concertgebouw music hall?

He was smiling like a kid with a secret he couldn't hold for much longer.

"Inside the Rijksmuseum!" he said, raising one forefinger.

For just a moment my mind was filled with crazy images of Mogi and his associates raising toasts to their Dutch hosts in front of magnificent Rembrandts and Vermeers, but almost immediately that absurd fantasy evaporated. Of course, one of the world's most famous museums has event halls and private meeting spaces to entertain special guests...

"It was amazing," he continued, looking off to one side as the scene played back in his mind. "There were about 500 people, including the Minister of Finance and many other celebrities, all of us standing right there in front of *The Night Watch*. It was an incredible experience, one that I will never forget."

My pen had stopped moving at this point. I was trying to imagine the scene. I had heard that the groundbreaking ceremony in Walworth was held in the middle of winter and was about 10 degrees below zero, a bad day to be standing outside on a frozen Wisconsin plain, listening to speeches. There were a couple of other big Kikkoman events that might not have motivated me to jump on an airplane and rush to see, but to attend a private reception in the Rijksmuseum in front of

Rembrandt's large, breathtaking canvas known in English as *The Night Watch*? For the first time I wished that I had done this research project a couple of decades earlier. I also took to heart his point about receiving exceptional cooperation from the local authorities.

I looked at my watch. Hardly any time left, and I still had so many questions to ask. I remembered that almost everyone I had met referred to Mogi as a visionary, and my research supported that claim. He not only literally embodied the company's DNA, but had imprinted his own character on that DNA — a refusal to be satisfied with yesterday's status quo and a deep desire to always be looking for the next challenge. Where did that leave his company today? I decided to wrap up our talk by looking at the future. Some people would say that you should only ask an octogenarian about the past, not the future, but in Mogi's case I knew it was a topic he relished discussing. He transformed this company by constantly thinking about the future, and I doubted that age had made him change his ways.

"Mr. Mogi, according to my research, Kikkoman is one of the most globalized companies in Japan. Most Americans think of Sony and Honda and Toyota, but yours was the very first Japanese company to set up a manufacturing business in the U.S., and it was years later when the others followed. More than that, you took an extreme approach to localization that I think none of the other companies copied, or at least not as successfully. Mick Neshek told me that Walworth became the template for your expansion around the world, and that makes a lot of sense. What you did there really was a kind of business and social miracle in many ways. You must be very proud of that success, and very happy to see how Kikkoman has grown. But what will happen to Kikkoman in the coming decades without new frontiers left to explore? And what will happen to your home market here in Japan?"

He sat back in his chair, frowned at me for a moment, trying to decide where to begin, and then started to speak, clearly yet softly: "Yes, I am very proud of what this company has achieved. And yes, we are one of Japan's most globalized companies. Roughly 55 percent of our sales come from overseas, and 85 percent of our operating profit. The Japanese market may grow or it may not. We have new products to introduce and new approaches to engage with consumers. But the company's real growth potential is not here. It's overseas.

"As you know, our North American business was our first overseas venture, and it has grown tremendously. Will it continue to grow? I believe it will. As more people discover how to use Kikkoman sauces creatively in cooking, and as we introduce all sorts of new products, sales in the U.S., Canada, and Mexico will keep expanding. People who have never used Kikkoman will try it, and people who have used it before will want to use it more.

"Our European business is already very healthy — it has been growing in double digits for some time, and I think it still has a long way to go. Europe will continue to grow strongly far into this century. And Asia? Like Europe, Asia is not one market but many. However, just to make things simple, let's talk about an 'Asian' market. It's a *huge* market for soy sauce, one where our brand is well known but we are not yet everyone's first choice. The reasons have to do with tradition, tastes, and price.

And yet, as the entire region continues to develop economically, more and more people want the best things in life. Cooking with the world's best *shoyu* is one way to do that, and for a very reasonable price. I think if you look at Asia in fifty years, you will be astounded to see how much Kikkoman has grown."

I was taken aback.

"So, you're saying that all your markets — America, Europe, and Asia — are going to keep growing?" On the face of it, that sounded like an unrealistically optimistic stance for any senior executive. I guess my expression showed my doubts, for he immediately responded.

"Perhaps that sounds naive. I assure you, Russell-san, we are not naive. We are constantly looking at business realities, political realities, and economic realities, always watching for changes that could affect our growth. Kikkoman's reality is this: we are a foods business; we are not in luxury goods or trendy electronics or automobiles. The—" he paused, perhaps searching for a term from his business school days "—fluctuations of the markets are not a big threat for Kikkoman. On the contrary, our total Group sales seem to keep growing regardless of economic trends. I feel comfortable in saying that Kikkoman will continue to grow throughout this century."

Thinking of all the big companies that had come and gone in the past century, his view seemed at first glance like delusion. A list of famous names that once seemed "too big to fail" immediately floated to mind — Standard Oil, Pan Am, RCA, Enron, American Motors, Lehman Brothers, Baring Brothers, and dozens more. How could Mogi talk seriously about his company continuing to grow for the next century? That seemed like pure fantasy.

Then I remembered a resourceful samurai's wife named Shige Maki who refused to sacrifice herself and her child, and then overcame enormous odds to survive and to start a new life, and then turn it into something altogether different. That was 400 years ago. In the centuries that followed, Kikkoman, like its progenitor, had survived, thrived, and successfully transformed itself into an ever-stronger player. Four centuries of growth — why not a fifth? But would there be enough markets to support that growth? Mogi was already following my train of thought and seemed to be waiting at the station when I finally arrived.

"We are already doing business in the Mideast, and I expect that business will continue to grow. We're selling in Mexico and have started operations in Brazil. I see great potential in South America, a market we have only begun to tap. And then there is Africa, a huge, unexplored market. Between those two continents, I think we have many challenges and also tremendous growth ahead. I only wish I could be around to see it!" He laughed out loud in his usual, good-natured way.

The way he put it made it all sound so inevitable. Perhaps if I were an institutional investor with nothing but computer data in front of me, I would doubt it. But having traveled the world and seen what it is that makes Kikkoman the unique organization that it is, I believed him.

There was a soft knock at the door, then a female assistant came quietly into the room and handed Mr. Mogi a note. He looked at his watch just as I was looking at mine — he had given me much more than the half hour he'd promised.

We both stood up, he shook my hand warmly, and then said something that took me by surprise.

"Russell-san, thank you for your interest in Kikkoman. I appreciate your efforts, as an outsider, to try to get to know this organization worldwide in just a very short time. As you have seen, we are a big, global company, with so many operations in so many markets, so many products and activities, I don't think any one person can grasp the whole thing, not even me. My advice to you is not to pay too much attention to the details, the 'what's new' in Kikkoman. Instead, look at what *doesn't* change; look at the essence, the things that make us what we are. Then you will understand our past, our present, *and* our future."

He stepped back slightly, bowed to me politely, and in a moment he was gone.

I turned to Narusawa.

He had just confirmed a vague notion that had been growing in the back of my mind since I first visited Walworth.

"That's it, isn't it?" I said absent-mindedly. Narusawa looked blank.

"All this traveling I've been doing, the factory visits, the pages of notes I've got on production techniques and container sizes and the ancient history of soy sauce — none of it really matters. It's the spirit of the company, that odd mixture of contradictory drives — to preserve centuries-old traditions while at the same time taking up new challenges — and always with a focus on quality. That's what Kikkoman is really all about. That's what he was trying to tell me. Understand that and you understand our company in any country, in any era."

Narusawa looked at me. "Perhaps that is what he wanted you to understand."

"So, maybe I wasted a lot of time," I said. "I should have just come to Tokyo, gone out to Noda, and talked to Mr. Mogi. That's all I needed."

"No. You needed to discover what you called the 'spirit' of the company, and that spirit is a living thing, passed along from one member of our family to another. Of course, Mr. Mogi embodies that spirit, but that's probably true of the heads of many companies in Japan. What was more important was for you to see that same spirit in factory line workers and managers, in secretaries and chefs and lab technicians all over the world. Even people outside the company — a governor, a mayor, two PR agents, a famous lawyer, and so many others — all sensed that same spirit, they felt it and understood it at some level. By meeting all of them you have seen one of the things Mr. Mogi is most proud of — that Kikkoman is not a Japanese company but a truly global company. And you have seen that this company spirit — the DNA, I think you call it — is very much alive, not only in the Mogi family, but in every corner of every firm in our worldwide Group. It is what makes us who we are.

"Yes, you could have flown directly to Tokyo and perhaps you would have had a chance to talk to Mr. Mogi." He paused. "But you would not have understood his message. Now, because of your travels and your experiences, I think you do."

Damn, I thought. I hate it when the people I interview are smarter than me. And that happens all the time.

THE MAGIC SEASONING

Epilogue (by Yuzaburo Mogi)

First and foremost, I want to thank Mr. Russell for taking the time and showing the interest to research and write this book about our company. Only one other foreign journalist has made that effort, and that was many years ago. As the Kikkoman Group continues to grow and expand, I feel it is essential for people around the world to understand us better, to see what we do and to understand why we do it. In this respect, Mr. Russell's book is a very welcome addition to the foreign-language literature on Kikkoman.

When this project began, our staff explained to me that an American writer wanted to investigate our company and write an independent book about our history, products, factories, overseas offices, management philosophy, and so on. Some of them were worried that an independent third-party portrait of any company could be unflattering, and that it might be better for us not to cooperate unless we could be sure of some direct control over the text. But I have worked with foreign journalists long enough to know that you cannot tell them what to write or how to do their job any more than they can tell us how to make *shoyu*. Where was the risk? I said. We have nothing to hide. If the writer does his job even reasonably well, the book will show what a good company Kikkoman is, both in Japan and around the world. So I advised our PR Department to cooperate with Mr. Russell as much as possible and get out of his way. Of course, there was always a chance that he would misunderstand or misrepresent something vital to our business, but he came to us well recommended, and I have always been one for taking calculated risks.

Thus, I was happy to see that his book did such a good job in examining our operations, looking at so many important areas, and explaining much of Kikkoman's business to people overseas. However, no work such as this is completely without shortcomings, as I'm sure Mr. Russell would be the first to agree. There are gaps in the description of our Group businesses and even minor misunderstandings where I think the author focused too much on less important parts of our story, particularly my role in it. For the record, it is foolish to say that one man or one manifestation of "corporate DNA" created what we know today as Kikkoman. Our remarkable success in the past half-century is due to the efforts of thousands of hard-working people around the world. I am proud of my role in that process, but I was just one of many who contributed to the company's growth.

Nit-picking

Among other minor complaints I have with this work, I wish that the author had devoted a little space to what we call *shoku bunka*, or "food culture." At Kikkoman, we are all very much aware of the wide diversity of traditions and customs involving eating, serving, and entertaining with food. We believe that food culture is one of the most important elements

of our multi-cultural global village that needs to be actively pre-
served. In Japan, we have seen the sudden influx of Western and
particularly American eating habits displace many valuable and
healthy domestic traditions. In the space of just a generation
or two, dietary habits have shifted radically: Young people who
used to start their day with rice and grilled fish now prefer
toast or sweet rolls and other pre-packaged foods. Today's busy
housewives find it much easier to drop a couple of pieces of
white bread into a toaster than to cook a traditional Japanese
breakfast for their children, and even those who make the effort
to preserve the healthy traditions of their grandparents discover that their husbands and kids would rather grab a quick
bite of something as they run out the door than sit down and
eat a proper meal.

Throughout the world, "progress" and modernity are threatening the diversity of food culture in much the same way that
industrial progress is threatening biodiversity and the global
environment. What is easy is not always what is best, and what
is good for one country is not necessarily a good template for the
entire world. At Kikkoman, we respect and rejoice in the wonders of global food culture, and we work to support it. Building
a safer, happier, healthier world through good food and good
nutrition is one of the pillars of our business philosophy.

Our traditional Japanese food culture is called *washoku*,
and in 2013, UNESCO added *washoku* to its list of Intangible
Cultural Heritage assets. Since then, there has been a visible
washoku boom around the world, and its popularity has continued to grow. Of course, as the world's No. 1 producer of soy
sauce (*shoyu*), which is the ideal condiment to accompany

Japanese food, we are delighted with that trend. However, we have also been working tirelessly for decades to show people around the world that *shoyu* is an ideal seasoning for just about any kind of cooking, that it is in no way limited to Japanese food. Although this point is made in Mr. Russell's book, I would have been happy to see a wider discussion of both *washoku* and global food cultures and the ways that *shoyu* can play a supporting role in dozens of types of regional and ethnic cooking. In fact, one part of our long-term management plan, A Vision for the Future of the Kikkoman Group, is to see our *shoyu* become a truly *global standard seasoning*. That involves understanding and responding to the food cultures of 100 different countries and using *shoyu* to create new and exciting tastes that resonate with those many different cuisines. Our goal, simply put, is to see a small bottle of soy sauce on every kitchen table around the world.

While we're on the subject, I am surprised that Mr. Russell did not mention the "little red bottle," one of the world's most iconic containers. That little five-ounce glass teardrop soy sauce dispenser with the red plastic cap was designed by Kenji Ekuan, one of the most famous and most decorated industrial designers in the world. It was introduced back in 1961, the year I graduated from Columbia University, and has won numerous awards around the world since then. A bottle now sits on display at the Museum of Modern Art in NYC. Of course, I know that a bottle is a very small thing to mention, yet to me it is much more — it symbolizes Kikkoman's commitment to simple, timeless, consumer-friendly quality. That little bottle has become our ambassador, our symbol to the world.

Old and New

As I read this text, I am actually quite impressed by how different our perspectives are. If my staff had created this book, I'm sure it would have had a very different perspective. Perhaps in the end that is the true value of this book: It looks at Kikkoman from an outsider's point of view, not from a corporate point of view. Mr. Russell sees some things in exactly the same way that we do, and other things from his own perspective. In no case would I say that his view is absolutely wrong. Rather, I would remind readers that his perspective and particularly his interpretation of things is highly personal. This is a very personal book, something our own staff would never imagine doing. In that respect, I am very grateful to him for creating a new and original portrait of an old company.

While we're talking about "old," I noticed that the author likes to refer to our "400-year-old tradition." I want to clarify that exaggeration: It is true that our earliest ancestor was making *shoyu* in the village of Noda in the 17th century, and we can trace our business back to those early roots, but our business as a business has not been around in any form for 400 years. I would be more comfortable thinking of our total history as "approximately 350 years," and our history as a prominent business as only half of that. The forerunner of what is now Kikkoman was only registered as a corporation in 1917, so in that sense we are only celebrating our 100th anniversary.

More than the numbers, I fear that the constant focus on our history distracts readers from what is really important. Yes, our traditions are extremely important to us, but Kikkoman did not grow to its current size by thinking only of yesterday's traditions. The company has always innovated, it has responded to successive waves of social change, and it has developed many new products and entered new business fields. Rather than focus on the traditions filling our rear-view mirror, I like to see Kikkoman as always looking ahead, always moving forward, never afraid to take up new challenges so long as they are in line with our basic company philosophy. I believe it is precisely this adaptability that is the major reason why our business has been able to continue for so long — we are enriched by tradition, not limited by it.

Of course, we will continue to manufacture the world's finest soy sauce, as well as to expand our range of offerings with other sauces and related products, and we will continue to grow our other businesses as well. Later in this century, Kikkoman may celebrate 400 years as a family enterprise, and I haven't the slightest doubt that this will be just another milestone on a very long road. I expect that both the parent company and the Group will still be healthy and growing well into the next century.

In closing, let me say that it has been a pleasure to read an outsider's perspective on our Group. To most people, Kikkoman is essentially a one-product business. This perception is not completely wrong: We do focus on manufacturing one product above all others. However, our business is no longer limited to manufacturing. Our Group is the world's number one supplier of Oriental foodstuffs, and we have been gradually expanding into new products such as soy milk and a variety of health-related products as well.

Yet I find this "dry" analysis of our business both accurate and misleading at the same time. It is merely an objective, balance-sheet view of Kikkoman's "assets." We do not look at our business this way, the way a stock analyst might see it. Those of us in the Kikkoman Group believe that our mission is all about food and food culture. We exist not to achieve numerical growth or even simply to produce soy sauce, but rather, to promote the international exchange of food culture. Our main product happens to be a seasoning that complements and enhances all types of cooking, so we feel intricately connected with the amazing diversity of global food cultures. Helping people around the world to discover new and different tastes and to rediscover the pleasures of their own food culture is our sole *raison d'etre*. If readers can grasp that fundamental point from this book, then I am satisfied.

Yuzaburo Mogi
Tokyo, Japan 2017

End Notes

---

1 www.mattsonco.com — it turns out to be an interesting company.

2 *Kikkoman Chronicles*, by Ronald E. Yates; McGraw-Hill, New York, 1998.

3 I should point out that I don't normally ask rude questions directly in front of company's VP. In this case, I had previously told Dick what kind of things I wanted to ask Kikkoman employees, even if my line of questioning might seem inappropriate from management's point of view. He told me to go ahead, whether he was there or not, and ask anyone any question I liked. He seemed totally confident of what kind of responses I would get, which in itself spoke volumes about this organization.

4 http://www.kochschule-duesseldorf.de/ (in German, but worth a visit)

5 That's on a PPP basis, which is a measure used to compare living standards in different countries